MW00423371

Communism and Strategy

Communism and Strategy

Rethinking Political Mediations

Isabelle Garo

Translated by Gregory Elliott

VERSO

London • New York

This work received support for excellence in publication and translation from Albertine Translation, a program created by Villa Albertine and funded by FACE Foundation.

This work was published with the help of the French Ministry of Culture – Centre national du livre
Ouvrage publié avec le concours du Ministère français chargé de la culture – Centre national du livre

This English-language edition published by Verso 2023
First published in French as *Communisme et stratégie*,
Éditions Amsterdam, Paris, 2019
© Isabelle Garo 2023
Translation © Gregory Elliott 2023

All rights reserved

The moral rights of the author have been asserted

1 3 5 7 9 10 8 6 4 2

Verso
UK: 6 Meard Street, London W1F 0EG
US: 388 Atlantic Avenue, Brooklyn, NY 11217
versobooks.com

Verso is the imprint of New Left Books

ISBN-13: 978-1-83976-816-3
ISBN-13: 978-1-83976-823-1 (UK EBK)
ISBN-13: 978-1-83976-828-6 (US EBK)

British Library Cataloguing in Publication Data
A catalogue record for this book is available from the British Library

Library of Congress Cataloging-in-Publication Data
A catalog record for this book is available from the Library of Congress

Typeset in Minion by Hewer Text UK Ltd, Edinburgh
Printed and bound by CPI Group (UK) Ltd, Croydon CR0 4YY

Contents

Introduction: The Alternative in Shreds

How can we know if your communism according to the Book
Isn't going to be cancelled like the Sunday ball,
Because with the rain the orchestra is stuck in the mud?
                                Heiner Müller, *The Displaced Person*

Is there still time – or, indeed, is it already time – to revisit communism? There are reasons to doubt its survival. In these dire times, how can we be oblivious to the fact that global capitalist domination and its crisis have, as their corollary, the unprecedented defeat of the forces of social contestation and, above all, of any alternative collective, majoritarian political project? In recent years, however, the question of communism has tended to re-emerge here and there, in theoretical and in some philosophical works. This modest return is paradoxical, given the profound and enduring disqualification of the radical political project to which the term refers. Since the late 1970s, Stalinism has been depicted as the very essence of a communism that is quintessentially totalitarian and murderous.[1] More than two decades later, François Furet's *Le Passé d'une illusion* and Stéphane Courtois's *Le Livre noir du communisme* seemed to bring the epoch of positive use of the word to a definitive close, replacing it with a criminalization pure and simple, and debate now focuses

---

1 See Michael Scott Christofferson, *French Intellectuals against the Left: The Anti-totalitarian Moment of the 1970s*, New York: Berghahn, 2004.

exclusively on the millions of deaths attributed to it.[2] Deliberate use of the term did not disappear for all that, though. Preserved within parties and organizations that continue to identify with it – despite their weakness and marginality – it has also remained alive thanks to critical theoretical works. Located on the margins of classical engagement, the latter have sought to explore and redefine the fertility of the term in an original, striking fashion.

The Return of the Communist Question

The current uncertain and unstable meaning of the word 'communism' therefore derives from a long history and a recent conjuncture. From the late 1980s, the fall of the Berlin Wall and the disappearance of the communist bloc helped gradually free the term from the charge of totalitarianism, while serving to bury the idea of a viable alternative to capitalism more deeply than ever. If the word thus became available for positive usage – certainly minoritarian but, to some extent, reviving the hope of which it was once the bearer and confronting violent, reactionary neoliberal policies – it remains uncoupled from any concrete political perspective. Now it is a question not so much of politically preparing the transition to communism, understood as the supersession or abolition of capitalism, as of evoking it in a way that combines the desire for change with oppositional practices, critical radicalism with academicism. Accepting this marginality, contemporary use of the term, when positive, attests to a continuing aspiration to reconstruct alternatives which, if not concrete, can at least be named, preserving them as hypotheses while the social conditions and political forces for their reactivation are wanting. This is how we might understand the philosophical return of the communist question in France and its resonance, in particular, via the works of Alain Badiou, Antonio Negri, Jean-Luc Nancy, Jacques Rancière or the Invisible Committee – alongside those Marxist authors who never stopped identifying with communism and reworking its meaning, but whose readership

---

2 See François Furet, *The Passing of an Illusion: The Idea of Communism in the Twentieth Century* (1995), trans. Deborah Furet, Chicago: University of Chicago Press, 1999; and Stéphane Courtois *et al.*, *The Black Book of Communism: Crimes, Terror, Repression* (1997), trans. Jonathan Murphy and Mark Kramer, Cambridge: Harvard University Press, 1999.

is more limited, such as Lucien Sève, André Tosel, Jacques Bidet and Daniel Bensaïd.

Notwithstanding their differences and divergences, it is striking that the great majority of post-Marxist approaches to communism situate themselves on a philosophical terrain which they attempt to redefine and which they find disconnected from the issue of socialism – traditionally a major site for reflection on the moments and transitions of political and social transformation – when they do not directly reject its terms. How should we understand this new situation? Does it fundamentally alter the post-capitalist perspective? The aim of this book is to analyse this situation while being involved in it. Rather than venturing a strictly descriptive, general panorama of intellectual debate on the left, we shall dwell on a few authors who broach key questions of socialism and communism from an original, prospective angle, each of them stressing a particular dimension of the alternative: Alain Badiou (on the state and the party); Ernesto Laclau (on the conquest of power and strategy); and Antonio Negri and theorists of the common (on labour and property). Sharing a similar commitment to theoretical and political intervention, which resonates strongly even outside activist circles, they strive to renew this tradition while revisiting its fundamentals.

These authors have another essential feature in common: it is in confronting Marx and Marxism critically that they contribute to a revival of reflection on the alternatives to contemporary capitalism. In so doing, they engage in two striking tendencies. On the one hand, they illustrate the fragmentation of the projects outlined, which are incompatible with one another, focusing on certain themes of the socialist, communist or anarchist tradition to the exclusion of others. On the other hand, they embody an attempt to repoliticize theory, but on the terrain of theory itself. Such repoliticization remains dependent on the philosophical displacement of politics, updated in line with the critique of Marxism in the 1960s, '70s and '80s,[3] which all these authors represent. Remaining more convinced than others of the need for radical social change, they are distinguished by their claim for a power peculiar to theory in this regard.

---

3 See Isabelle Garo, *Foucault, Deleuze, Althusser et Marx. La politique dans la philosophie*, Paris: Démopolis, 2011.

At the same time, the social and political urgency of an alternative comes directly up against an inability to build it collectively alongside the serial defeats of the labour movement, whereas capitalism, having entered its authoritarian neoliberal phase, not only adds to its misdeeds, but multiplies its disasters upon one another: exploding inequalities, increasing exploitation, combined forms of domination and oppression, the clash of imperialisms, unbridled financialization, general militarization, the ransacking of nature, ideological domination and so forth. This destructive sequence, on an unprecedented scale, arouses anger and rebellions, social struggles and multiple challenges, without it being possible in the short term to envisage a radical transformation of the mode of production as a whole, despite the growing urgency to do so. Given this, the resurgent contestation on the philosophical and, more broadly, theoretical terrain should be regarded as an admission of weakness, but it is also an asset, one of the ways of countering a neoliberal ideology unduly convinced of its omnipotence. Evidence of such contestation in search of new political roads helps in its own way to reopen space for an intervention at once critical and activist.

To revive collective reflection on the question of an alternative to capitalism, beyond its critical dimension, we must therefore begin by taking these theoretical propositions and interventions seriously, starting from the paradox of a politics both projected and impossible, referred to as 'communism', which is once again an emblem of the problematic links between a project of emancipation and its realization. But rather than adding a further option to the patchwork coat of scattered alternatives, or attempting to reconcile fundamentally divergent hypotheses, this book opts to broach them from the angle of what is missing in contemporary political critique and contestation alike: a strategy, in the strong political sense of the term, that enables the collective construction of a project of general, mobilizing, radical transformation by the exploited and dominated. Over and above ways to win power, the term refers to the invention of mediations that go beyond such a conquest, aiming to escape state control and the conversion of means into ends. Strategy concerns forms of collective mobilization to be organized on an enduring basis, but it also designates critical reflection combining historical analysis with the development of a shared, democratic, dialogic consciousness, the latter escorting political intervention to control and readjust it to ends that are likewise elaborated en route.

What we need most urgently today is a strategy of this exacting kind. Amid the present conjoint crisis of capitalism and of the alternative to capitalism, this strategic angle fully emerges once we proceed to compare contemporary formulations of the communist hypothesis with what was, and remains, its crucible: the conception developed by Marx in his time, which is contemporaneous with a revolutionary sequence that defined political modernity in its essential contradictions between 1848 and 1871. Hence the anti-chronological approach adopted here, which consists in rereading Marx from a strategic angle on the basis of the questions raised by today's theoreticians. As well as enabling us to rediscover the oeuvre of the author of *Capital* in a way that restores the dimension of theoretical and political intervention *en situation*, this approach opens up the prospect of a strategic reactivation of the critique of capitalism at a time when this critique is rediscovering its relevance but struggling to reconstruct its political – and not merely its critical – radicalism. This explains why I have opted to bypass the strategic debates within the Second and Third Internationals, which are merely glanced at in the introduction, despite their richness. Rereading Marx in the light of a different, more recent posterity makes it possible to adduce the features of a reflection powerfully shaped by the revolutionary turbulence of its time but not gripped by the urgency of the tasks of revolutionary leadership in the tragic circumstances of the First World War and the Russian Civil War. Furthermore, the decline of the labour movement and the erosion of its mass organizations since then re-create a relative kinship with its inception amid an unbridled, deregulated capitalism, which in some respects is ours once again.

For while it is well known that Marx nowhere defines communism in its detailed modus operandi, and while it is often accepted that his analysis of capitalism, by dint of its generality, retains (or regains) its relevance today, it has rarely been emphasized that it advances an essentially strategic approach to the issue of communism. His scholarly study of the contradictions of capitalism aims above all to merge with social struggles and irrigate the protracted process of a radical social transformation. In Marx, 'communism' and 'communist' specifically refer to this search for a revolutionary road during a period (1840–80) that contained its promise and sought to construct it. Conceiving communism as general social reappropriation and historical control wrested at last, Marx's originality was to rethink political mediations from the angle of this reappropriation and this reappropriation subject to the development of historical mediations. Such is the dialectic that must be revived.

In light of this reflection, and without seeking any universal lessons in a sphere that contains none, it becomes possible to restore critical and political potency to the communist question. It is active not as some ultimate perspective, but as the patient, aggressive re-creation of the mediations and transitions required for a political exit from capitalism. Today, it is on the terrain of the forms and means of this reappropriation that the alternative, whatever name we give it, is to be rethought, without making the word *communism* a term as grandiloquent as it is impotent. Confronted with certainties and impatience, with the fetishization or rejection of electoral logic, it involves reflecting and working on the mediated, and mediating, invention of a vigorous counter-offensive, resolutely geared to a democratic redefinition of the functions confiscated by the state, the socialization of wealth, the abolition of all forms of domination, the development of individual and collective capacities and the reconstruction of a sustainable metabolism with nature. Such an initiative involves rethinking and rearticulating the traditional perspectives of socialism and communism, far removed from any scenario in stages, while inscribing their renewal in the aftermath of a history from which, for better and for worse, they remain inseparable.

Rereading Marx in light of twenty-first-century concerns that were not his also makes it possible to add to the classical questions tackled by Laclau, Negri, Badiou – dimensions they have had a tendency to neglect, being themselves the inheritors of a Marxism much more closed to those realities than was Marx himself. Consideration of these aspects is imperative for a strategic revival today: struggles against colonialism, racism and sexism, but also ecological concerns, are now the sites of the unity to be re-created or they become, alternatively, its tomb. The contemporary rise of these demands, which do not spontaneously coalesce with one another or with the class struggles from which they are inseparable, requires us to construct their emancipatory convergence theoretically and politically, to articulate them without subordinating them to one another or to a causal *prius*, while maintaining the fundamental character of the capital/labour contradiction. For the peculiarity of strategy is to know how to distinguish a historical causality from the specific logic of political intervention, avoiding forms of determinism as well as false universals.

Strategy and Politics

But what is strategy? The term 'strategy' has become one of the buzzwords of sport, marketing and neoliberal management.[4] Being a strategist today involves practising the art of guile and cunning without questioning either the established rules or the intended goal, like the highly neoliberal game theory that purports to model supposedly immutable human behaviour.[5] Faced with this purely instrumental conception, the 'eclipse of strategic reason' analysed by Daniel Bensaïd persists. It concerns the development of a concrete alternative to capitalism that involves the means and conditions of its realization and is capable of constantly readjusting to them.[6] For strategy, in the full sense of the word, is a theoretico-practical reflection, always set in singular, concrete circumstances and which seeks to define the goals and mediations of political action by one another. At the antipode of the strategy of the dominant, the strategy of the oppressed covers the whole field of politics, which it tends to remodel, because politics does not boil down to electoral success but concerns the radical transformation of the totality of social relations.

Greek in origin, the term *strategy* refers to the conduct of an army (*stratos*) and, more generally, the means that make it possible to secure victory over an opponent in concrete historical circumstances which, by definition, cannot be predicted. These contingencies delimit the specific space of decision-making, individual or collective, capable of exploiting a propitious moment to dramatically change a historical situation. From Sun Tzu to Pericles, from Machiavelli to Lenin, from Rosa Luxemburg to José Carlos Mariátegui and Amílcar Cabral, strategists are theorists at

---

4 Lawrence Freedman points out that occurrences of 'enterprise strategy', rare before the 1960s, have proliferated since the 1970s to the point of overtaking references to 'military strategy' from the 2000s onwards (*Strategy: A History*, New York: Oxford University Press, 2013, xiii).

5 Developed in the mid-1940s on the terrain of mathematics, game theory studies individual interactions, including their cooperative dimension. It has bearing on board games, involving gains and enabling the players' observation of their respective choices. From the 1980s onwards, the neo-classical economists who colonize it expelled the cooperative dimension, backing the model of perfect competition and the thesis of rational individuals as, in essence, 'maximizers'. See Bernard Guerrien, *Dictionnaire d'analyse économique*, Paris: La Découverte, 2002, 515–18.

6 Daniel Bensaïd, *Éloge de la philosophie profane*, Paris: Albin Michel, 2008, 44.

the same time as they are men or women of action. And such a strategic conceptualization must confront both the issue of effectiveness and that of legitimacy as a means to achieve the concrete construction of an alternative, over and above the mere victory to be won against an opponent.

On a world scale, collective ripostes from the oppressed have not been wanting throughout history. Strategic thinking for a long time merged with a military art of the poor, who reacted to injustice with anger, rioting, revolution, egalitarian projects, millenarian hopes and magnificent utopias in the face of ferocious repression and merciless class warfare. From Spartacus to peasant *jacqueries*, via the major popular insurrections that punctuated the history of China, establishment of an armed relation of force has been a primary, vital concern. Aiming to win power, this armed relation has risked being conquered in turn by its fundamentally unaltered logic. Gradually, an independent political strategy was invented, the French Revolution marking a break in this regard: a radical transformation of social relations, based on a broad popular mobilization, it faced a powerful state in the process of being centralized, while being the inheritor of the rationalist thought of the Enlightenment and its controversies over the popular will and equality, slavery and the status of women. These features broadened horizons and enriched views concerning the means and forms of mobilization of different social strata involved in the revolutionary process, even if there remained a tendency to separate reflection on the modalities of action, imprisoned in empiricism, from ultimate ends, which embraced an institutional logic or glimpsed a more radical social and political overhaul. For a time, the Napoleonic epic tended to narrow revolutionary horizons to the war of conquest once again, but without extinguishing the egalitarian, seditious flame of which Babeuf's conspiracy was the outlier and model for decades. Hesitating between wider mobilization and plot, for a long time it established the coordinates and difficulties of a political strategy of the oppressed.

From this epoch, contradictions have run through modern revolutionary thinking, from the seizure of power and transformation of politics to the conditions of insurrection and sustainable forms of organization, from the skilful handling of circumstances and the goals of the revolution to renewed hierarchy and reinvented democracy. Perfectly logically, the strategic question has been the centre of the contrast between the proclaimed alternative and the world as it is, but it is also the refraction of that world's logics in the structures and consciousness of those seeking to overthrow it. The reflections of nineteenth-century socialists and communists – Cabet, Dézamy, Saint-Simon, Proudhon, Bakunin, Hess, Marx, Lassalle, to name only them – would explore these issues in conjunction with the revolutions that punctuated the century, before the first mass organizations of the labour movement were built.

Once these organizations emerged – especially the powerful German social democracy – the term *strategy* changed meanings and referred predominantly to the conquest of state power. The whole problem then meant successfully linking this immediate prospect to a more distant horizon of social transformation, which was incompatible with using institutions as they were. Very schematically, we might say that the Second International was to be the centre of this perspective of electoral conquest of the state, at the risk of integrating into a labour movement that had become a counter-society and intermediate body rather than an active mediation between working-class mobilization and social revolution. Despite their divergences, Eduard Bernstein and Karl Kautsky both ended up envisaging achieving power without popular revolution, with the numerical expansion of the industrial working class nourishing faith in an inevitable electoral victory.

A proponent of the thesis of a 'passive accumulation of forces', Kautsky was, however, the only one to reflect on the concrete conditions of a victory never won in advance, which he broached in terms of military strategy. This strategic reflection would initially influence Lenin, before he redefined the role of the party as a major actor in the social and political correlation of forces. Once the October Revolution had been launched, a broader conception of strategy renewed the art of popular insurrection, rethought activist intervention, fuelled debate on the respective structuration and roles of the party, soviets and trade unions, questioned political and social alliances but also that of workers' control, and broached issues of national aspirations, anti-colonial struggles, women's liberation, teaching and culture.

In the situation of Russia's military encirclement, and given the economic and social chaos, however, the debate soon came to a close: the militarization of social life in a context of world war and civil war, rapidly rising bureaucratization and disagreements among the political leadership eclipsed the democratic dynamic.

Once Stalinized and in service of a bureaucratized party-state, the Third International would everywhere impose its options and persecute its opponents. The irony of history had it that Marx's notion of the 'dictatorship of the proletariat' – distorted from its original meaning as well as an erroneous reading of the *Critique of the Gotha Programme* in terms of fixed phases, socialist then communist – served to justify this state control. Amid these developments, supporters of strategic conceptions initiated by Trotsky tried to construct a different way, while, from fascist jails, Gramsci maintained the imperative of renewing strategic thinking in the context of a now unfavourable balance of forces. Each in their own way, they sought to understand the blockage of revolutionary momentum and the rise of fascism.

Subsequently, the Chinese and Cuban revolutions and Yugoslav self-management would open up new horizons, their failures or impasses not erasing the scale of this fresh momentum. The revival of strategic thinking in the 1960s was the product of Third World revolutions and anti-imperialist movements, of the international wave of challenges to the established order in 1968, of the struggles of Blacks in the US, of women, gays and lesbians. The reflections of Charles Bettelheim, Samir Amin, Nicos Poulantzas, Mehdi Ben Barka and Angela Davis attest to this resurgence of political thought. Promoters of Eurocommunism set out in search of a new anti-capitalist way; the theme of self-management seemed capable of renewing social democracy and possibly subverting it, while international solidarity persisted in a context where social gains, albeit relative, nevertheless seemed secure. Nonetheless, the revolutionary perspective subsequently receded inexorably, along with the strategic thinking that lived only at the point of contact between theory and struggles, inasmuch as both were vectors of alternatives to capitalism. The virulent ideological campaign of the 1970s – anti-communist in the name of anti-totalitarianism – ended up discrediting and demonizing any revolutionary perspective, gradually equating the terms *communism*, *Stalinism* and *Nazism* and reducing the definition of socialism to the labelling of social-democratic parties and their projects, which initially were redistributive but then offered nothing but a 'social' accompaniment to neoliberal policies in ever more rhetorical fashion.

An exceptional time in terms of strategy, the twentieth century was also, and ultimately, an era of defeat and retreat: the crushing of the Spanish Republic and the Greek partisans, the Sétif and Madagascar

massacres, colonial dirty wars, the coup d'état in Chile and the failure of
the Portuguese Revolution. The decades that followed the close of the
Second World War were thus characterized by the tragic involution of
the hope born in 1917. The thematic and lexical inventions peculiar to
revolutionary strategic thinking in these years – insurrectionary general
strikes, dual power, hegemony, united fronts, protracted people's wars,
urban guerrillas and so on – would not prevent the ebbing of the revolution and would end up losing their meaning in the process. What
survives today of this reflection on transitions, from the capture of the
Winter Palace to the debate on self-management, from the issue of the
vanguard party to the definition of 'new managerial standards'? Not
only have the words aged, but the perspectives have been disqualified, to
the point of rendering the terms *socialism* and *communism* – even *capitalism* and a fortiori *imperialism* – unpronounceable, while the democracy that is supposed to have triumphed worldwide designates nothing
more than the prolonged defeat of the labour movement and the reign
of the market.

Reviving Strategic Debate

From the 1980s onwards, the neoliberal sequence of capitalism imposed
brutal policies of social regression. While this strategy of re-conquest
developed from the interwar period onwards, the crisis of the early
1970s afforded an opportunity and justification to embark on dismantling a Fordist compromise conceded by default. The financialization of
capitalism allowed the dominant classes to restore the profit rate,
combining pressure on wages, destruction of redistributive social
conquests and competition between workers on a world scale.
Perspectives on a concrete alternative to capitalism tended to collapse,
even though the contradictions of capitalism were accentuated and its
global instability grew, offering a glimpse of nothing but new financial
crises, social convulsions and endless military interventions, aggravated
social and environmental damage bringing humanity ever closer to
barbarism as the prospects of socialism and communism receded.

Today, the crisis of the labour movement seems at its height. While
small organizations preserve the strategic grid of the 1920s without
being in a position to render it operative, the parties of the institutional

left try to find a second wind while remaining prisoners of short-term electoral logic, which increasingly reduces strategy to alliances without any content and ruptures those alliances without any perspective, fostering the detachment of broad sectors of the popular electorate from such politics. This occurs against the backdrop of an ascent of the extreme right, whose theses are now relayed by the majority of other political forces and by a rising institutional racism. Like the term *strategy*, which has shifted onto enemy ground, the notion of mediation now refers to nothing more than supposedly neutral legal arbitration, while that of transition, characterized as ecological, holds out the promise of a 'green capitalism' after having served to describe the brutal, pervasively mafia-style restoration of capitalism in the former socialist countries.

However, history is not over. The grand narrative of the victory of democracy is coming undone, and the promise of general well-being by yesterday's liberals is giving way to the threat of something worse brandished by neoliberals; this is occurring in a world rendered gangrenous by exploitation and oppression, generalized competition, wars and environmental devastation. Alternatives without roots abound in this barren soil, only to wither, striving to escape past failures by circumventing the state or denouncing the 'party-form', rediscovering the early-nineteenth-century labour movement's inspirations – sometimes unawares, sometimes while dreaming of revitalizing them. Persistent aspirations to radical transformation bear the burden of defeat, often severed from knowledge of its history and its victories. Logically, it is by shifting onto the terrain of the search for original initiatives and new ideas that these aspirations endeavour to constitute themselves as a coherent project. In them the urge to change the world is seeking to rediscover its collective, solidaristic dimensions, while theorists, activists and political forces ponder the viability of new social models based on free access, sharing and a sustainable reorientation of growth.

This effervescence proves that neoliberal practices and homilies cannot uproot a spirit of revolt profoundly nurtured by a sense of injustice and real forms of oppression. But we have to give a material shape to this awakening beyond the numerous incompatible hypotheses that leave hanging the issue of the agents of the transformation – to repoliticize a project collectively and democratically constructed in direct connection with social and political mobilizations. For if philosophy can conserve and propagate political critique at a time when revolutionary prospects are ebbing, it is also one of the forms of the cleavage studied by Marx that separates a collective activity from its fixed, specialist forms, wrenched from the social dynamic. For him, the state and philosophy share this alienating characteristic – the source and legitimation of a dispossession, a sterilizing separation pitted against that which is a collective and individual reappropriation of separated powers, radical democratization of the state and theoretical elaboration of the alternative. In this book we shall explore the way these two reappropriations not only converge, but are in fact a precondition for one another, the only means of reactivating a blocked dialectic and rethinking, at the same time as the communist question, the possibility of a revolutionary politics in our time.

Chapter 1 is devoted to Alain Badiou, a committed philosopher in an original sense. His work beckons us to linger over the philosophical migration of the communist question, at the same time as it raises the problem of the state – whether to attack it or bypass it – as well as that of the party or organization. These questions, which are more central than ever, bear on the forms and ideas of politics but also on the concrete conditions of radical transformation. As regards the last, Ernesto Laclau, whose theses are discussed in Chapter 2, is one of the major contemporary theoreticians of strategy, who, for his part, rejects any communist hypothesis and instead focuses on the construction and reconstruction of an alternative hegemony to the dominant social order. His approach, at once pragmatic and expressly rhetorical, makes it possible to tackle the issue of political and social power, as well as the hegemonic role of ideas, from a different angle. What he endeavours to develop is the external character of political intervention, promoting strategy as the construction of a political offer capable of unifying disparate social demands. Chapter 3 examines the theory of the common and, in particular, the version of it proposed by Antonio Negri and Michael Hardt. They tackle the question, likewise crucial, of property, this time from the perspective of the immanence of the alternative to the dynamics of contemporary capitalism. These four authors thus explore the major classical axes of the critique of capitalism while separating them from one another, to the point of constructing profoundly incompatible alternatives. However, despite their divergences, they align in a reviving of polemical discussion with Marx and Marxism, thus inviting us to reread Marx in the light of their own lines of enquiry. This rereading is the object of Chapters 4 and 5, which examine Marx's thematic of communism as the site of a reflection fundamentally strategic in kind, closely bound up with the history of Marx's moment and activist engagement. Following these analyses, and on their bases, the sixth and last chapter explores the conditions for a contemporary reconstruction of an alternative to capitalism from this strategic, as opposed to programmatic, angle.

1

The Eruptive Communism of Alain Badiou

Alain Badiou is one of the principal proponents of the return of the idea of communism, associated in his work with a continuous critique of Marxism and a violent rejection of existing political forms – parties and trade unions, institutions, states. He revisits these issues, which are at the heart of the alternative to capitalism, in an original way: the cleavage between socialism and communism has from the start revolved around the relationship to the state, whether as regards its conquest, perspectives for its transformation or its abolition. It is also on the problem of the state that all twentieth-century revolutions failed, for want of having attempted to shatter its class logic – or for not having succeeded in so doing and wrongly believing it possible to utilize it differently. Given the history of socialist and communist organizations, but also because of the diversity of doctrines and theories, the spectrum opened up by this issue ranges between resolute statism and radical anti-statism, the latter condition raising the question of whether a different political form must replace the state and, if so, which.

We should add that left-wing forces – political, trade union or associational – necessarily confront the state and its institutions in three ways, which are at once contradictory and combined: when they use or challenge state power such as it is; when they defend some of its components – public services – and its social role; and when they are integrated to varying degrees into the state apparatus through the party-form, as well as political and union representatives who intervene through state bodies.

Despite its complexity and what is at stake, this question remains largely neglected by contemporary theoreticians of communism. Yet it was at the heart of Marxist thinking, starting with Marx himself, and central in debates within the Internationals.

It seems clear that, amid the current crisis of representation and, more profoundly, accelerating de-democratization, the reopening of these theoretico-political issues is crucial to a larger political and activist revival. In the absence of such a resumption and readjustment to circumstances, a big gap opens up between fixed options: some advocate smashing the state and permanent revolution, rejecting any centralization, any form of organization even, while others devote themselves to existing institutional operations. It might be thought that this divorce, and the symmetrical impotence of these two options, is one of the causes of the rejection of the party-form in general, which erases the diversity of experiences covered by this notion depending upon the epochs, projects, traditions and structuration peculiar to each of them.

This general rejection, when combined with the defence of communism, is often formulated in favour of movementist and spontaneist logics which, for want of generating alternative democratic forms, soon succumb to the defects of the very delegation of power and 'verticality' they sought to dispel, enabling the most skilful orators and licensed speakers to impose their point of view. It remains the case that hierarchical and bureaucratic phenomena have never spared the labour movement. That is why it is important to discuss as such the various strategic options present and to re-raise the issue of the state as not separate from, but dialectically involved in, all those forms treated in the other chapters of this book. It is this articulation that has to be analysed, contrary to the tendency to single out the institutional question, regardless of the analysis of it proposed. From this point of view, several recent theoretical interventions warrant discussion, in that they continue or renew the debate on these subjects by relating them to the contemporary questions of socialism and/or communism. Alongside Badiou's approach, even confining ourselves to France, mention should be made of those of Jacques Bidet, Lucien Sève, Jacques Rancière, the Invisible Committee, Daniel Bensaïd, Emmanuel Terray, Éric Hazan, Michael Löwy and André Tosel.

It seemed logical to devote the first chapter of this book to the oeuvre of Alain Badiou, because he vigorously presents one of the most seductive options today – a resolute anti-statism, now associated with the idea of a non-party politics, inseparable from the redefinition he suggests for the role of philosophy and the communist question. He writes: 'To be brief, let us say that I shall call emancipatory politics any politics that strives to bring about a truth of the collective in the broadest sense of the term, in a modality that is not a state modality. This is the most abstract and most general definition.'[1] Author of a demanding, systematic philosophical oeuvre, which might be deemed monumental, he is one of the most widely read and remarked contemporary French thinkers, but also one of those who evince constant engagement, never renounced. By this token, he is definitely one of the theorists who have proved capable of preserving the activist dimension of a theoretical argument that is never cut off from what is going on in the world and never strays from the desire to intervene in it.

The Hypothesis of a Politics

The following analysis is organized around one question: is Alain Badiou the thinker of a rejuvenated politics and updated communism, reopening the prospect of an exit from capitalism, in the context of our collective crisis? Answering this question involves revisiting the very meaning of the term *politics* in Badiou's oeuvre. Several commentators have stressed the contradiction between the metaphysical orientation of his work and its desire to renew political intervention. Daniel Bensaïd writes: 'detached from its historical conditions, pure diamond of truth, the event according to Badiou . . . is like a miracle. The politics without politics that it commands veers towards negative theology and the aesthetics of politics.'[2] This comment correctly points out Badiou's refusal to have any confrontation with the state and existing institutions and his rejection of the party-form. But it also targets his singular relationship to real history, from which he only adopts certain sequences, the 'strong singularities' or 'events' that punctuate its course, counterposed with the contemporary passion for history and memory. Can these choices be regarded as pertaining to a metaphysical, even theological, transposition of politics?

---

1 Alain Badiou, *Entretiens I*, Paris: Nous, 2011, 230.
2 Daniel Bensaïd, 'Badiou ou le miracle de l'événement', 2001, danielbensaid.org.

We must start by registering Badiou's own response: 'under the rubric of event, my philosophy is also a secularization, a rationalization, of the religious notion of miracle. In this sense, yes, I believe in miracles.'[3] Obviously, every word there acquires new meaning and is inseparable from a radical redefinition of faith as a political or meta-political category. Further, Badiou attributes to Saint Paul's writing 'a new possibility, still not effective for all'.[4] By dint of an identical semantic torsion, the term *politics* likewise changes its meaning: Badiou radicalizes and firms up Marx's distinction between politics in the institutional sense and its revolutionary subversion – a radicalization that in return undermines the ordinary meaning of the word. He writes: 'every communist politics strives for its own disappearance by striving to abolish the separate form of the State in general, even the State that declares itself to be democratic'.[5] At the same time, communism, which has become a 'philosophical, hence eternal, concept of rebellious subjectivity',[6] does not include the roads to its realization, for 'it is not relations of force that count, but the practical processes of thought'.[7] Abandoning the classical question of transitions and the modalities of historical transformation, as well as economic and social contradictions, Badiou opts to bypass existing political forms.

The thesis defended in this chapter is that, far from abandoning the political question in favour of a philosophical retreat, such a rejection of mediations, which is resolutely anti-representative and anti-programmatic, is above all a determinate political option, as well as a redefinition of militant action. Both of these belong to the tradition of 1960s French Maoism, as well as the slipstream of the critical French philosophy of those years and the following decade, as indicated by the following statement: 'The militant figure of politics requires, in its very concept, the unmediated presence (in particular, without parliamentary or trade union mediation) in major sites – factories, housing

3 Alain Badiou, *Images du temps présent*, Paris: Fayard, 2014, 123.

4 Alain Badiou, *Saint Paul. La fondation de l'universalisme*, Paris: Presses Universitaires de France, 2015, 108.

5 Alain Badiou, *Metapolitics*, trans. Jason Barker, New York: Verso, 2005, 80.

6 Alain Badiou, *D'un désastre obscur. Sur la fin de la vérité d'État*, Paris: L'Aube, 1998, 14.

7 Alain Badiou, *Peut-on penser la politique?*, Paris: Éditions du Seuil, 2008, 104.

estates, etc. – of the working-class and popular event.'[8] At the same time, this proposal consists in a singular combination of political intervention and theoretical elaboration, which revisits and transfigures this militant past. It happens that this conception, associated with a high-flying mathematico-logical argument, a creative rereading of poetry and literature but also with a relatively conservative moral position, chimes today with resurgent libertarian tendencies. This composite, unexpected alliance accounts for the fascination exercised by an unclassifiable oeuvre.

An Intellectual and Political Trajectory

Alain Badiou belongs to the generation of French intellectuals active during the 1970s, even though, born in 1937, he is younger than most of them. Furthermore, his celebrity would come much later. His mother was a *normalienne* and an *agrégée de lettres* while his father, Raymond Badiou, was a socialist mayor of Toulouse. Himself a *normalien* and a mathematics graduate, Alain was a great resistance fighter. The young Alain joined the PSU (Unified Socialist Party), of which his father was a founding member, out of hostility towards the SFIO (French Socialist Party), which rallied with de Gaulle during the Algerian War. Alain Badiou stresses the war's significance for him (as for many of his generation) during the initial stages of his political and intellectual career.[9] As a pupil at the École normale supérieure (ENS), he was received in 1960 in the philosophy *agrégation*. At the time, Badiou was one of the young philosophers gathered around Louis Althusser. After 1968, he became one of the pioneering teachers at the young Vincennes University and began to develop an original, ambitious philosophical and literary oeuvre. Despite his relative marginality, he had numerous academic backers, including François Wahl, Georges Canguilhem, Michel Foucault and Michel Serres. By dint of solid institutional anchorage, Badiou obtained a number of prestigious accolades, albeit belatedly. He became co-director with Barbara Cassin of 'L'ordre

8 Ibid., 83.
9 See Alberto Toscano, 'The Name of Algeria: French Philosophy and the Subject of Decolonisation', *Viewpoint Magazine*, 1 February, 2018, viewpointmag.com.

philosophique' collection at Éditions du Seuil, founded in 1964 by Paul Ricoeur and François Wahl, and was appointed a professor at the ENS in 1999.

Alongside this intellectual trajectory, he was intensively militant. In 1969, when Althusser was endeavouring to link a renewal of Marxism with internal critique of the Communist Party, some of his students (including Badiou) set up the Union des communistes de France marxiste-léniniste (UCF-ML), of Maoist observance, which joined two other French Maoist organizations, the Gauche prolétarienne and the Parti communiste marxiste-léniniste de France (PCMLF). In 1985 he founded the Organisation politique with Sylvain Lazarus and Natacha Michel, which renewed this Maoist orientation. The group's manifesto claims that 'every correct idea, at the moment it appears, is borne by a very small number of people', and specifies that 'the militants of the Organisation politique do not stand in any election and do not vote, because this is a clear way of demonstrating that they are absolutely external to the distribution of positions of power in the state'. Registering the failure of the so-called socialist countries, this small organization would devote itself in particular to support for 'illegal' immigrants, while keeping its distance from all parties. The group ultimately dissolved in 2007.

From the 2000s onwards, a series of opuscules entitled *Circonstances* would win Badiou a wider readership and a certain media notoriety. In these short, scathing essays, which are more accessible than his major works but consistent with them, he tackles the politics of Nicolas Sarkozy, the return of the 'communist hypothesis', the evolution of ethics and international political issues. At a time when the revolutionary history of the past has become a deterrent, Badiou continues to identify with some of its episodes, the Chinese Cultural Revolution remaining 'the most promising experience of the twentieth century' even while he acknowledges its failure.[10] With Jacques Rancière, Badiou is one of the last French philosophers born in the interwar period who succeeds in addressing both a specialist audience and a much wider public in search of theoretical and political radicalism.

By virtue of this distinctive itinerary, and despite the divergences and polemics that pitted Badiou against some of his contemporaries (in

---

10 Alain Badiou, *Quel communisme?*, Paris: Bayard, 2015, 8.

particular, Gilles Deleuze and Félix Guattari),[11] for political and theoretical reasons alike (especially over the issues of the subject, the dialectic, truth, as well as relationships to Plato, Hegel and Sartre), we may say that he shares with them the project of redefining relations between philosophy and politics, at a remove from traditional engagement and the academic philosophy of old. On this flank of French intellectual life, politics and philosophy commingle and debate, their confrontation occurring on a terrain where theory helps to fashion both a certain kind of engagement and a rejection of classical activism. The issues of inspection, power, subjection and ideological apparatuses are occasions for advanced theoretical elaboration, in proximity to certain struggles that this philosophy sets out to register, rework and, above all, displace. In this sense, we may consider a certain thread of French philosophy in the 1970s not merely a substitute for an absent practice – and this is especially true of Alain Badiou. His works retain the oppositional, creative spirit of the period, converted into a power of conceptual invention, amid a profound crisis for the whole left.

From this point of view, and despite their differences and divergences, Badiou belongs with the French philosophers of his generation who politicize philosophy at the very point they philosophically refine political questions much more than they undertake their conceptualization. This operation is inseparable from a critical relationship to Marx and Marxism – and this for at least two reasons. The first is that the Marxist tradition, bound up in France with the labour movement, whose intellectual, cultural and political presence remains strong, struggled to take on social and political issues that came to the fore: feminism, anticolonialism, struggles by gays and lesbians, the condition of youth. The second is that this situation induced a crisis in Marxism of both its waning analytical power and especially the proclaimed link between theory and practice, which ossified in its turn. Notwithstanding the calibre of a number of its intellectuals, the Communist Party was at the heart of this divorce between strategic options and theoretical research, without the organizations of the extreme left succeeding in opening up

---

11 See 'Contre Deleuze et Guattari', in *La Situation actuelle sur le front de la philosophie*, 1977, lesmaterialistes.com/files/images/img13/ucfml9.pdf. Badiou subsequently moved closer to Deleuze and devoted a book to him, *Deleuze: The Clamor of Being* (1997), trans. Louise Burchill, Minneapolis: Minnesota University Press, 1999.

new routes. Ultimately, hopes for a political revival took refuge among some of the most brilliant philosophers of the time (Foucault and Deleuze, but also Althusser), fuelling an alternative, paradoxical politicization that accompanied the decline of the labour movement.

This philosophical tradition blossomed in a complex context, which combined contradictory features: the continued power of the Communist Party at the point when the growing discredit of the 'socialist' countries hit it hard; the very real presence of Marxism (albeit small compared with the hegemony frequently attributed to it) when violent questioning of it got underway; the revival of the non-communist left and the French Socialist Party, whose hostility to communism was in no way diminished by the development of the Common Programme for government; the rehabilitation of the old collaborationist elites and technocratic-liberal modernization of French capitalism; significant social mobilizations and long-term depoliticization; liberation wars and neo-colonialism; and widespread rejection of all forms of domination and inequalities of class, race and gender. This landscape, in a state of upheaval when the 'Fordist' sequence seemed to promise lasting stability and growing social equality, helped discredit any revolutionary perspective, replacing it with the thesis of a capitalism permanently pacified and matched on its edges by recharged social contestation. It was only logical that new theoretical perspectives offered themselves for exploration, whereas all earlier theorizations seemed outmoded or in the process of becoming so.

The most original and widely recognized critical philosophers of the moment – particularly Gilles Deleuze, Michel Foucault, Alain Badiou and Jacques Rancière – were positioned outside of traditional parties and on the margins of the university system. They enjoyed media and academic recognition as the former began to replace the latter, in a process that condemned allegedly less-attractive creative Marxists and critical activists to obscurity.[12] The conceptual renewal initiated by these authors who were most visible, while never divorced from political and social investigations, breaks radically with more classically engaged trajectories. It is precisely this concern with a relationship to reality, displaced but invoked, that accounts for the success of more recent

---

12 We might mention Louis Althusser, despite the resonance of his work, and Henri Lefebvre, but also Georges Labica, Michel Verret, André Tosel and Lucien Sève. The major figure who became repellent was Jean-Paul Sartre.

books, especially Badiou's. Adjusting to the present political situation without being merely descriptive, having registered the defeats of the labour movement and the decay of the French left without abandoning opposition to the established order, they revive aspirations and anger that are more than ever in search of perspectives.

For want of an alternative project, or instead of it, Badiou's books encapsulate this political moment and its contradictions with great skill. In short, it is as if a certain French philosophy, elaborated in a period of downturn, had made itself the repository of aspirations and protests which, reawakening and reviving today, recognize themselves in it and are once again looking to it. In Badiou's case, his distinctiveness consists in his engagement in a certain French Maoism that remains the matrix of his theoretical work. A rhetorical politicization, even over-politicization, of theory is thus protected in a dazzling mathematical and logical frame which preserves and displaces its initial strategic principles. That is why we must stress that Badiou's philosophical politics does indeed remain a politics, even if it edulcorates and euphemizes it. It remains to spell out what it consists in.

Theory and Politics of French Maoism

Badiou's very first books shed light on his subsequent oeuvre: *Théorie de la contradiction* and *De l'idéologie* (co-authored with François Balmès) were published by Maspero in 1976. The first text elevated two of Mao's assertions: 'it is right to rebel against reactionaries' – one of the maxims of the Cultural Revolution – and 'one divides into two', a formula stated in 1957 by Mao during an international conference of Communist parties in Moscow. Both texts affirm a certain unity of politics and theory that immediately distinguishes Badiou's thought, by virtue of the pride of place accorded to the dialectic, at the very time it was being violently denounced by non-Marxist philosophers, particularly Deleuze and Foucault. This loyalty to the dialectic survives in Badiou's oeuvre today, at the cost of its formalization and transfer to the terrain of a 'prospective metaphysics',[13] allowing him to reaffirm the project of a

---

13 Alain Badiou, *Logics of Worlds: Being and Event, 2* (2006), trans. Alberto Toscano, London: Continuum, 2009, xxii.

'materialist dialectic'[14] with a nod to 'dialectical materialism': the inversion of Engels's formulation, as well as the adoption of Marx's terms, indicates both the primacy of a reconstructed dialectic and the rectification of a key category of Second and Third International Marxism, also employed by Mao Zedong.

The core of his mathematical and ontological formalization here is Maoism, and the theses of the first two volumes of *Being and Event* can be read as the metaphysical transposition of his political assertions. Thus, the statement that 'one divides into two', by virtue of its extreme generality, can pass from the register of tactics to that of an already implicit ontology. Explanation of the latter leads Badiou to affirm that 'deciding always means filtering the infinite through the two'; in other words, 'to refer the infinite evaluation of nuances back to the simplicity of a choice'[15] connects the scholarly description of a never self-enclosed world to the subjective decisions that it makes possible and demands. Next, this theoretical reprise of politics is authorized through an assertion by Mao himself, framing the 'decisive, principal role' of theory in some cases. This thesis, which echoes the Althusserian concept of 'theoretical practice', chimes here, obviously, not so much with the particular strategy of the Chinese leader as with the readjustment of this Marxism to French intellectual life. It should be stressed that before being activist, this intellectual life is academic and institutional, even if Badiou calls for the disappearance of the state and a revolt against the 'reactionaries of the PCF' and the 'creeps of the CGT'.[16] One way of overcoming this contradiction is once again to invoke Mao's dialectic, whose distinction between principal contradiction and secondary contradictions can encompass every switch in the Chinese political line. In France, it was a key statement of the time, for it made it possible to promote intellectual intervention as full-blown political action, requiring no other form of involvement. Badiou is not the only one to over-politicize philosophical work, in a gesture considered part of the shadow cast by a tendency, which began in the 1960s and departed from the previous period, towards profound depoliticization, impacted by the legacy of the

---

14 Ibid., xix.
15 Ibid., 437.
16 Alain Badiou and François Balmès, *De l'idéologie*, Paris: François Maspero, 1976, 83.

Resistance and large-scale working-class struggles. May '68 only tempo-rarily interrupted this tendency.

Thus, French Maoism, in its very marginality and by dint of its essen-tially intellectual dimension, became the matrix of Badiou's philosophical output in the mid-1970s – an anchorage all the more formative theoreti-cally as it ceased to correspond to any concrete strategic orientation. Almost surreptitiously, this sublimated politics inflected and filled in the formalism of Badiou's philosophy. It authorizes and suggests the striking historical examples suggested by the most abstract, mathematized texts. Reviewing the sequence he baptizes the 'red years' (1966–76), Badiou stresses that, right from the start, reference to Mao was situated on the theoretical terrain and bound up with the resonance in 1960s France of the text *On Contradiction* written by Mao in 1937: 'I would say that basi-cally I found in Maoism something where there was no longer any antin-omy between what mathematics can convey by way of formal and struc-tural transparency, on the one hand, and the protocol of constitution of the subject on the other.'[17]

However, we should note that, alongside this fundamental consist-ency on the most directly political issues of party and state, Badiou's thought has changed considerably since his original publications. This shift is proof that political involvement and attentive analysis of a chang-ing conjuncture are at the heart of his philosophical output, including theses seemingly the most far removed from such concerns. Thus, *De l'idéologie*, at the height of the construction of French Maoism and the diffusion of Chinese Maoism, affirmed the importance of the party along with theory: 'the circuit of revolutionary knowledge, which proceeds from the masses to the masses, comprises at its centre media-tion by the party'.[18] Associated with this assertion was recourse to the notions of ideology and representation, subsequently doomed not merely to disappear, but to be repudiated: 'it is because a practice exists which cannot be represented in the dominant ideology (class revolu-tionary rebellion) that the latter is intelligible as representation'.[19]

How should we take the subsequent rejection of the notions of ideology, representation, mediation and party, the last three terms

---

17 Interview with Bruno Bosteels, *Failles* 2, 2006, 70.
18 Badiou and Balmès, *De l'idéologie*, 120.
19 Ibid., 42.

being subject to violent denunciation? We may find the cause of this reversal in the rapid decline of French Maoism, which collapsed without any hope of broadening its social base while leaving intact a denunciation of rival structures and of the state that is not peculiar to this tradition. For if these execrated notions pertained to a strategic road that was henceforth barred, this political failure, transposed onto a theoretical plane, was converted into an impetus prompting the redefinition and reinvention of some elements of the earlier analysis, rendering them consistent with the thesis of 'communist invariants' that likewise dates from 1976. Badiou would also retain the claim that Marxism is not predominantly a class philosophy, but a party philosophy, with the idea of party subsequently losing its initially positive connotations from his pen. In a sense, if it is true that 'proletarian organization is the body of the new logic',[20] the new logic is the theoretical equivalent of proletarian organization in the era of its recession. It thus seems that, by virtue of this very political failure, Badiou's first books provide the momentum and agenda for a large-scale philosophical reconstruction. The oeuvre that emerges effects a successful ontological construction of this failed politics, even if, ten years after these initial reflections, the Organisation politique will attempt to restore their concrete activist relevance.

That is why we can maintain that the power of Badiou's oeuvre derives from this principle of generating his own theses – a principle located at the intersection of theoretical ambition and a will to political intervention. However, his originality consists less in the displacement of politics onto philosophical ground, which characterizes a number of trajectories contemporaneous with his, than in the constant, crucial maintenance of authentically political concerns, which continue to inhabit his driest books. It must be added that the utterly distinctive dynamic of Badiou's intellectual output has become opaque to present-day readers, redoubling the fascination people can experience in reading an oeuvre that is occasionally precious and hermetic but which retains a staggering capacity to speak powerfully of history and the present, as well as a widely discredited revolutionary perspective. This initiative has precedents: Marx analysed in Hegel – one of Badiou's major philosophical reference points – the speculative tour de force that consisted in

---

20 Ibid., 107.

deducing the real fruit from the idea of Fruit, precisely because the Idea had previously and surreptitiously been abstracted from reality.[21] Badiou's treatment of the questions of state and party, communism and representation, attests to this logic of intervention internal to the work itself, at the same time as it allows him to deal with contemporary political questions and issues in an extremely acute way.

Communism against the State

The relationship to the state is one of the main axes of division between the various projects of social transformation, debated in the Marxist tradition since its inception. This issue retains a pronounced theoretical and strategic dimension. It involves explaining the capitalist state, its transformations and its contradictions, but also spelling out the strategic project in its conquest, radical transformation or destruction, in conjunction with recasting the totality of the forms and objectives of social organization. In contemporary critical theory, we are witnessing the rise of libertarian options, all the more readily restored to fashion in that they correspond to the decline of comprehensive political projects and the adoption of the old accusation of statism levelled against Marx by Bakunin.[22] This approach skirts the fundamental discussion about the functions and transformation of the neoliberal state and the prospect of its replacement by a democratic reorganization and planning of economic and social life. What prevails is the thesis of its pure and simple circumvention, proposing to *Change the World without Taking Power*, as the title of John Holloway's successful book has it.[23]

However, three main points render it urgent to reopen this discussion. First, this legacy is simplified and impoverished, Marx and Marxism being credited with a crude statism conducive to their

---

21 See *The Holy Family*, in Karl Marx and Friedrich Engels, *Collected Works*, Vol. 4, London: Lawrence & Wishart, 1975, 57–61.

22 Michael Bakunin, *Statism and Anarchy*, trans. and ed. Marshall Shatz, Cambridge: Cambridge University Press, 1990. For an analysis of the clash between Bakunin and Marx in the First International, see Mathieu Léonard, *L'émancipation des travailleurs. Une histoire de la Première Internationale*, Paris: La Fabrique, 2011.

23 London: Pluto Press, 2002.

misrecognition and dwindling of their influence. Second, subsequent discussions of the subject, informed by the historical experiences of the twentieth century, are generally forgotten or discredited despite their richness. Finally, the state is today the target of neoliberal theorizations and policies, which primarily denounce the welfare state. They compel the labour movement to defend old gains while experiencing the utmost difficulty in redefining the missions of political and social institutions offensively and innovatively. The degraded social and ideological balance of power obstructs renewal of their analysis along with the project of their radical transformation.

At once inheritor of this situation and original, Badiou's treatment of the issue of the state encapsulates his conceptions of politics and communism as well as his relation to Marx and Marxism. Already in *De l'idéologie*, he included among the 'communist invariants' the contradiction between 'the masses and the state', which indicated that these invariants had 'no definite class character'.[24] However, refusal of the state soon came to be presented as an alternative to struggle against the state. Faced with receding revolutionary prospects, systematic circumvention of the state became the key maxim of a post-Maoist politics, which was basically redefined by this attempt at evasion, formalized as an operation of subtraction: 'politics is what attempts operations of subtraction, even if local, from the dominion of the state, or what attempts to establish in the space of collective action a distance defended and secured from the super-power of the state'.[25] Here, Badiou gravitates towards theorizations by his contemporaries, notably Foucault's challenging the centrality of the state and endeavouring to think on the diffraction and social diffusion of power, or Deleuze and Guattari's defining the state as a trans-historical 'machine' seeking to block and channel the flows that incessantly flood it. However, on this point as on others, Badiou creates his theoretical distinctiveness around his own abiding political options: his critique of the state has as its matrix the campaign launched in 1966 by Mao against Communist 'bureaucrats'. According to Badiou, the Cultural Revolution aimed to maintain and relaunch the popular movement conceived as a sustainable dynamic and as an immediately political mode of existence of the

---

24 Badiou and Balmès, *De l'idéologie*, 67.
25 Badiou, *Entretiens, I*, 230.

social body, far removed from any mediation or representation, which are in essence deadly.[26] This analysis aligns him with the Sartre of *Critique of Dialectical Reason*, who defined the 'practico-inert' mode of degeneration of popular political intervention, once collective mobilization gives way to a structuration that blocks it and then rebounds against its initial momentum.[27]

Badiou's critique of the state sticks to rejecting all ossified structures of domination, adopting an already old denunciation of bureaucracy as an uncontrollable tendency immanent in any organization. But it must be stressed that at no point did he join the anti-authoritarian tradition on the rise in France at the time, which developed this critique and linked Nazism, Stalinism and Communism via the notion of totalitarianism – a powerful weapon of ideological warfare. Badiou makes it clear that 'it must be clearly recognized that the socialist states, which advocated global communism, are not the same thing as people who advocate the superiority of the German race over all others'.[28] The relative decline of anti-totalitarianism today, on account of the disappearance of the socialist camp and the profound discredit into which neoliberal state institutions have fallen, explains why political positions like Badiou's, worked out in a different historical context and in a tiny minority in their time, can now resonate with the concerns of readers seeking new analytical tools capable of nurturing original political perspectives. According to Badiou, this relevance stems from the acuteness of his earlier analyses: 'we . . . are the contemporaries of the problem revealed by May '68: the classical figure of the politics of emancipation was ineffective. Those of us who were politically active in the 1960s and 1970s did not need the collapse of the USSR to teach us that.'[29] In short, the detours of history in recent decades supposedly ended up confirming

---

26 According to Badiou, Mao thus initiated a fundamentally anti-bureaucratic movement, despite the fact that the campaign precisely spared the top leader of the Chinese Communist Party and state, the only one in a position to launch it and stop it as and when he decided. This second thesis is defended by Lucien Bianco in *Les Origines de la révolution chinoise 1915–1949*, Paris: Gallimard, 2007, 373.

27 Obviously, the critique of bureaucratization is older. In particular, it was developed by the Left Opposition to Stalinism, but also by Robert Michels, pioneer of the analysis of oligarchical tendencies in modern political parties.

28 Badiou, *Quel communisme?*, 89.

29 Alain Badiou, *The Communist Hypothesis* (2009), trans. David Macey and Steve Corcoran, London: Verso, 2015, 47.

the analyses produced by the Organisation politique, bearing in particular on the failure of the Cultural Revolution and, more generally, on the relationship between mass movement, party and state.[30]

In this optic, the statist drift crowns the failure of emancipatory politics, suffocated by the parliamentary and bureaucratic logic of socialisms, unlike a communism redefined as incessantly resurgent event, as revolution at once permanent and intermittent, with Badiou casting himself as the thinker of the infinite resilience of insurrectionary communism. The socialist states are the primary targets of this approach, whereas analysis of the capitalist state and its transformations remains neglected: 'People referred to the "socialist" states. This figure reminds us that communism is first and foremost a movement. Perhaps Mao said it most clearly: "without a communist movement, no communism". Hence communism cannot be a form of power strictly speaking, but must be a movement.'[31] But praise for enduring momentum quickly turns into systematic denunciation of every structure of the labour movement, be it party or trade union, defined as representatives in the narrowly delegated sense – a denunciation accompanied by an apologia for local experiments, out of synch with the general analysis from which it flows. This rejection of the state takes the form of its theoretical circumvention, skipping analysis of its specific contemporary reality as well as the conditions of concrete intervention in the existing political field. The declaration of the principles of the Organisation politique states that it 'is not an oppositional organization, it is not on the left of the left, or on the extreme left. In our view it is impossible to oppose this politics from within this politics.'[32] Local activism and ontological elaboration remain the only two feasible ways of absolute dissidence.

In the course of this analysis, Badiou naturally comes to the theme of the 'smashing of the state', placed by Marx at the heart of the communist project. What he develops is the critique of this thesis, tacitly adopting

---

30 Article 12 of 'Qu'est-ce que l'Organisation politique?' claims: 'a politics that is fashioned starting from people, from the idea that people think, is organized (politics is always collective and organized). That is why there is an Organisation politique. But it is not a party. We do not seek any position of power or place in the opposition waiting to replace the current government. We never stand in any election. We work in real situations, such as workers' hostels or factories, or certain international situations, or certain debates.'

31 Badiou, *Quel communisme?*, 60.

32 'Qu'est-ce que l'Organisation politique?'

the reading advanced by Raymond Aron – a reading of which one finds the manifest trace, never avowed, among a number of left-wing critical readers of Marx from this generation.[33] Following Aron, Badiou affirms the composite character of Marx's oeuvre. According to him, the part concerning economic categories 'does not pertain to politics',[34] with the result that analysis and revolution remain separated.[35] The theme of smashing the state is thus separated from the rest of Marx's analysis, in particular from two of its essential parts. On the one hand, the issue of the formation of the capitalist state as a specialist functional instance is eliminated. Its separation from civil society no longer corresponds, as in Marx, to a way of specializing and confiscating the political function, while as a minimum regulating the chaos of private interests and class struggles – and that in the interest of the dominant class, as Nicos Poulantzas stressed – is reduced to an aberrant autonomization. On the other hand, and consequently, the issue of the maintenance and radical redefinition of a central, public decision-making body, conceived as a non-state but democratic coordinating instance, disappears. It is only logical that the episode of the Paris Commune should be at the heart of the debate, inasmuch as for Marx it embodied the project of an alternative organization of this kind, whereas for Badiou, it constitutes the quintessential counter-statist, anti-representative event. According to him, Marx's analysis of the Commune proves that, for want of being utterly consistent, Marx ended up relapsing into statism. Criticizing the Commune for its 'statist incapacities: its weak military centralization; its

---

33 Raymond Aron writes: 'The objectivist vision which invokes the laws of history involves the essential difficulty of declaring an undated and unspecified event to be inevitable; the dialectical interpretation can assert neither the necessity for revolution nor the nonantagonistic character of postcapitalist society nor the all-embracing character of historical interpretation' (*Main Currents in Sociological Thought*, Vol. 1, trans. Richard Howard and Helen Weaver, New York: Routledge, 2019, 156). Following this, Aron attributes these options to a Kantian school and a Hegelian school within Marxism. For his part, Badiou describes 'the war between analytical and dialectical, which was the war internal to Marxism, between those who thought that the economy enjoyed primacy . . . and those who thought that political action had primacy' (*Quel communisme?*, 49). This analysis, which clearly presents certain political debates after Marx's death, while simplifying them, is retro-projected onto Marx's oeuvre, attributing to him a basic inconsistency that would be the source of the war internal to political Marxism.

34 Badiou, *Entretiens, I*, 147.

35 Badiou, *Quel communisme?*, 43.

inability to define financial priorities; and its shortcomings concerning the national question',[36] Marx revealed himself to be an uneasy thinker of the rupture with the state, whose hesitations and ambiguities paved the way for the party structure as theorized after him by German social democracy and then by Lenin.

The Curse of Representation

Badiou is therefore seeking to be more consistent than Marx, but in and through basic fidelity to the latter's original inspiration, as revealed by Badiou's early works: the triple rejection of state, programme and representation, whose triad evokes the contours of communism. This critique targets the nature of the bourgeois state apparatus but also, more indirectly, any central instance of control and administration, any democratic structure, even federal. In *The Communist Hypothesis*, written in 2009, Badiou claims, amazingly, that Marx's analysis leads to the definition of the party as 'free in relation to the state and in a position to exercise power'.[37] This state 'bears the thematic of a new state, the state of the dictatorship of the proletariat'.[38] Yet Marx does not at any point define the 'party' in the modern sense of the term, which did not exist in his day. In addition, it is the mature Marx who was most insistent on smashing the state and abandoning the perspective of its mere 'withering away'.[39] In *Quel communisme?*, written in 2015, Badiou corrects the first point in his analysis: 'There is a very precise passage in Marx's *Manifesto* that I always recall. Marx says that the communists are not a separate part of the general working-class movement.'[40] Badiou concedes that 'the idea of a party of the proletariat is certainly not an idea of Marx's',[41] and this because for Marx the proletariat is 'what could not be represented'.[42]

---

36 Badiou, *The Communist Hypothesis*, 135.
37 Ibid., 136.
38 Ibid., 137.
39 See Stathis Kouvélakis, 'La forme politique de l'émancipation', in Jean-Numa Ducange and Isabelle Garo, eds, *Marx politique*, Paris: La Dispute, 2015, 59.
40 Badiou, *Quel communisme?*, 92.
41 Ibid., 91.
42 Ibid., 105.

The next chapter, devoted to Ernesto Laclau, will confirm this point: following the thread on representation – which is seemingly subordinate but, in reality, located at the intersection of theoretical and political questions – makes it possible to identify a point of bifurcation between two strategic options. What do these two ways consist of? For Marx, the Commune was at once a proletarian revolution and a new conception of politics, and therewith of representation, redefined as a political form situated outside the narrowly parliamentary framework: 'If the Commune was therefore the genuine representation of all the healthy elements in French society, and therefore the genuine national government, it was at the same time a working-class government',[43] and by that same token, of international significance. Marx next evokes the 'genuine representatives' who emerge in any revolution.[44] Between 'representation' and 'genuine representation' is established not an unbridgeable gap but a process – that of the democratic transmutation of politics, enabling a transition from the capitalist state to workers' 'self-government'. This process radically reconfigures representation, transforming it into the relay of local decisions, under the control of the working class and the people, in accordance with a federal construction whose model is furnished by the Commune.

For his part, Badiou develops a general, radical critique of representation that coincides with his definition of politics. In effect, his definition of representation, strangely de-dialecticized and regressive compared with the critique Hegel had made of it,[45] reduces it to a systematically deadly, paralysing dynamic, whereas, by contrast, 'proletarian political capacity, called communist, is absolutely mobile, non-statist, unfixable. It is not open to being represented or drifting from the order that it exceeds'.[46] Politically, rejection of representation chimes with valorisation of the event, which is never structured but always reborn out of its ashes. The main concrete consequence of this analysis, and thus in truth

---

43 Ibid., 71.

44 Ibid., 74.

45 For Hegel, representation pertains to the thought of understanding, separating producing images from its objects. It is destined to be overcome by reason and its living recapture of the whole. However, understanding is a constitutive moment in knowledge, a 'labour of the negative' that is itself worked from within by the necessity of the transition to the concept and to reason. Dismissing it leads only to romantic illusions of immediate, sentimental fusion with the world.

46 Badiou, *Peut-on penser la politique?*, 25.

its origin, is the rejection of any electoral procedure and condemnation, in principle, of any institutional structuration, conceived systematically as the blockage of an original movement, the hijacking of an emancipation that is underway. Envisaged as permanent mobilization, communism only exists as historical convulsion, not as an established alternative. This conception abuts a fundamental historical pessimism.

This universal thesis pertains to an ontology of history. Bound up in power dynamics, the demonization of representation reconnects with its Platonic, rather than its Rousseauist, origin. But this critique prevents thinking about non-delegated forms of representation, associated with the control and revocability of elected officials. Remote from any investigation of what the collective, radically democratized institutions of communism might be, Badiou develops a critique of democracy that mingles philosophy and moralism, with his neo-Platonism occasionally approximating some of the theses of contemporary conservative thought: 'the democratic norm is the paradigmatic youth and the old man in joggers who runs behind'.[47] Badiou proposes the term 'capitalo-parliamentarianism'[48] to designate what he deems to be a fatal subordination to 'the autonomy of capital, property-owners, the market'.[49] But in equating the dominant relations of production with political forms that are irreducible to them, because they are engendered by class struggles that have imparted an emancipatory significance to them, it becomes impossible to think democratization as one of the major issues of contemporary political struggle. Retreat to exclusive denunciation of commodification, added to the abandonment of concrete issues of labour, exploitation and domination, authorizes and conceals this circumvention.

The recourse to philosophy is the other side of this abandonment, leading, on occasion, to the adoption of Heideggerian accents: 'democracy and totalitarianism are the two epochal versions of the fulfilment of politics, in the dual category of the bond and representation'.[50] In each case, political reflection on the conditions of, and roads to, self-government is abandoned, in favour of increasing abstraction that at

---

47 Badiou, *Images du temps présent*, 81.
48 Alain Badiou, *Second manifeste pour la philosophie*, Paris: Flammarion, 2010, 115.
49 Badiou, *D'un désastre obscur*, 36–7.
50 Badiou, *Peut-on penser la politique?*, 17.

once simplifies and accentuates cleavages, dramatizes and euphemizes them, politicizes and ontologizes them: the philosophical transmutation of the questions of party, state and event aims to authorize their axiomatization. Badiou writes: 'the essence of politics is to exclude representation and never to have as its figure the programmatic consciousness. Its essence consists wholly in fidelity to the event as it materializes in the network of interventions.'[51] This critique, developed in the first volume of *Being and Event*, counterposes presentation and representation while affirming the ontological character of mathematics or, more exactly, with the idea that 'mathematics . . . pronounces what is expressible of being qua being.'[52]

Immediately installing this statement on the terrain of philosophy and its history, Badiou opposes to Heidegger's theses 'the radically subtractive dimension of being, foreclosed not only from representation but from all presentation.'[53] Appearances notwithstanding, there is a direct link between this statement and political issues. For Badiou's thought does not move from politics to metaphysics, as his critics frequently allege, but from politics to politics via its metaphysical purification and ontological guarantee, which serve as substitutes for practical validation. It is then scarcely surprising that the main categories of politics inherited from Maoism – intervention, investigation, subject, truth and so on – often find an exact correlate on the ontological plane, where they are reworked but also renewed in their initial political sense, magnified and strengthened by this transmutation. As for communism, its definition as Idea is in line with this work where ontology and politics are mutually supportive. Whereas Marx envisaged an 'exit from philosophy' at the same time as the construction of a 'true democracy' on the ruins of the capitalist state, Badiou returns to philosophy the better to dismiss any concrete reworking of the democratic form and replaces it simply with the perspective of a 'subtraction from the state'.

This ascending dialectic, in the Platonic sense (from reality to the Idea), combines with its descending moment (from the Idea to reality) abstractions and invariants connecting with their real correlates and

---

51 Ibid., 82.
52 Alain Badiou, *Being and Event* (1988), trans. Oliver Feltham, London: Continuum, 2006, 8.
53 Ibid., 10.

seeming to generate them in quasi-demiurgic fashion. Far from being the historical illustration of a debatable thesis, any revolutionary upsurge becomes the embodiment of a principle demonstrated by the example. Badiou adopts an inversion of metaphysics that retains its procedures: 'Ordinarily, conceptual construction is reserved for structures whilst the event is rejected into the pure empiricity of what-happens. My method is the inverse.'[54] Consequently, the singularity of the event is in no way incompatible with its universality – on the contrary, Badiou's dialectic is constructed here in the vicinity of Hegel's *Science of Logic*, but also Saint Paul's preaching, and it is far removed from its Marxist inversion.[55] It is not based on an analysis of concrete historical contradictions, but formulated in the formal, mathematical terms of a theory of the unprecedented event: 'a multiple which is an object of this world . . . is a "site" if it happens to count itself in the referential field of its own indexing.'[56]

Crisis of Foundations and Ontology

The question of form becomes the core of a new dialectic, authorizing in an original fashion the connection between abstraction and revolution, mathematics and politics: 'the proletariat is the greatest formal power in history', Badiou wrote in 1976.[57] This unprecedented enterprise of formalizing revolutionary political thought calls for its justification. It is precisely at this point that a philosophical construct founded on its own theses becomes self-contained and disseminates this self-foundation to history, basing itself on a philosophical reinterpretation of set theory. Marx had sought to invert Hegelian logic and Badiou inverts this inversion, using mathematics as a means for a metaphysical reworking that does not speak its name, while invoking a materialism that is itself radically redefined. Communism thus takes the place of Hegel's rational state, while finding itself detached from the Hegelian conception of the Whole in favour of the promotion of the local and singularity. Thus, Badiou's anti-statism can be an ontological position at the same time as

54 Ibid., 178.
55 Badiou, *Saint Paul*, 16.
56 Badiou, *Logics of Worlds*, 363.
57 Badiou and Balmès, *De l'idéologie*, 96.

a political thesis: 'we share with Hegel a conviction about the identity if being and thought. But for us this identity is a local occurrence and not a totalized result.'[58] Set theory converts the Hegelian totality into pure multiplicity, making it legitimate to think decision and truth, action and event, together. The first of the decisions is to proclaim that the event is a 'pure cut in becoming'[59] and to attribute effectivity to this assertion.

Within this construct, Badiou diametrically opposes situation and form, event and representation, movement and power, without ever considering their various actual historical articulations. The upshot is that communism is not a different mode of production, but this very break, 'better understood as an operation than as a concept.'[60] Referring to the Marx of the 1844 *Manuscripts*, Badiou writes: 'every communist politics strives for its own disappearance by striving to abolish the separate form of the State in general, even the State that declares itself to be democratic.'[61] For Badiou, the state only ever appears as a parasitic excrescence, essentially coercive, even a police state, just like parties, which are mere machines enslaved to electoral logic, in contrast to being popular practices that are supposedly recalcitrant to any structuration and institutionalization.

Given this, a politics that does not refer to the state is both possible and necessary, the only kind that makes it possible to rediscover politics in its essence. Even if we set aside the schematic character of the contrast between mobilization and institution, we can criticize Badiou for evading the issue over which the revolutionary processes of the twentieth century, China included, faltered: that of the modalities and moments of a transformation of state power, which is necessarily long-term, taking the form of a process of transition that combines de-statization and radical democratization. In its stead we find a radical critique of Marxism. In *Peut-on penser la politique?*, Badiou describes the condition of Marxism in ways that are once again quasi-Heideggerian: 'Marxism is not dead today, it is historically destroyed. But there is a being of this destruction. More precisely, it is possible, and necessary, to stand in the immanence of destruction.'[62] He reiterated the point in

---

58 Badiou, *Logics of Worlds*, 143.
59 Ibid., 384.
60 Badiou, *The Communist Hypothesis*, 178.
61 Badiou, *Metapolitics*, 80.
62 Badiou, *Peut-on penser la politique?*, 52.

2017: 'if "Marxism" designates a politics, it does so in the singular complication that it designates it as the process of its own disappearance'.[63] In that it is 'the life of a hypothesis',[64] Marxism does not have to be 'defended' as a corpus, being no more than 'statist survival, an apparatus of big parties, big unions, politically monstrous and philosophically sterile'.[65]

Pitted against this strange vision of a monolithic Marxism, institutional and dogmatic, 'its own Hegelianism',[66] which dispenses with discussing its many versions and consideration of its internal debates, is the possibility of its strictly political reactivation, in the sense given the term by Badiou. It involves a radical distancing from any critique of political economy, including in terms of style and concepts:

> [E]conomics, the critique of which was to weave what exceeds it absolutely in a singular point, was the bias whereby Marxist politics, which is the interpretative precarity of working-class consciousness, which is the release, in a vulnerable cleavage, of a previously unseen political capacity, found itself nailed down in the form of a particular doctrine of the political.[67]

If this sophisticated formulation seems enigmatic, its target is clear: it involves opposing politics and economics, as action and doctrine, as a poeticized ontology of becoming faced with a vulgarly prosaic description of the state of things.

This point is particularly important: in denouncing a post-Marxian economism, which was sometimes especially neglectful of political questions in favour of a determinist reading of history, Badiou sets about rejecting any critique of political economy *en bloc* – that is to say, avoiding an analysis of capitalism in its modus operandi, its dynamics and contradictions. The definition of the word *politics* is what is at stake, leading to a dichotomy between a conception of insurrectionary

---

63 Alain Badiou, *Qu'est-ce que j'entends par marxisme?*, Paris: Éditions Sociales, 2017, 27.

64 Badiou, *Peut-on penser la politique?*, 53.

65 Ibid., 54.

66 Ibid., 61.

67 Ibid., 14.

intervention, even 'revolutionary civil war',[68] and reflection on the articulation between tendencies of the capitalist process, social mobilization,
political struggles and the invention of genuinely democratic forms of
collective life. To justify this cleavage, rendered absolute, Badiou recalls
that for Mao 'political decision is not fettered by the economy'[69] and
affirms the absence of any 'political subject' in what is called Marx's
'economic' oeuvre: 'Marx stopped *Capital* at the point he reached the
concept of class'[70] – an assertion of Althusserian provenance to which a
number of objections might be adduced.[71]

In his opuscule of 2017 devoted to Marxism, Badiou takes up this
thesis, stressing the importance of practice and opposed to academic
definitions of Marxism but also its dimension of positive knowledge:
'Marxism is not lodged in ready-made compartments, like "philosophy",
"economics" or "political theory". In truth, for me Marxism is the
constantly renewed invention of a practice of politics.' As a result, curi-
ously, 'the essence of politics is the meeting.'[72] This welcome repoliticization, on a reduced scale, has as its largely invisible converse the essential
distance taken from analysis of capitalism and its concrete contradictions – an analysis abandoned by Badiou's oeuvre and replaced with an
ontology directly connected to a politics whose categories it reformu-
lates while hypostasizing them. The result is a promotion of the 'communist idea'. Whereas for Marx communism is the always concrete political
construction of an exit from capitalism, based on its contradictions and
gains but also on knowledge of a specific kind, communism as Badiou
conceives it is, above all, a break and organizing practice, independent
of the construction of a new mode of production and new configuration
of the economic and social world. Paradoxically, its status as Idea
expresses the profound caesura introduced by Badiou between political
project and theoretical critique, despite the repeated assertion of the
identity of thinking and acting.

---

68 Alain Badiou, *Théorie du sujet*, Paris: Éditions du Seuil, 1982, 33.
69 Badiou, *Logics of Worlds*, 23.
70 Badiou, *Quel communisme?*, 43.
71 See Chapter 4.
72 Badiou, *Qu'est-ce que j'entends par marxisme?*, 61.

Communism, Which Idea?

A different active politics is therefore implied by the hypothesis of the existence and persistence of the communist Idea as Idea. It does not involve establishing the pre-eminence of the Idea over, and against, reality, despite frequent objections to that effect. According to Badiou, the Idea is not a norm external to the historical process, but an immanent norm whose resurgences punctuate history at the same rhythm as its repeated failures. Thus redefined, the term *communism* refers to 'everything in politics that concerns the emancipation of humanity as a whole, and hence the possibility that something of collective life has a universal value'.[73] The modality peculiar to the Idea is not realization but manifestation, defeats not preventing but guaranteeing its eternal return – and its eternal rout. Despite the gap between the programme of deconstruction and the development of a formalized ontology, here Badiou is close to that other philosopher of the event, Derrida, whose resolutely messianic conception permits and heralds an effective occurrence: 'the effectivity or actuality of the democratic promise, like that of the communist promise, will always keep within it, and it must do so, this absolutely undetermined messianic hope at its heart, this eschatological relation to the to-come of an event *and* of a singularity, of an alterity that cannot be anticipated'.[74]

Three major books, monumental and difficult, apply themselves to the construction of this 'prospective metaphysics'.[75] The first, *Theory of the Subject*, published in 1982, reaffirms the validity of the notion of the subject contrary to its general deposition by the philosophy of the period and the whole structuralist tradition in the social sciences. From the angle of the political subject, this reworking leads Badiou to propose a rereading of Hegel and Lacan (himself a great reader of Hegel), which by the same token outlines anew the contours of the dialectic and the communist question. *Being and Event*, published in 1988, defines philosophy as the exploration of truth procedures of an eventful kind, beyond the epistemological dimension in which the term *truth* is

---

73 Badiou, *Quel communisme?*, 55.
74 Jacques Derrida, *Specters of Marx*, trans. Peggy Kamuf, New York: Routledge, 1994, 81.
75 Badiou, *Logics of Worlds*, 7.

generally imprisoned. Consequently, what Badiou identifies with is a unique 'Platonism of the multiple'.[76] The second volume of *Being and Event*, entitled *Logics of Worlds*, is presented as a study of coming-into-being, or being-there, the logic of being taking over from the ontology of being developed in the first volume, in accordance with divisions adopted from the Hegelian system.[77]

In *Logics of Worlds*, Badiou further clarifies his definition of history, in conjunction with the conceptions developed in *Theory of the Subject*, so that he can affirm that 'there is a subject only as the subject of a truth'[78] or that 'the faithful subject is nothing but the activation of the present of the truth under consideration'.[79] At the heart of this systematic philosophical construct, Badiou outlines an analysis of subjectivation with ethical accents. Against what he calls 'democratic materialism', the contemporary culture of bodies, relativism and scepticism, he aims to reinvent a 'materialist dialectic' whose core proposition is that 'there are only bodies and languages, except that there are truths'[80] – a thesis whose inscription in the tradition of materialism may be regarded as less than self-evident, and this is so even if the notion of truth is now broached in its connection to a definite world: 'I give the name "truths" to real processes which, as subtracted as they may be from the pragmatic opposition of bodies and languages, are nonetheless in the world.'[81] Badiou repeats that '"mathematics" and "being" are one and the same thing' and that it is a question of showing that '"logic" and "appearing" are also one and the same thing'.[82]

The book ends with a meditation on the question 'What is it to Live?', proclaiming magnificently: 'we will only be consigned to the form of the disenchanted animal for whom the commodity is the only reference-point if we consent to it. But we are shielded from this consent by the

---

76 Alain Badiou, *Manifesto for Philosophy* (1989), trans. Norman Madarasz, New York: State University of New York Press, 1999, 103.

77 As this book was being written, the third and final volume of *Being and Event* was about to appear. See now Alain Badiou, *The Immanence of Truths: Being and Event, III*, trans. Kenneth Reinhard and Susan Spitzer, London: Bloomsbury Academic, 2022.

78 Badiou, *Logics of Worlds*, 50.

79 Ibid., 72.

80 Ibid., 4.

81 Ibid., 9.

82 Ibid., 100.

Idea, the secret of the pure present.'[83] Yet Marx's positing of the subject as an individual aspiring to emancipation disappears, along with the issues of the social alienation of the producers and social relations of sex and race. Instead of a concrete analysis of the modes of constitution of individuality, we find a typology that combines subjects and truths, distinguishing three general figures of the subject – faithful, reactive, obscure – differentiated by their specific relations to politics, love, art and science. No contradiction haunts these subject types, whose relation to labour and social relations is of no import and whose schematic character stands in stark contrast to the subtlety of the analyses conducted.

General considerations of the 'true life' follow that strangely extend the dominant norms by dint of capitalism's putative capacity 'to fashion a subjectivity that corresponds to it'.[84] Thus there allegedly exist 'fashionable sexualities', which ignore the fact that 'sexual duality' makes 'the multiple appear before the Two of a choice',[85] this thesis outlining a critique of homosexuality that is not ethical but ontological. More classically, Badiou argues that the risk of 'de-symbolization' is increasing, old refrain of reactionary ideologies: 'the exit from tradition, as realized by capitalism . . . does not in reality propose any active symbolization, but only the brutal, independent operation of the economy, the neutral, a-symbolic reign of what Marx magnificently called "the icy water of egotistical calculation"'.[86] This peremptory anthropology is formulated affirmatively and under the cover of Lacanian authority, whose essentializations might be reckoned as dubious as they are decidedly non-emancipatory:[87] 'We shall adopt the logic of the Two, of the passing-between-two as what defines femininity. This femininity is opposed to the strong assertion of the One, of the single power, which characterizes the traditional masculine position. Masculine logic is encapsulated in the absolute unity of the Name of the Father.'[88] This

---

83 Ibid., 514.

84 Alain Badiou and Alan Finkielkraut, L'explication, Paris: Lignes, 2010, 143.

85 Badiou, Logics of Worlds, 421.

86 Alain Badiou, La Vraie Vie, Paris: Fayard, 2017, 44–5.

87 See Éric Delruelle, 'La "bonne nature" du Symbolique: sur quelques équivoques de l'anthropologie française contemporaine', in P. Durand and S. Simalco, eds, Le Discours néo-réactionnaire, Paris: CNRS, 2015, 219ff.

88 Badiou, La Vraie Vie, 103.

proximity to certain neo-reactionary theses, notwithstanding Badiou's visceral attachment to equality,[89] leads him to partially concede to Alain Finkielkraut his critique of democracy, as well as that of May '68, quartermaster of the 'general substitutability of opinions, objects and bodies',[90] but without compromising on the rest.

The Event against Causality

All told, this project leads Badiou to pursue an imposing and complex formalized analysis of politics, one which is often more intimidating than genuinely convincing. His thesis, based on the unproven assertion of the ontological nature of mathematics, struggles to persuade us that the basic ontological question 'why can a body exist in this world?' could truly clarify a strategic question like the one raised by Mao on 5 October 1928: *Why Is It That Red Political Power Can Exist in China?*[91]

Understanding Badiou's analysis is not automatic. It assumes a sustained, profound reading of an oeuvre that demands a solid philosophical and mathematical culture. In addition, it involves conceding the possibility and utility of two operations: an ontologization of the political and a mathematization of ontology. Politics and its redefinition are at the heart of this theoretical construct, combining proximity to and distance from Marx.

Thus, when it comes to revolutionary history, Badiou proposes to reserve the term 'event' for cases of strong singularities whose consequences are 'maximal', far beyond the brief duration of the Communard insurrection itself, to cite a recurrent example of Badiou's. It creates distant, belated echoes and reprises – in October 1917 in Russia, during summer 1967 in China or in May '68: 'commencements are to be measured by the re-commencements they enable'.[92] An event of this kind, despite the repression of the Commune and its failure, consists in the destruction of 'the political subordination of the workers and the people. What was destroyed was of the order of subjective incapacity'.[93]

89 Badiou and Finkielkraut, *L'explication*, 122–5.
90 Ibid., 138.
91 Badiou, *Logics of Worlds*, 493.
92 Ibid., 375.
93 Ibid., 379.

And this event lives on: 'it is this destruction that the Paris Commune carries out for the future, even in the apparent putting to death of its own over-existence'.[94] As a pure interruption in becoming, an event is 'neither past nor future. It presents us with the present', which comes down to saying that it is neither cause nor effect, but 'act' or 'actant'.[95]

Badiou names such a singularity – which breaks with any linearity and, above all, consists in a mutation in the logic of the existing world – 'event'. To define this logical rupture, Badiou resorts to set theory and Russell and Zermelo's paradox, without ever justifying the parallel thus established between the mathematical crisis of foundations and its transposition to political history. Doubtless, this lack of justification weakens his thesis, but it likewise poeticizes it, by virtue of the unanticipated analogy it introduces between two disparate orders of thought. This way of doing things allows Badiou to exploit the formidable power of modern and contemporary mathematical thought, knowledge of which, not widespread, is inversely proportional to the respect and awe it elicits. Paradoxically, neoliberal economists and Badiou join in banking on its legitimizing power, which confers a superior aura on their hypotheses without actually shoring them up.

Redefined as a 'paradox of being',[96] the event no longer has anything of the simple fact about it, interlacing causes and effects in the impure mode typical of any concrete, and hence contradictory, process. According to Badiou, the event can only be conceived starting from the more encompassing notion of 'site'. As 'ontological figure of the instant',[97] the site eludes linear causality and, above all, shatters it: it is 'the ontological support of its own appearance'.[98] Or, again, 'a site supports the possibility of a singularity, because it summons its being in the appearing of its own multiple composition'.[99] It is precisely against a classical definition of the event that Badiou deploys a mathematical conceptuality, which contrasts starkly with the causal logics of natural or social sciences, the major absentees from these analyses. On the other hand, and paradoxically, Badiou is close here to Arendt's conception of action,

---

94 Ibid.
95 Ibid., 384.
96 Ibid., 378.
97 Ibid., 369.
98 Ibid., 363.
99 Ibid.

severed from any social determination and conceived as fundamentally unpredictable, irreversible commencement: 'since the site is a figure of the instant, since it only appears to disappear, true duration can only be that of consequences'.[100] To a certain Marxism, one which asserted a direction to history and the necessity of revolution, Badiou objects that 'the idea of an overturning whose origin would be a state of the totality is imaginary'.[101] While an event cannot be deduced, it is not unconnected to the eventful site where it is generated. That, Badiou makes clear, is why '[o]rdinarily, conceptual construction is reserved for structures whilst the event is rejected into the pure empiricity of what-happens'.[102] Dwelling on the French Revolution, an example dear to the Sartre of the *Critique of Dialectical Reason* – to whom Badiou shows himself to be just as close here as he is to the Hegel of the *Science of Logic* – Badiou specifies that even if it is interpreted as a series of events by 'historical retroaction', it is nevertheless 'supernumerary to the sole numbering of the terms of its site, despite it presenting such a numbering': 'the event is thus clearly the multiple which both presents its entire site, and by means of the pure signifier of itself immanent to its own multiple, manages to present the presentation itself, that is, the one of the infinite multiple that it is'.[103]

Here, once again, we must reject the objections invariably addressed to Badiou. While the event is not the mechanical resultant of its conditions, nor is it a sudden irruption, unconnected to what we shall trivially call its historical context. With a view to blocking the objection focusing on the radical absence of cause, Badiou pre-emptively denounces the 'speculative leftism' of that option, which according to him is that of theoreticians of the multitude as well as partisans of the absolute beginning, spontaneity and autonomy, whose seductive power is growing again today: 'speculative leftism imagines that intervention authorizes itself on the basis of itself alone; that it breaks with the situation without any other support than its own negative will'. Consequently, 'what the doctrine of the event teaches us is rather that the entire effort lies in following the event's consequences, not in glorifying its occurrence'.[104]

---

100 Ibid., 369.
101 Badiou, *Being and Event*, 176.
102 Ibid., 178.
103 Ibid., 180.
104 Ibid., 210–11.

This is the point at which a theory of history and historical intervention that thinks in terms not of commencement, but of recommencement, is constructed: 'the possibility of the intervention must be assigned to the consequences of another event. It is eventual recurrence which founds intervention.'[105] And this trans-historical recurrence excludes the articulation of political intervention with present circumstances, with concrete social mobilization as well as existing forms of organization, political or trade union. Badiou aims to define politics not as realization but as 'creation of the possible'.[106] And it is precisely on this political terrain that definition of the event rediscovers its eschatological, even Christ-like, significance, in the incarnation of the truth: 'a truth is a vanished event whose unforeseeable body the world causes to gradually appear in appearing's disparate materials'.[107]

Communism versus Strategy

In spite of Badiou's skill in foiling unduly hasty refutations, the objection that immediately arises is that such an approach verticalizes history by disconnecting politics from the social, that 'neurosis of politics'.[108] In this regard, Badiou's definition of politics once again approximates Arendt's, for whom the major error of the French revolutionaries was to mix political demands with economic and social concerns which, according to her, adulterated their import. This definition of politics, which uncouples it from any economic and social dimension, is a transverse thesis that paradoxically links the liberal tradition and Maoism in opposition to Marx's endeavour to articulate them. This explains why the contrast between socialism and communism is, according to Badiou, so complete and so far removed from the meaning assumed by these two terms in the past.

Refusing to recognize any history other than that rare and convulsive, of the exceptional moments he selects and the rebellious subjectivities

105 Ibid., 209.
106 Badiou, *Images du temps présent*, 189.
107 Badiou, *Second manifeste pour la philosophie*, 85.
108 Badiou, *Théorie du sujet*, 159.

he heroizes, Badiou perfectly logically detaches communism from socialism conceived as a relapse into representation and mediations, and into state power: 'The primitive universality of the communist idea has been dialectically converted into its opposite, and the operator of this reversal is, I'm convinced, the idea of representation.'[109] Conversely, communism construed absolutely exists as militant tenacity which, from one age to the next, repeats 'the egalitarian passion, the idea of justice, the desire to break with the accommodations of the property department, the deposing of egotism, intolerance for forms of oppression, the desire for the cessation of the state. The absolute pre-eminence of multiple-presentation over representation.'[110] Despite the conceptual and political destitution of representation, paradoxically, communism is turned into an icon, a banner with glorious arms, as sumptuous as it is inoffensive, nostalgia decked out for eternity.

More story than history, this communism is only tenuously linked to real history by the embroidery of heroic figures who ballast it with a bit of reality. This paradox is not so much an interpretative hypothesis as a noticeable tension between scarcely compatible assertions: 'I call "Idea" that from which an individual represents the world, including herself, to herself, so that, by incorporation into the truth process, she is linked to the faithful subjective type', we read in the *Second Manifesto*,[111] whereas dialectical thought is recognizable 'by its conflict with representation'.[112] Elsewhere, however, Badiou does not hesitate to call upon fiction and symbols: 'the Idea exposes the truth in a fictional structure',[113] 'the Idea presents certain facts as symbols of the real of truth'.[114] In short, narration precedes the history that it reconstructs:

> Why this glorious Pantheon of revolutionary heroes? Why Spartacus, Thomas Müntzer, Robespierre, Toussaint Louverture, Blanqui, Marx, Lenin, Rosa Luxemburg, Mao, Che Guevara and so many others? The reason is that all these proper names symbolize historically – in the guise of an individual, of a pure singularity of body

---

109 Badiou, *Quel communisme?*, 93.
110 Badiou, *D'un désastre obscur*, 13.
111 Badiou, *Second manifeste pour la philosophie*, 99.
112 Badiou, *Peut-on penser la politique?*, 88.
113 Badiou, *The Communist Hypothesis*, 179.
114 Ibid., 184.

and thought – the rare and precious network of ephemeral sequences of politics as truth.[115]

Such a conception is indeed political in its way, at least as much as the Byzantine debate over icons was in its time.

The consequences of this re-exploration of communism are multiple. On the one hand, Badiou holds high the standard of rebellion, refuses to abandon the term *communism* and renounce the revolutionary perspective, at a time when the ideological offensive to discredit any form of challenge is at its peak. Nevertheless, his political theses authorize only a local activism, motivated by hopes for its proliferation and sudden expansion:

> And that is one of the Idea's functions: to project the exception into the ordinary life of individuals, to fill what merely exists with a certain measure of the extraordinary. To convince my own immediate circle – husband or wife, neighbours and friends, colleagues – that the fantastic exception of truths in the making also exists, that we are not doomed to lives programmed by the constraints of the State.[116]

It should be added that Badiou also evokes political meetings 'in a hostel of workers from Mali, for example, or at the gates of a factory',[117] but always outside of the least unitary perspective and, in accordance with the principles of the Organisation politique, without paying attention to the initiatives of trade union and political organizations. Thereby spurned is the complex, turbulent history of the labour movement, but also any elaboration of an alternative project and any perspective of a general reorganization of social and economic life beyond 'small kernels of local political experimentation'.[118] Ultimately, Badiou decides to re-adopt the old neo-Kantian thesis of communism as a 'regulative hypothesis'.[119]

In terms of concrete politics, the communist Idea thus replicates the micro-politics dear to Deleuze and Foucault, as well as their definition

---

115 Ibid., 187.
116 Ibid., 190.
117 Ibid., 191.
118 Badiou, *Quel communisme?*, 61.
119 Badiou, *Second manifeste pour la philosophie*, 126n16.

of the plebs against the working class, the latter adjudged to have been definitively integrated into capitalism, even if Badiou recombines this local definition with a persistent general revolutionary perspective. We may challenge the relevance and effectiveness of such an approach, but not the fact that it is indeed a political option. This politics, Badiou writes,

> begins at the level of the real, with a practical alliance with those people who are in the best position to invent it in the immediate: the new proletarians who have come from Africa and elsewhere, and the intellectuals who are the heirs to the battles of recent decades. The alliance will gradually expand, depending on what they are able to achieve.[120]

This politics 'at the level of the real', peculiar to periods of political downturn, benefits from its seeming realism.

Thus, blending limited projects with persistent ambitions, conceiving communism as Idea, means stating and preserving an active essence, a revolutionary motor in the absence of any real revolutionary process. The Idea is not the name for a renunciation of politics, but its reassertion at the cost of circumventing its real complexity, the outline of a politics at once absent and magnified. For Badiou, a disappointing history never extinguishes the hearth of its unspoilt potential, which is regularly reactivated. Compatible with the miniaturization and idealization of communism, the absolute refusal to compromise with reality as it is confers on communism à la Badiou its character as an absolute, causing its eternal promise to glow above the real history of revolution and its defeats: 'proletarian political capacity, called communist, is absolutely mobile, non-statist, non-fixable. It does not allow itself to be represented or to be derived from the order that it exceeds.'[121] Communism becomes the name and symbol for this escape from the limits of the conceivable, beyond any kind of representation and any mode of organization. Valorising the communist thematic in this paradoxical fashion, which preserves it from history while risking its severance from the same, Badiou intervenes as a philosopher but also as a militant for a clearly

---

120 Badiou, *The Communist Hypothesis*, 75.
121 Badiou, *Peut-on penser la politique?*, 20.

defined view of politics. He rejects all those strategies that conceive the
state as a specific site of social conflict and refuses any participation in
institutional logics: 'the militant figure of politics requires, by virtue of
its very concept, unmediated presence (in particular, no parliamentary
or trade-union mediation) in major sites, factories, estates, etc. of the
working-class and popular event'.[122] We may reckon that, in Badiou
specifically, philosophical labour is neither a precondition nor an
outcome, and still less an escape from reality, but the form adequate to
this pure, resolutely minoritarian politics, which compromises with
nothing – especially not 'circumstances' that no strategy targets. The
'power of thought' is politics itself, ensuring the preservation of an initial
conviction. In an interview with Peter Hallward, Badiou says: 'Obviously
we're no longer Lacanians or Maoists. But Lacano-Maoism remains as a
possible figure of thought, deployed in the philosophical conceptual
space, but also practical and political. Today, I embody this tendency.'[123]

How to Read Badiou?

All told, Alain Badiou's thinking is among the most stimulating and
creative of recent decades, not afraid to tackle political issues in partisan, divisive fashion. The success of his books proves the pertinence of
an intervention that maintains its radical, revolutionary course in periods of downturn and ideological jamming. His multifaceted oeuvre
combines ontological reflection, logical analysis, literary interventions,
and historical and political considerations. We may deem this extraor-
dinarily sophisticated philosophical construct needlessly technical and
formalistic and find a sometimes hermetic and precious style off-putting.
But it is inseparable from a political conception so imperturbable that it
becomes its theoretical blueprint, subtracted from the vagaries of its
confrontation with real conditions and contradictions. Badiou moreover revives one of the key features of communism: the prospect of a
radical break with the world as it is. The construction of this perspective

---

122 Ibid., 83.
123 'D'une théorie de la structure à une théorie du sujet: un entretien avec Alain
Badiou', comments assembled by Peter Hallward, in *Concept and Form: The 'Cahiers
pour l'analyse' and Contemporary French Thought*.

does not take the path of utopia, still less that of a programme, but the much less frequent road of a dialectical reflection on the possibilities of intervention inherent in human history and on the trace left to this day of certain past events, vectors of truth beyond the moment of their irruption.

In the present context, characterized by the comprehensive capitalist conquest of the former socialist countries, the retreat of left-wing forces, the deep crisis of capitalism, and persistent but diffuse and fragmented social protest, the invocation of communism, along with the publication and wide distribution of books that articulate this identification, is always a political, constitutive gesture. In this sense, Badiou's oeuvre and its audience refer to a real contradiction, which it would be wrong to reduce to an escape into the concept and out of history. Badiou is the only theoretician to propose a negative view of institutions, of parties in their entirety and ongoing mobilizations, which in one and the same move helps to amplify the tendency to depoliticization and to nurture the spirit of rebellion. The redefinition of communism by Alain Badiou concentrates all these dimensions in contradictory fashion, conferring on his oeuvre its quirky incandescence, a doctrinaire rigidity from another era managing the exploit of converting itself into a robust, incisive philosophy that perseveres in maintaining the momentum of the revolution in its very absence.

2

Laclau and the Spectre of Socialism

In the political and theoretical culture of the labour movement, the question of strategy was once as central as it is today marginal. Neglected theoretically in favour of a more philosophical approach, politically it often boils down to the development of lines and programmes narrowly subordinated to the electoral calendar. However, while it always included the problems of class and party alliances, the past strategic reflection of the labour movement proved capable of going considerably beyond these limits. Whether considering the electoral or insurrectionary road, or their potential combination, more generally, it concerns the means and stages of social transformation and emancipation, addressing in the process the issues of the state, work and property but also popular mobilization and its structuration. Inseparable from the definition of a transformative objective and an emancipatory project, strategy consists in investigating their particular mediations and temporalities, as well as the many obstacles and dangers they have to confront. These questions were conceptualized, in particular, in the late nineteenth century and during the early decades of the twentieth century in the context of the Second and Third Internationals, faced with global historical situations marked by armed confrontation, the First World War, the October Revolution and the Second World War.

In the postwar context, the perimeter and stakes of strategic reflection were significantly reduced in the capitalist countries of the centre, under the framework of consolidated parliamentary states and fresh economic growth. Fordism, and the comparatively redistributive social policies resulting from the balance of forces constructed in the context of projects for abolishing capitalism, seemed to discredit it. Principal left-wing forces consequently settled into electoral competition and gradually renounced the perspective of a radical transformation of social life. From the late 1970s, the economic crisis and the ensuing ideological reversal made a formidable class revenge possible, paving the way for the victorious assault of neoliberal policies. The ideological reversal was structured around anti-totalitarianism, born during the Cold War. At a time when its main promoters – Hannah Arendt, Zbigniew Brzezinski and Carl Joachim Friedrich – were tending to limit its scope, the theme was taken up and amplified in France on the occasion of French publication of Solzhenitsyn's *Gulag Archipelago*. This campaign, which denounced communism and any alternative to capitalism, was powerfully relayed by such publications as *Esprit* and *Le Nouvel Observateur* and contributed to the emergence of intellectuals of a new kind – pamphleteers and polemicists like André Glucksmann and Bernard-Henri Lévy – alongside more traditional theoreticians like François Furet or Claude Lefort. It is from Lefort that Ernesto Laclau was to borrow the main elements of his redefinition of democracy.

From the 1980s, faced with the increasing violence of policies of social reaction, the global reign of financialized capitalism and the absence of a political alternative, popular protest took increasingly diverse and patchy forms. It initially renewed forms of social mobilization, stimulating reflection and the formulation of original political hypotheses – which ultimately proved incapable of obstructing the neoliberal steamroller intent on undoing social conquests and the common political culture that rendered them conceivable and possible. Alternative collective projects were gradually supplanted by mass abstention, a proliferation of fronts of struggle, but also retreats and withdrawals, endlessly fracturing the camp of the exploited and the dominated. At the same time, political strategy tended to be redefined as a mere technique of communication and electoral tactics, helping to accelerate a mass depoliticization. Faced with the rise of incredibly diverse anti-systemic forces, which frustrated the schemas of alternation, limited democratic functions, once conceded by the dominant classes, found themselves under threat from the authoritarian liberal turn and the concomitant growth of neo-fascism, and then from the proliferation of governments adopting all or part of their nationalist and xenophobic agenda.

Such is the context in which the term *populism* has enjoyed increasing favour, an echo of the ongoing dislocation of the political landscape formed in previous decades. This ambivalent notion was notably theorized by Ernesto Laclau from the 1980s onwards. Resonating in the first instance with the orientation of certain progressive governments in Latin America that emerged in the early 2000s, it now informs various left-wing political currents in Europe, which are in search of a new political road in light of the discrediting of traditional parties, without renouncing the electoral conquest of power. This option wagers on the charisma of leaders projecting themselves as the voice of the people, bypassing all intermediate structures to discover a logic of embodiment, which, in reality, is simply the acme of delegated representation combined with its denegation. At the same time, given a pejorative connotation, the term *populism* is employed as a synonym for *demagogy* to denounce and equate all political projects deemed simplistic, which are invariably imputed to the popular classes, validating an amalgam between extreme right and radical left.[1] For his part, Laclau explores only the positive and innovative import of the term. It is therefore important to connect this original theoretical reworking of the strategic question with its associated project, in order to clarify the critical analysis of communism and socialism that supports it, as well as the argument with Marxism inseparable from it.

An Argentine Itinerary

Ernesto Laclau is one of the rare contemporary thinkers committed to re-exploring the strategic question, to maintaining and redefining social and political antagonism, in the context of a fresh reflection first on socialism, then on emancipation, and finally on radical democracy, reworking the notion of populism throughout this trajectory. In this regard, he can be linked to an old tradition that has become residual: that of activist intellectuals engaged in a project of radical social

---

1 On the term *populism*, see Ugo Palheta, *La Possibilité du fascisme*, Paris: La Découverte, 2018, 19ff.

transformation. His initial political engagement positioned him on the Argentine extreme left, Laclau then distancing himself from it on account of his divergent political itinerary and involvement in a different tradition – academic critical thought and political theory, which he taught at the University of Essex from the 1970s. His theoretical work is to be situated in the context of a certain kind of return of the political as a question that was initially activist and subsequently developed philosophically, but with a view to rediscovering a political relevance that remained Laclau's main concern.

Despite its originality, Laclau's oeuvre typically evinces the paradox of contemporary political thought: the proliferation of innovative research, distinguished by sophisticated styles, goes hand in hand with their relative uniformity, bound up with common themes and references, based on kindred political options. Thus, the poststructuralism and post-Marxism Laclau identifies with often share the same rejection of totalizing analysis, the abandonment of issues of work and production, the thesis of the disappearance of the working class and class confrontation, as well as the foregrounding of ideological and cultural questions, of the role of contingency, of linguistic philosophy and discursive procedures. Erudite and eclectic, Laclau multiplies references to a large number of theoreticians, sometimes in dizzying fashion. In addition to its role as aggregator of prestigious academic markers, his work informs an original prospective and strategic reflection, registering the failures of the left as well as the crisis of capitalism, and enrolling Laclau in the prestigious tradition of critical philosophers of the 1970s.

Laclau's continued dialogue with Marx and Marxism, at a time when this debate had generally been regarded as closed since the 1980s, indicates the desire to rehabilitate a perspective of political transformation, at a distance, however, from its construction as an alternative to capitalism. This resonates with the projects of various current political tendencies, at grips with the crisis of the party-form and democracy in the neoliberal era. In this respect, Laclau is clearly demarcated from other contemporary theoretico-political options that address the political question by opting for a flight towards local and interstitial alternatives (John Holloway, Erik Olin Wright and others); for a return to political philosophy connected with actuality (Alain Badiou, but also in a different way Claude Lefort, Norberto Bobbio and others); for reflections of an ethical-juridical kind (Alasdair MacIntyre, Michael Walzer, Axel

Honneth and others); or for procedural theorizations of democracy that expel antagonism from it (Jürgen Habermas, Robert Dahl and so on). Starting with a recasting of the notion of socialism, Laclau was to undertake a continuous critique of the term. Abandoning the communist thematic from the outset, this critique retains the perspective of an inventive popular democratic politics enlivened by social conflictuality, which remains to be oriented. The assertion of a radical autonomy of the political is based on the thesis of the fundamentally amorphous, dispersed nature of social life, but also on a philosophical claim intended to link this social theory to a political strategy: 'that is why we conceive of the political not as a superstructure but as having the status of an *ontology of the social*.'[2] Declining, in the name of political pluralism and the critique of totalitarianism, to challenge liberal institutions, Laclau invokes a certain kind of break with the dominant order, relying on collective mobilizations and struggles, especially by minorities.

Laclau's stress on strategy, in the broad sense of the term, endeavours to make good one of the shortcomings of contemporary political reflection. At the same time, the radicalism he proposes to regenerate consists in a predominantly methodological proposal, issuing in a reflection that might be characterized as 'meta-strategic', uncoupled from any perspective of determinate transformation, from any alternative construed as a transformative social objective. While he is one of the theoreticians most in tune with contemporary attempts to reconstruct left-wing forces intent on winning hegemony, Laclau ultimately remains an enigma. And, no doubt, it is this enigmatic character, this constant veering between professed radicalism and an apologia for institutions, between concrete proposals and self-referential scholarly constructs, that explains the success of his theses among an audience in search of repoliticization and officials anxious for doctrinal renewal, both of them registering the decline of the historical alternatives to capitalism and inheriting the increasing distrust of traditional political formations.

Laclau's trajectory, which took him from Perón's Argentina to post-Marxist populism, clarifies the entry and exit points of his analysis. Born in Argentina in 1935, he became politically active in the late 1950s. Initially a member of the Socialist Party, he joined the Partido Socialista

---

2 Ernesto Laclau and Chantal Mouffe, 'Preface to the Second Edition', in *Hegemony and Socialist Strategy: Towards a Radical Democratic Politics*, London: Verso, 2001, xiv.

de la Izquierda Nacional (PSIN) at the start of the 1960s. The PSIN, Trotskyist in culture, was one of the protagonists in the lively debate within the Argentinian left over the nature of Peronism and the strategy to be adopted towards it. While the Socialist and Communist Parties opted for struggle against Perón, the extreme left in the PSIN supported the nationalist camp. For this group, in contrast to the rest of the Argentinian left, Peronism was not a form of fascism but the starting point for an anti-imperialist revolution, which remained to be extended in the direction of socialism. Laclau entered the leadership of the PSIN alongside its founder, Jorge Aberlardo Ramos, and edited the organization's journal.

Ramos is the author of a standard text, *Historia de la Nación Latinoamericana*, published in 1968, which analyses nationalist movements as well as the role of *caudillismo*, in connection with what the author refers to as the semi-colonial societies of Latin America. As regards Argentina, he writes:

> Under Perón's regime, the major conquests of working-class legislation derived from the regime's need to obtain the domestic support that was indispensable in order to resist the exactions of foreign imperialism. The working-class itself enthusiastically supported Peronism, which symbolized its own access to political life, a high standard of living, and the defeat of the oligarchy.[3]

In the pages that follow, Ramos dwells on the role of industry and agricultural prices in relation to international capital and class conflicts in Argentina. This approach is presented as resolutely Marxist. However, because it is detached from a general analysis of capitalism and focuses exclusively on Argentine circumstances, this reflection on an anti-imperialist national strategy furnishes the matrix of Laclau's political reflection. Peronism provides the model for what Laclau would subsequently define as 'articulation': a creative, voluntaristic operation of composition between distinct, even divergent, popular demands

---

3 Jorge Aberlardo Ramos, *Historia de la Nación Latinoamericana*, Buenos Aires: Ediciones Continente, 1968, 379–80. A leading Argentine intellectual, Ramos was the founder of the PSIN before distancing himself from the left to the point of becoming an ambassador for Carlos Menem until 1992.

(nationalist, social, liberal, democratic and so on), organized under the primacy of one of them, but also, and more problematically, as legislation generated at the heart of state institutions.

Laclau's political thought was thus engendered in a distinctive political history – that of Argentina in the 1960s – and the debate it prompted around the very definition of the political, linking established politics to popular mobilizations. After the 1966 coup d'état, his career became essentially academic, without repudiating this complex strategic culture. In the interview he gave in 1988 to *New Left Review*, Laclau even stated that, ultimately, his political standpoint had scarcely changed since his initial engagement.[4] And, indeed, many of the political options subsequently developed by Laclau seem to be consistent with his original strategic thinking. They always involve building a broad alliance, beyond the boundaries of traditional classes, in the framework of a popular front including organizations of the liberal bourgeoisie, with a view to pressing on to the conquest of the state. Subsequently, Laclau would abandon this perspective of conquest in favour of integration into liberal institutions. Here is where the radical break with Peronism paves the way for original strategic research, at once against any revolutionary option and against the conquest of state power, replaced from the late 1980s by an appeal for a 'deepening' of existing democratic dimensions.

Of what does this 'deepening' consist? Laclau ends up defining it as the result of the attention that is (or should be) paid by elected leaders to social demands, principally those 'formulated *to* the system *by* an underdog of sorts'.[5] This relative institutional realignment attests to Laclau's distancing from his initial engagement and socialist perspective, while retaining the fundamental choice to get involved in existing logics the better to change them. Thus, his originality attaches both to his activist involvement, rooted in Argentine political life, and to his ability to switch this political option onto the theoretical terrain and universalize it, constructing it as an original emancipatory perspective of relevance beyond Argentinian and Latin American borders. This would enable him to reconnect with contemporary political reality forty years later as

---

4 Ernesto Laclau, *New Reflections on the Revolution of Our Time*, New York: Verso, 1990, 199.

5 Ernesto Laclau, *On Populist Reason*, London and New York: Verso, 2005, 125.

an intellectual of world renown. From 2008, Laclau gave his support to the 'populisms' of Bolivia, Ecuador, Venezuela and Argentina, with some of whose leaders – particularly Argentine president Cristina Kirchner – he rubbed shoulders. The considerable resonance of his work dates from this third period, when theory and politics reconnected, but in a new shape, crossing the figures of the fellow traveller and the advisor to the prince.

Epistemology and Politics

Like a number of theoreticians active during the 1960s and '70s, Laclau constructed his oeuvre as a continuous debate with Marx and Marxism, but in profoundly altered circumstances. This initial critical dialogue, directly linked to the mutation of the intellectual and political landscape of the time, would open up a new theoretical and political space for a left that was neither Marxist nor communist. From the 1980s, critical discussion of Marxist conceptions receded in favour of violent denunciation, compounding the eviction of Marxist researchers from academic and editorial milieus; ignorance of Marxism, and rejection of it on principle, succeeded its crisis. Laclau's ongoing dialogue with Marx and Marxists between 1980 and 2010 is thus a feature that distinguishes him, even though he never concerned himself with a precise analysis of Marx's texts.

Politics and Ideology in Marxist Theory, Laclau's first important book, published in 1977, inaugurated this discussion with Marx and Marxism in a characteristic way: it positioned itself on epistemological ground, attributing significant political stakes to it. Referring to Louis Althusser and Galvano Della Volpe, addressed above all as theoreticians of ideas, Laclau defined theory as a link established between concepts that are not necessarily linked by themselves and which are only valid when articulated in a paradigm, a mental construct to be carefully distinguished from reality. According to Laclau, this was true of Marxism as of any other theory, except that, in the case of Marxism, the 'socialist political practice' combined with it, taking words for things, had contaminated 'Marxist theoretical practice'.[6] This would explain why

---

6 Ernesto Laclau, *Politics and Ideology in Marxist Theory: Capitalism, Fascism, Populism*, London: New Left Books, 1977, 10.

the concept of 'capitalist' had come, for Laclau, to be confused with an actually existing 'agent', an error entailing 'class reductionism'[7] with its train of disastrous strategic and theoretical effects. The imperative was to proceed to 'an increasing theoretical formalization of Marxist categories', enabling the working class to perform its role as a hegemonic force, realization of the ability to unite other social categories having as its necessary condition the abandonment of 'any narrow class perspective'.[8]

If this argument seems at first to spare Marx, rejecting only certain interpretations of him, it puts in place all the elements of a radical critique of Marxism whose principle is to separate concepts from reality and ideology from the economic and social world. Just as, in Laclau's view, capitalism is a process without a subject, so Marxism is a theory that does not imply any politics, a theory like any other, subject to the exigency of a constructed coherence rather than of verifiable knowledge. Laclau underscores this in the ensuing chapters. Adopting Althusser's distinction between real-concrete and concrete-in-thought, he asserts that 'the area of empirical confrontation of a theory's system of propositions is not external, but internal to the theory'.[9] Ideas being clarified solely by their own internal, formal rules of construction, ideologies cannot be connected with class interests or objective logics. That is why, discussing Nicos Poulantzas's analysis of fascism, Laclau criticizes him for thinking that 'social classes have "pure", "necessary" or "paradigmatic" ideologies',[10] Marxist-Leninist ideology supposedly being the ideology of the working class and liberalism that of the bourgeoisie. Refutation of this conception, which, in truth, neither Marx, nor Lenin, nor indeed Poulantzas defended, paves the way for the converse assertion – equally schematic, in fact – of an absence of class anchorage of fascism and the radical autonomy of ideologies.

To the putatively Marxist thesis that, by definition, fascism could meet with no support in the working class, Laclau responds that 'fascism, far from being the typical ideological expression of the most conservative and reactionary sectors of the dominant classes, was, on the contrary, one of the possible ways of articulating the popular-democratic

---

7 Ibid., 12.
8 Ibid.
9 Ibid., 61.
10 Ibid., 94.

interpellations into political discourse'. He does not hesitate to stress the point: 'that popular-democratic interpellations have no precise class connotation and can be incorporated into quite distinct political discourses, is something of which fascism provides eloquent proof'.[11] Such an ahistorical reading of fascism as a fundamentally contingent construct raises numerous problems, starting with the adjective *popular-democratic* applied without further ado to the ultra-nationalist, racist and xenophobic theses of fascism, which become here mere expressions of a sudden social demand, which, whatever it may be, needs to be registered. This approach enables Laclau to stress what will form the core of his own strategic re-elaboration: *'ideological "elements" taken in isolation have no necessary class connotation, and . . . this connotation is only the result of the articulation of those elements in a concrete ideological discourse'.*[12] Fascism as hegemonic construction of a 'mass regime'[13] invites us to pit against it a counter-hegemony, generated symmetrically and basically analogously – even if its aims are quite different – in wholly conjunctural fashion.

Nevertheless, in this book, Laclau still preserves a certain type of weak social determination of political representations by evoking the 'class overdetermination' of any demand. Althusser had borrowed the concept of 'over-determination' from Freud to refer to the way that secondary contradictions condition the principal contradiction, which is economic in kind. Dismissing any historical determinism, Althusser thus stressed the relative autonomy and real efficacy of the ideological and juridico-political superstructure, drawing direct inspiration from Mao's theses. In *For Marx*, he underscores the necessity, if the principal contradiction is to issue in a revolutionary process, of an accumulation of 'circumstances' and 'currents' that '"fuse" into a *ruptural unity'*, resulting in 'the immense majority of the popular masses *grouped* in an assault on a regime which its ruling classes are *unable to defend'*.[14] Laclau's thesis consists in analysing class struggle as a secondary contradiction of the capitalist formation, while isolating it from any 'determination in the last instance'. The operation leads to redefining Althusserian

---

11 Ibid., 111.
12 Ibid., 99.
13 Ibid., 88.
14 Louis Althusser, *For Marx*, trans. Ben Brewster, London: Verso, 1979, 99.

'interpellation' as articulation: *'the popular-democratic interpellation not only has no precise class content, but is the domain of ideological class struggle par excellence'.*[15] The distance between the two authors is therefore considerable, even though Laclau ultimately pushes the logic of 'relative autonomy' to disintegration.

Alternatively put, classes only exist through their struggles – a fundamentally Marxian thesis, except that for Laclau these struggles are not linked to concrete economic and social interests, nor to an emancipatory project as a bearer of universality. Their success depends on a strategy developed externally to them, effective in ad hoc circumstances, without knowing who exactly is able to proceed to this strategic elaboration. The great leader is the one who imposes himself, outside of any causality, as the demiurge of the unifying political transmutation of a social world that is by definition fragmented. Transformed into a general strategic method, this approach is illustrated by disparate historical examples from English Chartism to Boulangism, from Mao via Tito to Hitler, without Laclau introducing any equal sign between such options, at a time when he still identified with the perspective of a 'socialist populism'.[16] Such a strategy, which can be adapted to diverse situations and eras, is based on adjusting to social circumstances as they are and hence to supposedly dominant popular ideas. It involves embracing the contours of a conjuncture independently of the goals of its transformation, by striving to organize a people beyond classes and class discourses on the basis of their own tendencies, which it misrecognizes in existing only through non-reflexive adhesion to one of them. The effectiveness of this pragmatic option depends exclusively on the judicious selection of one demand or 'interpellation' among others, depending on its potentially catalytic virtues as regards the set of existing demands. Thus, it is through a formal process of unification of the diverse, Kantian in ancestry, that interpellation will be in a position to buttress all forms of contestation. It becomes a means of constructing a new hegemony, the latter being redefined as a device for access to a pre-existing social and political power, remote from its Gramscian sense.

In this text from 1977, Laclau's analysis thus consists in making Marxism at once a largely old-fashioned theory and a reservoir of ideas

---

15 Laclau, *Politics and Ideology*, 108–9.
16 Ibid., 174.

that remain indispensable, on condition that they are wrested from their
alleged essentialism, for the purposes of developing a new political
project which is at once more consistent and more modest. While the
democratic thematic is still combined with that of socialism, it is
predominantly directed against a Marxism that only knows how to
instrumentalize democracy as a way of establishing its ultimate goal: the
dictatorship of the proletariat.[17] By making the momentary Marxist
name for a simple form of transition its goal – communism – and playing on the sinister echoes of the term *dictatorship* in the twentieth
century, Laclau is well aware that he can count on a general ignorance
of Marx and Marxism, as well as the failures and reputation of state
socialism. Against such aberrations, which are easy to stigmatize, revolutionary strategy is redefined as fabrication of an effective subterfuge, a
unifying myth, proximate to the much earlier conceptions of Georges
Sorel. It allocates a decisive role to the ingenious elaboration of a 'popular-democratic interpellation' that 'not only has no precise class content,
but is the domain of ideological class struggle par excellence'.[18] In this
sense, Sorel is the veritable initiator of Marxism's 'tropological turn',[19] by
dint of his anti-statism and anti-Jacobinism, and despite his nationalist
and anti-Semitic turn. Laclau, uncoupling such a strategy from any
construction of a specifically social relation of force rooted in relations
of production, separates it from the capitalist historical formation and
its peculiar contradictions, starting with the conflict between labour
and capital, whose existence he revokes, the social being nothing but
'the infinite play of differences'.[20] The linguistic and rhetorical turn of
socialism has as its corollary the assertion of a basic fragmentation of
historical reality, a dispersion of its components. This authorizes strategic interventions which are all the bolder insofar as they presuppose a
fundamentally malleable, diffuse social reality, but one which, by definition, is blind to the discursive logics that structure it from without. Once
again, the thesis is validated solely by denouncing the converse position,
oversimplified and attributed to Marx, who is allegedly an adherent of

---

17 Ibid., 107n36.
18 Ibid., 108–9.
19 Ernesto Laclau, *The Rhetorical Foundations of Society*, London and New York:
Verso, 2014, 69. The neologism 'tropology' is coined from the word *trope*, referring to a
rhetorical figure.
20 Laclau, *New Reflections*, 90.

determinism and the representative of a philosophy of history that has never been overcome.

'There Is No *Aufhebung*'

This critique of the philosophy of history imputed to Marx is well-known: it consists in criticizing him for his continuing proximity to Hegel, while attributing to the latter a crudely finalistic vision of history. In the process, Laclau ends up making some concessions to perfunctory anti-Marxism and anti-communism. In *Emancipation(s)*, a collection of texts from the early 1990s when he had broken with any mention of socialism, Laclau proposes to the reader to 'remember' how Marx describes 'the emergence and development of antagonistic societies: primitive communism had to disintegrate in order to develop the productive forces of humanity; the latter's development required, as its historical and logical condition, the passage through hell of the successive exploitative regimes'.[21] Then arrives communism, which confers meaning on the past and realizes its promises. However, it is very difficult to 'remember' where Marx claimed any such thing. Having mentioned Hegel in mid-flight, Laclau does not hesitate to summarize the thesis he imputes to Marx in stunning fashion: 'seen from the vantage point of universal history, everything – slavery, obscurantism, terrorism, exploitation, Auschwitz – reveals its rational substance'.[22] In a similar register, he affirms that 'the Stalinist conception of the "objective sense" of actions is but the coarse expression and the *reductio ad absurdum* of something that was implicit in Marx's theoretical project'.[23]

Obviously, it is not irrelevant that these charges were levelled by Laclau not long after the fall of the Berlin Wall, the collapse of the so-called 'socialist' countries having been feted by virtue of a different philosophy of history, all the less visible in that it is only presented via its shadow: the putatively terminal defeat of the finalistic scenario assigned to Marx. Compounding the collapse of the socialist camp is the rallying of social democracy to liberal theses, completing the discrediting of the word

---

21 Ernesto Laclau, *Emancipation(s)*, New York: Verso, 1996, 10.
22 Ibid.
23 Laclau, *New Reflections*, 184.

socialism, but by the same token deserting a political space that Laclau undertook to reoccupy. That space was a moderate reformism, inspired by the more institutional wing of Eurocommunism,[24] reaffirming the role of political decision-making and the virtues of social dialogue while presenting itself as an alternative of a new type solely by virtue of the modalities of its construction. In this context, the post-Marxist project becomes more convincing to the extent that it radicalizes denunciation of a theory whose practical failure seems attested and definitive. In so doing, however, Laclau simply inverts the characteristics of the communist project he attributes to Marx: Marxist necessitarianism supposedly took as its ultimate goal a transparent, fully rational society in which the universal was synonymous with the crushing of singularity.

Faced with the general disavowal of communism as well as socialism in both variants – social democratic in the West, statist in the East – whose faults he gladly exaggerates, Laclau seeks to redefine what is at once a project and a method – 'radical democracy' – constructed as contingent, voluntaristic articulation of disparate demands. Fruit of a political decision detached from any concrete economic or social conditioning, it consists in the preservation of a pluralistic framework that renounces the aim of transcending antagonisms, whether political or social. It is presented as the idealized operation of existing systems and capitalism, which ultimately leads to an essentially ethical formalization of democracy: 'A society is democratic, not insofar as it postulates the validity of a certain type of social organization and of certain values vis-à-vis others, but insofar as it refuses to give its own organization and its own values the status of *fundamentum inconcussum*.'[25] Consequently, any emancipatory project can, simply by dint of the imputed or professed conviction of its rationality, find itself accused of seeking to resolve this ethical and political version of the crisis of foundations by force, of threatening the fundamental agnosticism that suffices to characterize contemporary democracy.

Belying its oppositional exterior, this alternative to the alternative quite simply proposes to take liberal democracy at its word. Laclau had

---

24 According to Bob Jessop, 'left'-Eurocommunism conceives its project in terms of a rupture based on broad social mobilizations, whereas 'right'-Eurocommunists call for increased parliamentary control of state and economy (*The Capitalist State: Marxist Theories and Methods*, Oxford: Martin Robertson, 1982, 14).

25 Laclau, *New Reflections*, 187.

begun by uncoupling socialism from communism: his twofold rejection of political mediations and an anti-capitalist objective led him to propose what we might call a 'post-socialism', political twin of post-Marxism, which is none other than bourgeois parliamentary democracy restored to its own abstract ideal. It is true that, at a time of ongoing political and social reaction, to recall the principles proclaimed by classical liberalism and counterpose them to contemporary neoliberal practices can, if not resemble an alternative, at least assume a subversive colouring. But in the process, does Laclau not circumvent the profound contemporary crisis of democracy rather than confront it? Many before him have constructed political thought out of the mourning of revolution. But they conceived it as a withdrawal from politics, or as politics displacing and euphemizing itself on the philosophical terrain, or again as a strictly local, micro-political escape. While Laclau inherits such options and remains close to them, he also seems to draw the lessons from their inability to materialize. His wager is different: it involves rehabilitating intervention in the institutional political field as it is, noting the mounting popular rejection of it while reaffirming it as an untranscendable horizon.

To do this, he sets about rehabilitating the idea of antagonism while shifting it onto discursive terrain, so that it can also be pitted against any prospect of transcendence of the capitalist mode of production and class domination, since in his view neither of these actually exists. 'There Is No *Aufhebung*':[26] the formula rings out like the philosophical version, unwittingly parodic, of the famous Thatcherite slogan 'There Is No Alternative'. At the same time, Laclau opposes both the tendency to political abdication and Jürgen Habermas's procedural theory of democracy, despite their seeming proximity. For Habermas, a perfected democracy involves an extension of public deliberation, which is free but organized within the framework of existing institutions, to be perfected by the creation of spaces and procedures of communication. Rational determination of the common good, by the body of equal citizens, must aim to overcome the contradictions between divergent interests. While the conception proposed by Laclau sticks to a kindred formalism, it rejects the idea of a rational, consensual resolution of divergences. It stresses that 'there cannot be a radical politics without

26 Ibid., 96.

the definition of an adversary. That is to say, it requires the acceptance of the ineradicability of antagonism.'[27] The return of antagonism without any prospect of transcendence, as co-existence of opposites, is therefore compatible with a rejection of the dialectic, attached to theorizing the abolition of class divisions. This rejection was one of the salient features of non-Marxist philosophies of the previous generation, which Laclau inherits while repoliticizing their approaches. The result is a sophisticated, offensive strategy for constructing hegemony.

Capitalism Disassembled

Before developing more fully in strictly strategic terms, Laclau's theoretical and political project involves radicalizing the critique of Marx's analysis of capitalism, a 'critique of political economy' intent on connecting the economic, social and political but also cultural dimension within a contradictory, dynamic totality: the capitalist social formation. Laclau's critique of a comprehensive approach of this kind rests on the assertion of the effective, observable disintegration of this totality, both at the level of social organization and from the standpoint of the production of wealth, so that the assertion of its unity, albeit contradictory and dynamic, is a theoretical *coup de force* as well as a political threat. We shall have to return to this thesis, which justifies Laclau's hegemonic strategy.

As we have seen, the idea that capitalism is ultimately merely a conceptual construct whose relevance is debatable makes an early appearance in Laclau's oeuvre: 'Marx remains within the idealist field – that is to say, within the ultimate affirmation of the rationality of the real.'[28] This critique presupposes the discrediting of any causal analysis, compounded by the assertion of the undivided sway of contingency in history. Promotion of a strategic conception of discursive power comes at a price: disassembling the totality, and converting the internal contradictions posited by Marxism into external negations, makes it possible to develop proposals that are radically foreign to the existing relations of production, while he links them to social and cultural demands that are

---

27 Laclau and Mouffe, *Hegemony and Socialist Strategy*, xvii.
28 Laclau, *New Reflections*, 108.

very real. The externality of the conflict to the structure it concerns is supposed to free the will to transform from the influence of any objective determination, from any link to the specific materiality of economic and social processes. Simply set down, this thesis justifies the assertion of the contingent and autonomous character of hegemonic construction and, above all, transfers the transformative dynamic of its former subject – the working class – to a new actor, leader or strategic leadership.

The leader, whose figure emerges in the later works, is the virtuoso analyst of circumstances and the master of slogans, the will of wills and the arbiter of rebellions, but also and above all a Machiavellian prince without ambition. His mission is to interpellate, and structure from without, a malleable 'people' bereft of self-consciousness and available for multiple projects profoundly and constitutively apolitical: 'Any transformation of capitalism opens up a range of possibilities that are not just determined by the endogenous logic of capitalist forms, but also by the latter's constitutive outside and by the whole historical situation in which those logics operate.'[29] The 'historical situation' therefore includes capitalism as a merely regional logic – an audacious thesis that Laclau does not develop but which relays his conviction that capitalism is merely an incorrect name and not a coherent concept.

To justify his abandonment of the critique of political economy as an outmoded theory and inadequate strategy, Laclau has to radicalize his objections to Marxism. Thus, where, for Marx, the rearticulation of knowledge and action is the condition and goal of the transcendence of capitalism, Laclau makes their renewed separation the presupposition of the constructivist hegemony he advocates, maintaining the specialization of roles and the division of labour in political forces which, in principle, work for the abolition of this division. That is why it is so important for him to reject the assertion of a basic antagonism between capital and labour, which is inherent in capitalism only if it is defined, mistakenly, as a mode of production. As a result, his analysis sets out to uncouple construction of the political alternative from study of the 'economic and social formation' (to borrow Marx's phrase), in a way that is ultimately close to Arendt's strict separation between social question and political intervention, an analysis of liberal pedigree widely adopted by the anti-totalitarian tradition. Consequently,

---

29 Ibid., 56.

[t]he rejection of privileged points of rupture and the confluence of
struggles into a unified political space, and the acceptance, on the
contrary, of the plurality and indeterminacy of the social, seem to us
the two fundamental bases from which a new political imaginary can
be constructed, radically libertarian and infinitely more ambitious in
its objective than that of the classic left.[30]

His own strategy being (according to Laclau) the only conceivable route
today to collective progress, it remains for him to show that there exist
no intrinsically anti-capitalist struggles, as vectors of a plausible radical
alternative capable of doing without the vertical construction of a strategic leadership over and above passive subaltern masses.[31] To this end,
the Argentine philosopher affirms that Marx, having failed to define the
role of class struggles, resolved to think a history motored by an anonymous, teleological logic – that of the productive forces. To demonstrate
the point, for once he mentions a specific text by Marx, which he even
cites at some length: the preface to *A Contribution to the Critique of
Political Economy*, written in 1859.[32] In it, Marx argues that 'at a certain
stage of development, the material productive forces of society come
into conflict with the existing relations of production or – this merely
expresses the same thing in legal terms – with the property relations
within the framework of which they have operated hitherto'.[33] These
few lines can certainly be counted among the most deterministic that
Marx wrote, even if they are not intended to summarize his analyses of
the subject in their entirety. But it happens that this text, a recap of his
earliest research results fifteen years later, was the object of a subsequent
fetishization by certain Marxists in the Second and then Third
Internationals, who thereby sought to legitimize their own historical
determinism, helping to turn this passage into a statement of dogma.
    Relying on this retrospective oversimplification, Laclau denounces a
Marxian analysis of history from which 'class struggle is completely
absent',[34] immediately extending this diagnosis to Marx's oeuvre as a

---

30 Laclau and Mouffe, *Hegemony and Socialist Strategy*, 152.

31 Laclau, *New Reflections*, 127.

32 See ibid., 5–6.

33 Karl Marx and Friedrich Engels, *Collected Works*, Vol. 29, London: Lawrence &
Wishart, 1987, 263.

34 Laclau, *New Reflections*, 6.

whole: 'it would doubtless be wrong to assume that Plekhanov or Kautsky, who devoted a considerable part of their lives to the study of Marx's work – and who were certainly not hacks – have simply misread Marx'.[35] However, it is commonplace to challenge the rigour of these interpretations, which are indeed profoundly determinist, issuing directly from their authors' strategic options. According to Laclau, Marx suggested to his readers two theses that are utterly incompatible: either there exists a contradiction between the productive forces and the mode of production – a hypothesis developed in *Capital* – or the contradiction is constructed between classes, the latter hypothesis only being encountered in the historical texts devoted to France. This is an analysis which forgets that, far from referring exclusively to the technical means of production and imparting to them an automatic, and automatically progressive, development, Marx's notion of productive force includes the workers themselves. In other words, the contradiction between the productive forces and the relations of production that endeavour to structure them exclusively in accordance with the capitalist logic of valorisation is indeed, in Marx's view, a social contradiction at the same time as a principle of potential politicization – not a blind mechanism. Laclau here adopts a thesis we have already met with in the previous chapter, which its repetition reinforces: the class struggle is simply a *deus ex machina* that Marx never succeeded in integrating into his analysis.[36]

Is Labour-Power a Commodity?

Laclau seems to deal a decisive blow to Marx's conception of communism with a more surprising, but (if valid) much more decisive, argument: Marx could justify his conception of 'the economy . . . as a mechanism of society acting upon objective phenomena independently of human action'[37] only by way of a 'fiction' in which labour-power is conceived as a commodity. In passing, we might be surprised to find the register of fiction being counterposed to that of truth here, in flagrant

---

35 Ibid., 181–2.
36 Ibid., 15.
37 Laclau and Mouffe, *Hegemony and Socialist Strategy*, 78.

breach of the constructivist epistemology to which Laclau adheres. His goal is to affirm that labour-power is by no means a commodity inasmuch as it concerns a purely political reality: purchasing it is insufficient, it has to be set to work – a process that is completely external (according to Laclau) to its constitution as capitalist labour-power. Ignoring the analyses in *Capital* devoted to the labour contract as the legal form of class domination that combines equal right, violence and resistance by wage earners to the transformation of this power into a simple capitalist commodity, Laclau forgets that, for Marx, the transformation of labour-power into a commodity is a tendency inherent in capitalism. But if it is indeed (according to Marx) bought 'like' a commodity, it is because, despite this transaction being imposed on the wage earner, the capitalist tendency to completely commodify social life can never be fully realized.

These issues, which are never strictly economic in the narrow sense of the term precisely because they include the dimension of consciousness and the possibility of a politics, are strategically decisive for Marx as for Laclau. But whereas Marx conceives the articulation between critical analysis of capitalism and the working-out of the means and ends of its abolition as organic or, rather, dialectical, the political choice of their essential separation made by Laclau is presented as a precondition that steers his theoretical refutation. This approach explains why his argument is, on the one hand, profoundly eclectic, heteroclite even, mixing the most diverse references from Kautsky to Barthes, Gramsci to Wittgenstein – no doubt in the image of the dispersion of the social word that it describes – while, on the other, highly coherent, supported by political and strategic options given in advance and which it is a question of illustrating and developing rhetorically. In this respect, when Laclau defines political intervention as discursive elaboration of a demand that pre-exists it, he certainly describes adequately what, above all, is the elaboration of his own theory.

It is therefore only on condition of a radical abandonment of the world of production and its logics that Laclau defines a strategy which makes the proclamation of its own autonomy a thesis and a choice that are in essence political, in the still-classical and specialist sense of the term. Thus, the redefinition of the social world and the thesis of its unquestionable, definitive dispersion are the necessary correlates of this politics posited before being justified and in order to be justified. On this level, Laclau's initiative consists once more in constructing his options by simply inverting the schemas for which he criticizes Marxism. For, according to him, the latter formulates a dual thesis, whose falsity it has become easy to demonstrate: on the one hand, the proletariat is the subject of the realization of history; on the other, the tendency to proletarianization is general and ineluctable. These two claims lead to an essentialization of the social and abolition of politics: 'What is now in crisis is a whole conception of socialism which rests upon the ontological centrality of the working class . . . and upon the illusory prospect of a perfectly unitary and homogeneous collective will that will render pointless the moment of politics.'[38] In reality, Laclau explains, the working class is the bearer only of a corporatist universal, a 'universal [which] is no more than a particular that at some moment has become dominant'.[39] That is why bourgeois democracy is instrumentalized by Marx in the service of a goal which, in the last instance, does not include it. Laclau once again mentions the term 'dictatorship of the proletariat' as sufficient proof of the authoritarian perspective whose project Marx would only avow now and then. He adds that in the Marxist view, 'democratic demands were inherently bourgeois, and essentially linked to the establishment of "liberal-democratic" regimes'[40] – in other words, they are to be completely abolished after having been unscrupulously manipulated.

This violent denunciation, resuming one of the commonplaces of anti-Marxism while targeting the abuses of an orthodox Marxism seeking to legitimize the absence of democracy in the so-called 'socialist' countries, enables Laclau to defend the project of deepening 'liberal-democratic ideology' more vigorously,[41] while reiterating the diagnosis of a fragmentation of any class structure and a splintering of struggles, 'position in the production process' having lost 'its centrality in the general definition of social agents'.[42] Rather than asserting the pure and simple disappearance of the working class and, with it, any subject of social transformation, however, Laclau proposes to replace it within a

---

38 Ibid., 2.
39 Laclau, *Emancipation(s)*, 26.
40 Laclau, *On Populist Reason*, 125.
41 Laclau and Mouffe, *Hegemony and Socialist Strategy*, 176.
42 Ernesto Laclau, Préface to *La Guerre des identités. Grammaire de l'émancipation*, Paris: La Découverte, 2015, 9.

broader set of social groups, structured differently from traditional class relations rooted in relations of exploitation: the point is to conceive 'agents' who are 'constituted *outside the relations of production*'.[43] This concept of agent, taken from neo-classical economic theory, involves a radical redefinition of social reality. The latter is neither the site of constitutive power relations nor the site of economic exploitation and capitalist accumulation: 'socialist demands simply take their place alongside other democratic demands',[44] obliging us to admit that the 'political usefulness [of the left–right distinction] has done nothing but decline since the period of anti-fascist struggle and Cold War'.[45]

It follows that the break must be consummated with past egalitarian demands and hence with what, since its origins, has defined the left as such: 'democratic discourse was traditionally centred on equality beyond difference. This is true of Rousseau's general will, as well as Jacobinism or the emancipatory universal class of Marxism. Today, by contrast, democracy is bound up with the recognition of pluralism and differences.'[46]

This assertion is decisive, 'pluralism' referring in Laclau not only to the diversity of political opinions, but also and especially to social 'differences' – inequalities – in the context of persisting class relations, which we can no longer envisage being made to disappear. It is on this ground that the rejection of the division between right and left is presented as the strategic consequence of the anti-totalitarian matrix which emerges behind the abandonment of equality and social justice.

Hegemony and Populism

The power of Laclau's thought stems from the fact that it does not confine itself to diagnosing Marxism's theoretical failure and political noxiousness – a thesis that became utterly banal during the 1990s. On the basis of this analysis, he advances a political proposal that breaks with Marx, but also with the apolitical retreat of the critiques addressed

---

43 Laclau, *New Reflections*, 126.
44 Ibid., 229.
45 Ibid., 227.
46 Laclau, Préface to *La Guerre des identités*, 8.

to Marx in the French philosophy of the 1970s. In this sense, Laclau's post-Marxism seeks to preserve and revive the aim of social transformation, while endeavouring to root it in the political and social reality of a world refashioned by the disappearance of the USSR and by neoliberal policies. But this ambition is to be conceived and elaborated as a construct free of any economic or social determination that might ground the socialist project in the dynamics actually at work and in their contradictions. This must be stressed, given how crucial a theme exteriority is in the thinking of Laclau, who hammers home the non-contradictory dimension of labour and capital in capitalist society. It is, in fact, their fundamental juxtaposition that undoes all causalities, paving the way for a decisionism close to the views of Carl Schmitt. The latter defines as 'constituent power' the decision whereby a political subject, people or nation posits itself as will and determines the form of its existence, instituting norms rather than being subjected to them. The state of exception is par excellence this founding moment of the will, against which no rationality of a legal, ethical or political kind can be adduced. Laclau has recourse to Schmitt's analyses, but without precisely discussing either the grounds or the conclusions of the theses of a figure who was the grand jurist of Nazism.[47]

We must therefore underscore the magnitude of the theoretico-political consequences that follow from the radical rejection of the idea of objective contradiction. For Laclau, capitalism functions smoothly as long as the workers do not oppose it: 'could it be argued that the relationship is intrinsically antagonistic because it is based on unequal exchange and because the capitalist extracts surplus value from the worker? The answer to this point is "No" because it is only if the worker *resists* such an extraction that the relationship becomes antagonistic.'[48] If workers suddenly take this decision, which is historically contingent, their reasons are conceived as necessarily being external to the relations of production. What could their motives be if they remain foreign to the terms and conditions of labour? For example, their frustration as

---

47 For her part, Chantal Mouffe criticizes his rejection of pluralism, arguing that 'Schmitt was unable to grasp that there was another alternative open to liberals, one that could render the articulation between liberalism and democracy viable': 'Carl Schmitt and the Paradox of Liberal Democracy', in Mouffe, ed., *The Challenge of Carl Schmitt*, New York: Verso, 1999, 51.

48 Laclau, *New Reflections*, 9.

consumers at a sudden fall in wages, replies Laclau.[49] Starting from this reading of social conflicts – launched by disappointed consumers, not angry workers – Laclau can maintain that the wages policy of capitalism does not pertain to class struggle; that no social demand could, in itself, target capitalism as such; and that classes have definitively given way to uncertain, fluctuating identities, destined to link up, or free themselves, in vaster ensembles that always remain to be defined and invented. The recast notions of hegemony and populism will designate the new conception of strategy which forms the political pendant of this scholarly construct. It postulates political agents remoulding, in voluntarist and pragmatic fashion, a social world that is fundamentally blind to itself, which is to be guided without ever informing it of the strategy being applied to it or entrusting its elaboration to it.

Thus, if democracy is valorised by late Laclau, its definition remains highly problematic, with the category of hegemony representing the red thread of a reflection that has become principally and specifically strategic. He is anxious to stress that 'the deconstruction of Marxist tradition [is] not its mere abandonment'.[50] Inherited from Gramsci and part of Russian Marxism before him, from Laclau's pen the category of hegemony finds itself recast and expanded. It comprises an indefinitely renewed critique of Marxism, a postmodern epistemology, a project of social transformation and the reassertion of a liberal-democratic perspective. As early as his book of 1977, Laclau assigns Gramsci a concept of hegemony presented as an alternative to the discourse of class, despite Gramsci's own views on the subject. Chantal Mouffe would develop this interpretation in her book *Gramsci and Marxist Theory*, published in 1979. Such a post-Marxist instrumentalization forms part of a long history: Razmig Keucheyan has highlighted the importance of the South American and, in particular, Argentinian reception, even if Laclau pertains to the tradition of the 'Anglo-American academic world' and the depoliticized rereading of Gramsci by certain cultural studies theorists.[51] In a sense, by repoliticizing this depoliticization, subsequent to the prolonged neutralization of the revolutionary dimension of Gramsci's notion,

---

49 Ibid., 15.

50 Ibid., 179.

51 Antonio Gramsci, *Guerre de mouvement et guerre de position*, ed. and introd. Razmig Keucheyan, Paris: La Fabrique, 2011, 19.

Laclau makes hegemony the name of an ethereal political construct that consists in unifying and connecting forms of contestation from without, in accordance with the stylistic model of metonymy, so that 'a *particular* social force assumes the representation of a *totality* that is radically incommensurable with it'.[52]

If, from 1977, Laclau begins to conceive politics as construction, some decades later, in the belief that 'dislocation is the primary onto-logical level of constitution of the social',[53] he ends up defining politics as rhetoric, the only thing capable of temporarily re-creating the coherence of a people, whose designers are aware of its fundamental fragility. In subsequent works, Laclau constantly refines the modalities of this construction, allocating an ever more central role to its linguistic dimen-sion and the process of discursive articulation, which generates from outside the social world the principle of its relative unity, which has always to be rebuilt: 'the subject is the metaphor of an absent fullness',[54] implying that 'the condition for the emergence of an imaginary is the metaphorization of the literal content of a particular social demand'.[55] It follows that 'rhetorical mechanisms . . . constitute the anatomy of the social world'.[56] It is 'increasingly extensive chains of equivalences'[57] between disparate 'social demands' that will enable the formation of a new kind of universality at the same time as the constitution of a people, the populist hypothesis replacing the terms *socialism* and *emancipation* employed previously, which are much too substantive and insufficiently formal.

If the term *populism* refers to the 'crystalliz[ation] of all differential claims around a common denominator',[58] and if it 'requires the dichoto-mic division of society into two camps – one presenting itself as a part which claims to be the whole'[59] – the political objectives identified by Laclau prove ever more evanescent and now skirt around the conquest of political power:

---

52 Laclau and Mouffe, *Hegemony and Socialist Strategy*, x.
53 Laclau, *New Reflections*, 44.
54 Ibid., 63.
55 Ibid., 64.
56 Laclau, *On Populist Reason*, 110.
57 Laclau, *New Reflections*, 229.
58 Laclau, *On Populist Reason*, 82.
59 Ibid., 83.

From this we can deduce that the language of a populist discourse –
whether of Left or Right – is always going to be imprecise and fluctuating: not because of any cognitive failure, but because it tries to operate performatively within a social reality which is to a large extent
heterogeneous and fluctuating.[60]

Redefining these categories within his own strategic apparatus, Laclau
renews the promotion of the 'plebs' and the 'excluded' against the notion
of the 'exploited' – a promotion already pitted against Marx's theses
during the 1970s by Gilles Deleuze, Michel Foucault and André
Glucksmann,[61] but also by Alain Touraine, André Gorz, Cornelius
Castoriadis and others. For his part, Laclau claims that 'all we know is
that [it] will be the outsiders of the system, the underdogs – those we
have called the heterogeneous – who are decisive in the establishment of
an antagonistic frontier.'[62] The only alterity capitalism now confronts is
its own internal margin, pointing to no exterior or hereafter.

The Rhetorical Turn of Politics

This rhetorical turn is accompanied by loans from psychoanalysis –
in particular, the theses of Lacan, for whom the unconscious is structured like a language. Dealing with the many figures of this specific
rhetoric, Lacan clarifies: 'Can one see here mere manners of speaking,
when it is the figures themselves that are at work in the rhetoric of the
discourse the analysand actually utters?'[63] Politics, according to
Laclau, is likewise a 'figure at work', realizing only in an invariably
temporary and fragile way a meaning that is destined to be undone.
In 1996, he wrote that 'all articulation and . . . the articulating moment
as such is always going to be an empty place – the various attempts at
filling it being transient and submitted to contestation.'[64] Having
become a 'discursive space', the social authorizes recourse to

---

60 Ibid., 118.
61 See Daniel Bensaïd, *Éloge de la politique profane*, Paris: Albin Michel, 2008, 290ff.
62 Laclau, *On Populist Reason*, 150.
63 Jacques Lacan, *Écrits*, trans. Bruce Fink, New York: W.W. Norton & Company,
2002, 433.
64 Laclau, *Emancipation(s)*, 59–60.

psychoanalysis to consolidate his theses and displace them onto the terrain of the symbolic and the affective: 'deconstruction and Lacanian theory have had a decisive importance in the formulation of our approach to hegemony'.[65] Borrowed from Lacan, and he from Claude Lévi-Strauss, the notion of the 'floating signifier' highlights the elective character of 'interpellation', where heterogeneous social demands are going to crystallize; it also indicates its undefined character, which is always available for other constructions. 'This operation of taking up, by a particularity, of an incommensurable universal signification is what I have called *hegemony*.'[66] Thus, 'the hegemonic identity becomes something of the order of an *empty* signifier, its own particularity embodying an unachievable fullness'.[67] Here, Laclau borrows Lacan's redefinition of Oedipal structuration on linguistic ground, while distorting it. It is via the intermediary of the patronym that the child undergoes the experience of the repression of desire and therewith accedes to prohibition and symbolization. Approximating to Lacan's theorization of the 'names-of-the-father', and the role of symbolic embodiment assigned the 'name of the leader', it is ultimately the figure of political paternalism – Caesarism, Bonapartism or *caudillismo* – that Laclau reactivates, far removed from any revival of the popular sovereignty from which the 'radical democracy' he desires distances itself.

Thus, to object to Laclau that the role he confers on language dematerializes reality is to obscure what is concretely at stake in this rhetorical turn. In other words, in proceeding to the unwavering dilution of all the criteria that have hitherto characterized left-wing politics, the analytical linguistic turn proves to be both political and theoretical, underpinning the assertion that 'rhetorical mechanisms . . . constitute the anatomy of the social world'.[68] And this deconstruction takes the form of a conception of the effective power of discourse as 'the primary terrain of the constitution of objectivity as such'[69] and power of fashioning the people. From one work to the next, 'the people' become an ever more indeterminate and artificial entity, existing only by means of such

---

65 Laclau and Mouffe, *Hegemony and Socialist Strategy*, xi.
66 Laclau, *On Populist Reason*, 70.
67 Ibid., 71.
68 Ibid., 110.
69 Ibid., 68.

a construction: 'the chain exists only in so far as one of its links plays the role of condensing all the others'.[70] Laclau adds that

> [i]n those cases, the name becomes the ground of the thing . . . The less a society is kept together by differential immanent mechanisms, the more it depends, for its coherence, on this transcendent, singular moment. But the extreme form of singularity is an individuality. In this way, almost imperceptibly, the equivalential logic leads to singularity and singularity to identification of the unity of the group with the name of the leader.[71]

At this point, the name is assigned the quasi-theological power of a fiat, transposing to the political plane the principle of absolute oversight of a sovereign will, undertaking the political fashioning *ex nihilo* of the mass into a people who have no essence other than what such a construction makes of it. Laclau enjoys recalling Kautsky's famous assertion that socialist consciousness must be brought to the working class from without. Far from aiming at a democratization of political and social life, populism evinces an autocratic slant, whose risk Laclau faces up to despite his defence of liberal institutions.

Thus, despite the preponderant role attributed to language, Laclau is not in fact a postmodernist. Remote from claims for a pure and simple fusion of reality and fiction, or the provocations of a Jean Baudrillard asserting the effective dematerialization of reality replaced by its simulacrum, he stresses the effectivity and quasi-demiurgic power of discourse, once it is embodied. As a result, 'the people' as defined by Laclau is at once an imaginary and a reality created by this shared belief. It is not the result of a protracted history of social conflict in a national context. Nor is it any longer analysed as a polysemic, ambivalent term whose usages oscillate between a logic of class extended to all the dominated and a reactionary nationalist definition. If this people is nothing but the momentary product of discursive procedures, striving to unify fundamentally divergent and juxtaposed demands, then the phrase 'radical democracy' simply names in emphatic fashion a project whose absent social dimension rules out envisaging effective democratization

---

70 Ibid., 100.
71 Ibid.

of capitalist production and social relations, beyond the existing institutions of representative democracy. A pious wish, the call for 'a profound transformation of the existing relations of power'[72] boils down to the formation of a unifying discursive framework whose radicalism remains strictly declamatory, close to linguistic elements in the redefined lefts whose excesses Laclau himself denounces. In line with a history that goes back to ancient Greek democracy, rhetoric as creative power is under constant threat from its double: deceitful artifice.

Is this hegemony without a foundation or project really doomed to remain empty? In passages that are few and far between, Laclau suggests some programmatic tracks which are striking for the ambivalence of their suggestions. Thus, he glimpses the advent of a 'social management' out of the ruins of any 'objectivist outlook'.[73] As against any economic planning, he proposes mixing public ownership and private ownership,[74] a commonplace of neoliberal politics. As for the assertion of the possibility of democratization inherent in existing institutions, it replaces any precise analysis of the contemporary capitalist state and the ongoing neoliberal transformation of its functions. On these issues, the trajectory of Laclau's thought leaves scarcely any room for doubt: while his first book still referred to 'the elimination of class exploitation'[75] as a condition of 'real democracy', the last texts tirelessly reaffirm an essential, ineradicable social heterogeneity.[76] In his last book, the objectives retain the initial ambition only by developing it in an ever more philosophical, and sometimes hermetic, fashion, outlining the curve of a discursive strategy which is ultimately nothing but that of the oeuvre itself, running the risk of placing itself at the disposal of all imaginable uses: 'If hegemony means the representation by a particular social sector of an impossible totality with which it is incommensurable, then it is enough that we make the space of tropological substitutions fully visible, to enable the hegemonic logic to operate freely.'[77]

---

72 Laclau and Mouffe, *Hegemony and Socialist Strategy*, xv.
73 Laclau, *New Reflections*, 55.
74 Ibid., 239.
75 Laclau, *Politics and Ideology*, 108n36 (cont.).
76 Laclau, *On Populist Reason*, 223.
77 Laclau, *The Rhetorical Foundations of Society*, 93.

The Spectre of Socialism

Unquestionably, Laclau's oeuvre attests to his attempt to react to the defeat of the left across its entire spectrum. In proposing a hegemonic strategy, whatever the limits of its definition, he revives the perspective of an alternative, however undefined, which breaks with resignation to eternally minoritarian positions, with a culture of defeat that rules out envisaging the possibility of a dramatic change in the present balance of forces. At the same time, he is one of the few contemporary thinkers to revisit the question of representation on the political terrain. To the extent that this issue of political representation is inseparable from wider strategic problems bound up with transition and mediations, and whereas systematic repudiation of it was at the heart of the philosophy of the 1970s and '80s, it plays a more central role than it appears in the formulation of a political alternative to capitalism.

Indeed, when he underlines the need to bring disparate struggles together without claiming to unify them, Laclau ends up proposing fresh reflection on the general category of representation, going in the opposite direction from a number of the standard authors he calls upon. For all that, far from being grasped as mediation and on the terrain of a post-Kantian dialectical critique of it, representation is thought in the rhetorical mode of metonymy, as we have seen. One specific demand must be selected and charged with the mission of representing all the others, expressing an antagonism that exists only via its intermediary. This does not depend on restructuring the political field and rethinking forms of delegation and control from below, but on the contrary thinking of representation as conceived and controlled from above, organizing a people considered as material to be structured and not as a sovereign will. Consequently, 'any popular identity has an inner structure which is essentially representative',[78] representation having no other referent than the very process of its construction.

It is this representation, de-dialecticized and undemocratic, that comes to replace the classical political mediations of the revolutionary tradition, which aimed for the self-government of the associated producers and were structured around programmes, alliance strategies and radical alternatives, renewed democratic forms. Once there is no longer

---

78 Laclau, *On Populist Reason*, 163.

any mode of production, capitalism is to be thought of as a pure 'system of power'.[79] Politics is thereby freed from any determination that would constrain it, but also emptied of its capacity to be developed as a global alternative starting from the totality of social struggles and protests, however disparate, whose fundamentally anti-capitalist significance it reaps and develops. In this regard, Laclau's politics resembles Kant's dove, convinced that it would fly better in a vacuum than in the air – a metaphor for the propensity of thought to seek to dispense with experience. Without anchorage in the social relations of production, imagining itself liberated from the gravity of real causality, such a strategy no longer has the slightest support in concrete contradictions, to the extent of making the term 'emancipation' a figure of speech that becomes superfluous.

This representative-metonymic conception of politics comes dangerously close to the procedures of an electoral marketing logic, adjusting an offer to 'demands' pertaining to a specific market but incapable of endowing itself with the political structure that protects and regulates its own free functioning at the margins, in line with the neoliberal definition of the role of the state. For the mediating function of classical political representation, which combines diversion of the popular will with its partial, submissive expression, Laclau substitutes not its democratization, but a supremely delegated confiscation, which conceals itself behind the feigned immediacy of the encounter between a discourse and a people. Feint in reality, the discourse alleged to be the people's voice is in fact eruditely constructed without their ever knowing who is working on the articulation of demands and handling the discursive procedures or to what end. Feint again, for, more than the providential man himself, it is the 'name' of the leader which, by artifice, becomes the other name of the people. The latter supposedly believe that they discover in it the reality of a substantive 'us' struggling against the 'them' of an illegitimate oligarchy or a discredited elite, whereas what is revealed in it is merely the void of a signifier, destined to synthesize an absent totality. Such a representation consummates the cleavage that presides over the confiscation of social power, banking on the low consciousness of the masses and their essential political impotence. Further still, it authorizes political strategy becoming the means solely of the electoral

---

79 Laclau, *New Reflections*, 56.

conquest of power, far removed from Laclau's own project but in line with a pragmatism of which, despite himself, he becomes the instrument as well as the theorist.

If the strategy ventured by Laclau is inscribed in the context of a general crisis of politics, it is not long before it in turn suffers from it, proving powerless to understand it as well as to overcome it. Does not the populist strategy risk ultimately being nothing but a magical formula for a hyper-politics, cut off from the reality of exploitation, social injustice and all forms of domination, based on nothing but itself, and ultimately aiming merely for its own perpetuation? But in that case, how can we account for the seductive power of Laclau's work for part of the radical left, despite his renunciation of the construction of an alternative to capitalism? There are several reasons. One, evidently, is the very abandonment, quasi-general on the left, of the construction of an alternative to capitalism. The power of Laclau's thought consists in its capacity to take on board the proliferation of struggles and present them from the positive angle of their political fertility, not in light of the failure, deemed fatal, of a transformative project. Furthermore, Laclau knew how to keep his distance from a sheer glorification of differences and dispersion in order to re-sketch a general perspective, even if he partially discredited it and immediately emptied it of any definite content: 'even though impossible, [unity] remains a horizon which, given the absence of articulation between social relations, is necessary in order to prevent an implosion of the social and an absence of any common point of reference'.[80] Finally, his resonance on the left also derives from his candid revaluation of antagonism, restored to the heart of politics, and directed against both old-style class struggles and the irenicism of tendencies that swear exclusively by consensus and procedural democracy – paths disqualified by the current authoritarian turn.

Nevertheless, in a sense this success remains surprising, when we think that Laclau says nothing about contemporary capitalism – its crisis, the financialization of the economy, the decay of democracy, growing inequalities and rising authoritarianism, environmental destruction and so forth. In these conditions, can we really appeal to a radical transformation and give up on constructing a comprehensive alternative, with a professed social element? Should we not rather admit

---

80 Laclau and Mouffe, *Hegemony and Socialist Strategy*, 188.

that, despite Laclau's project of overcoming or circumventing the opposition between liberalism and socialism, it continues to haunt his whole oeuvre, like a contradiction that is endlessly pursued? This, essentially, is what Laclau himself seems to have recognized at the end of his career. In 2001 he wrote that 'with the failure of its communist variant, it is the very idea of socialism that became discredited'.[81] In his last book, however, he asserted that 'to advance both in the directions of autonomy and hegemony is the real challenge for those who aim for a democratic future that gives real meaning to the frequently advocated "socialism of the twenty-first century"'.[82] We shall venture the conclusion that following communism, socialism has likewise become a spectre that continues to haunt part of contemporary political and strategic reflection. It remains to continue along the strategic road re-explored here, pondering the possibility of a political and social project attentive to the forms of its democratization as well as its emancipatory content.

---

81 Ibid., xiv.
82 Laclau, *The Rhetorical Foundations of Society*, 9.

3

Theories of the Common, or the Permanent Transition

The debate over the property question is once again one of the liveliest spheres in the reconstruction of an alternative. But this question, which represents a classical axis of the distinction between socialism and communism, has long contributed just as much to confusion and fragmentation in defining the two terms. While socialism has often been characterized as the progressive or partial socialization of the major means of production and exchange and communism as the result of this process, communism continues to be regarded as the 'real movement which abolishes the present state of things', with socialism cast as the lower phase of this transformation. What is more, the term *socialism* has been associated with audacious experiments in self-management, while the communist tradition has defended the political principle of workers' control, without the difference ever being clearly established. This confusion reflects the diversity of experience in the transformation of property relations, whose long history on a global scale has seeded complex debates over concrete alternatives to the private appropriation of collectively produced wealth.[1] It continues to fuel a highly dynamic critical and prospective literature. This renewed reflection on forms of property and allocation seeks to offer escape routes from the combined crisis of capitalism and a comprehensive political alternative, proposing a more or less radical transformation of lifestyles and working

---

1 See *Autogestion. L'encyclopédie internationale*, Paris: Syllepse, 2015.

conditions. But in recent decades, it has also been concerned with rede-fining knowledge and culture, as well as a new approach to forms of solidarity and our relationship with nature.

Revival of the debate on property is only logical. Faced with the assault of neoliberal policies on employment law and the dismantling of public services – school, health, transport – but also with the power of the legal and political agents that are their relay – national states, the European project, international treaties, financial institutions, global policies and so on – and the capitalist appropriation of nature, it makes it possible to once again explore ways of rooting the alternative in the conditions of the present, however unfavourable. Added to this is the fact that under contemporary capitalism property law throws up new issues, leading, in particular, to an unprecedented inflation of patents and the ascendancy of intellectual property rights to the exclusive bene-fit of major international enterprises, seizing hold of living things, collective intelligence and social activity in general. At the same time, the old waves of privatization that targeted basic needs, starting with water, have provoked popular mobilizations, particularly in the early 2000s in Latin America, epicentre of a new progressivism that is currently in crisis. To this must be added struggles for access to land and seeds, for sharing and free provision.

We could endlessly extend this list of the challenges to expanding capitalist property rights. In their wake, we have been witnessing a redi-rection of economic and juridical thinking, which strives to construct specific proposals, starting points for a possible re-conquest of social existence in its entirety: common(s) in the singular or plural, lifetime salary or universal allowance, cooperatives, degrowth, a reduction in working hours, taxes on financial transactions and so on. Thus, the theme of property re-emerges in a fresh form, after a prolonged eclipse and its abandonment by various political left-wing organizations. Theoretically, it leads to the reactivation of two related traditions – self-management and the common – as they present themselves in the form of a set of proposals at once concrete and theoretically elaborated. But do they constitute breaches that can be widened for the purposes of superseding capitalism? Or are we merely dealing with suggestions for local adjustment or perspectives that are doomed to remain utopian? By virtue of this examination of their status and significance, but also their long history, they offer unparalleled terrain for reflection, making it possible to concretely clarify the questions of communism and socialism.

Yet for want of genuine strategic elaboration and despite the high political stakes, discussion of property forms often remains at the level of local considerations, feedback on factual experiments or expertise mainly in accounting. Thus, the contemporary theme of property, which directly challenges capitalist logic, often serves to skirt the issue of its supersession. The aim of this chapter is to dwell on this paradox. It involves discussing a number of approaches to the common as such, but also linking them to other dimensions of the alternative to capitalism studied in earlier chapters. For reconnecting the issue of the common with those of the state, struggles and their organization, ideological and hegemonic struggle, and the reappropriation of work and production can all give meaning to the contemporary themes of socialism and communism by linking the general project of transformation, construction of concrete mediations and consideration of past experience. Because it has the merit of being explicitly articulated with the themes of socialism and communism, it is the only question that will be broached in the following pages, via discussion of two approaches that share a critical examination of the very idea of an alternative to capitalism: on the one hand, that of Antonio Negri and post-*operaismo*; on the other, that of Pierre Dardot and Christian Laval, who tackle Negri's conception critically and venture an original and detailed analysis of the issue.

Antonio Negri and the Self-Transcendence of Capitalism

Since the 1980s, Antonio Negri has been the author of an important, ambitious oeuvre that continues to have a powerful influence on a section of European intellectual life. His work is situated at the intersection of academic reflection and political intervention, demarcating itself from Marxism and the left as a whole while developing an original, profoundly paradoxical critique of contemporary capitalism. Negri's itinerary is well known: as a militant close to the Italian extreme left, an academic and a major protagonist in the Italian tradition of *operaismo* constructed against earlier Marxism, he was pursued by Italian justice on account of his presumed links with the Red Brigades. His

philosophical works bear on political issues, mingling classical references to Spinoza, Machiavelli and Hegel in particular. Actively involved
in campaigns by casual and temporary workers, supporter of universal
income, and militant of the commons, he also declared his support for
the decidedly liberal project of the European Constitutional Treaty of
2005, which he reckoned capable of obstructing what he calls Empire
and US neoliberalism, while contributing (positively according to him)
to the dissolution of any form of national sovereignty.[2] The trilogy
written between 2000 and 2009 in collaboration with American theorist
Michael Hardt develops the idea of a transformation of the working
class and, more generally, of a mutation in capitalism, rendering the old
socialist and communist options inoperative. Their work unfolded in
several phases. *Empire*, the first volume published in 2000, sets in place
several fundamental themes concerning the new order of the world and
the new forms of resistance it provokes. *Multitude*, published in 2004,
develops these issues in strategic and political terms. Then
Commonwealth, published in 2009, tackles the question of the common
in particular. Before attending more closely to the third work, we must
therefore briefly recall Negri and Hardt's general project.

　　Their objective in the texts is to rethink politics in the context of capitalist globalization, regarding the latter as a development ultimately
more positive and promising than disturbing, for those capable of identifying its underground tendencies. Foremost among those tendencies
is the ongoing disappearance of any form of political control over a
liberal logic that is emancipating itself ever more radically. According to
the authors, this control hitherto fell to nation-states and was ensured
by the apparatus of modern sovereignty, of which they are the reposito-
ries. Its defeat is good news, attesting to an irresistible process of decentralization and de-territorialization, to employ a category from Deleuze
– one of Negri's major theoretical references. This is a process that
promises the inevitable defeat of all forms of control: 'Empire manages
hybrid identities, flexible hierarchies, and plural exchanges through
modulating networks of command. The distinct national colors of the
imperialist map of the world have merged and blended in the imperial

---

2 Antonio Negri, 'Faire l'Europe dans la mondialisation', *Multitudes* 14, 2003, 60,
and 'Oui pour faire disparaître cette merde d'État-nation', *Libération*, 13 May 2005.

global rainbow.'[3] For Negri and Hardt, Empire is a planetary reality, which they contrast with Marxist theories of imperialism. While Empire possesses a real power of oppression, it above all affords potentialities for liberation that entail the expiry of old political hypotheses about the transcendence of capitalism, not because the cause is lost in advance, but, on the contrary, because the disappearance of the latter is already a fact: 'Empire pretends to be the master of [the] world because it can destroy it. What a horrible illusion! In reality we are masters of the world because our desire and labor regenerate it continuously.'[4] It is simply a question of registering the tendencies at work and 'reorganiz[ing] them and redirect[ing] them towards new ends'.[5] One can see how this radicalism, which involves no concrete engagement, could prove highly seductive. Many commentators have noted the spontaneism and fervent optimism that underlie the declaration. But one point is especially striking: while they wish to promote the power of a new subject – the multitude – Negri and Hardt paradoxically revive the historical determinism so often imputed to Marxism in general, allocating a leading role to technological changes, independently of any strategy and project.

Thus, it is at the heart of its chosen field – critical analysis of production and labour – that the expiry of Marxism is proclaimed, while the most mechanistic version of its prognosis is recycled. Negri and Hardt see a new general configuration taking shape, which integrates political, social and economic dimensions with one another, in contrast to their distinction and hierarchical ordering according to a historical causality rigidly determined by the economic base, in line with the vulgate attributed to Marxism in its entirety. The disappearance of any economic determination, even in the last instance, reveals the predominantly normative political and social logic of the 'society of control' theorized by Deleuze, 'in which mechanisms of command become ever more "democratic", ever more immanent to the social field, distributed throughout the brains and bodies of the citizens';[6] this logic connects production, politics and life itself. Negri and Hardt's 'biopolitics', extending its definition by Foucault, is defined by the emergence of a power

---

3 Michael Hardt and Antonio Negri, *Empire*, Cambridge: Harvard University Press, 2000, xii–xiii.

4 Ibid., 395.

5 Ibid., xv.

6 Ibid., 23.

that is no longer external, of a disciplinary kind, but immanent, now focused on the production and reproduction of life, penetrating consciousness and bodies, abolishing any relationship of mediation and representation at root.

It is precisely here that Negri takes up and alters Marx's analysis of the transition from 'formal subsumption' to 'real subsumption' in the 1857–8 manuscripts.[7] Marx's terms describe the capitalist remoulding of the productive forces (real subsumption) after this mode of production inherited those forces from feudalism, initially using them as such (formal subsumption). For Negri, the process of subsumption that characterizes Empire is quite different: it now concerns the absorption of civil society by the state, attested by the decline of the old social institutions he lists – the school, the family, the hospital, the factory, the prison.[8] Their discipline, formerly imposed from without, gives way to diffuse, direct, ubiquitous control. But this higher level of integration immediately induces an explosion and proliferation of singularities which become central and 'active in the center of a society that opens up in networks',[9] escaping their previously imposed coordination in the framework of civil society.

In these circumstances, oppositional power is as immediate and immanent as the control that enfolds it (the thesis is Foucault's) but above all is more fundamental and decisive than that control (by contrast, Foucault never said this). Its victory is assured not by dint of a risky political prophecy, but by a proclaimed ontological truth. That is why philosophy once more plays a leading political role, through its capacity to identify subterranean processes invisible to the great majority. According to Negri and Hardt, these processes are unprecedented and the present understanding of biopower requires us to go beyond Foucault's 'structuralist' theses. The latter are incapable of grasping a complex dynamic, demanding recourse to the 'poststructuralist'[10] analyses of Deleuze and Félix Guattari, centred on a social ontology of flows. However, these approaches must in turn be superseded by analysis of an unequalled power of creative production impacting societies today. It is

---

7 See 'Appendix: Results of the Immediate Process of Production', in Karl Marx, *Capital Volume 1*, trans. Ben Fowkes, Harmondsworth: Pelican/NLR, 1976, 1019ff.

8 Hardt and Negri, *Empire*, 329.

9 Ibid., 25.

10 Ibid., 28.

from Italian post-*operaismo* that Negri and Hardt draw their fundamental inspiration to account for the 'immaterial labour' and 'general intellect' that characterize contemporary capitalism in its own right. To it they add the new importance of the productivity of bodies and the manipulation of affects, irreducible to the classical analysis of immaterial labour exclusively on the terrain of communication, inasmuch as they engage the very living individuality of the worker.

In short, the development of biopower is 'paradoxical', as Negri says, anxious to banish the Marxist dialectic and to supersede all past approaches, deemed unduly simplistic: 'Our analysis has to descend into the jungle of productive and conflictual determination that the collective biopolitical body offers us.'[11] Linking up with Deleuze's thesis that there is no longer any outside to capitalism, Negri rediscovers the positions of certain Frankfurt School thinkers and various sociological traditions asserting the integration of the working class into capitalism, contrary to its definition as the quintessential force of resistance to it. But above all, according to Negri and Hardt, who here adopt the theses of *operaismo*, it is proletarian movements and struggles that were the motor of the transformations of contemporary capitalism,[12] in the knowledge that today's proletariat is precisely no longer the working class of yesteryear. The systemic, totalizing character of the imperial machine has as its quid pro quo the presence within it of tendencies which, without being secessionist, re-create a space for innovative struggles that 'destroy the traditional distinction between economic and political struggles': they are 'constituent struggles, creating new public spaces and new forms of community'.[13]

Determined to confront the left's strategies for social transformation, the authors do not hesitate to affirm that the victory of liberal commodification was, in fact, impelled by capitalism's most substantial opponents:

The globalization of markets, far from being simply the horrible fruit of capitalist entrepreneurship, was actually the result of the desires of Taylorist, Fordist, and disciplined labor power across the world . . .

---

11 Ibid., 30.
12 Ibid., 208.
13 Ibid., 56.

The movements of desiring subjectivities forced the development to go forward – and proclaimed that there was no turning back.[14]

The major political turn attendant on this analysis concerns the nature of social conflict and, more fundamentally still, the Marxist thesis of class struggle, replaced by the theme of the multitude. This redefinition of social confrontation – likewise at the heart of Ernesto Laclau's approach and numerous other authors' – takes up theses developed from the 1960s to the 1990s which counterposed increasing social homogeneity to class analysis.[15] This assertion, defended despite all subsequent sociological works contradicting or complicating it, aims to bolster the assertion of the disappearance of the working class as a social and political reality. The perspective of an exit from capitalism is replaced by an appeal for a reorientation of its management and by a desire to amplify its immanent tendencies. While the latter hypothesis is more than plausible, the anticipated emancipatory effects are more than dubious. The traditional question of property is in turn posed in an original way, assuming that 'the foundation of the classic modern conception of private property is thus to a certain extent dissolved in the postmodern mode of production'.[16] It then only remains to construct the new institutional forms, envisaged as being automatically consensual.

Thus, at the same time as class structure disappears, the project of a different mode of production is sunk in euphoric fashion, in sharp contrast to the habitual registration of failure and consequent political pessimism. The critique of the dialectic, commonplace in 1970s philosophy, lies at the heart of this re-foundation. Negativity, which Hegel defined as the movement of negation of a positive term, a negation destined to rebound against itself in turn and generate a new positivity, is part of all dialectical conceptions of history, idealist and materialist alike, even if they differ fundamentally. Negativity, reduced to a

---

14 Ibid., 256.

15 Theories of the growth of the middle class were developed by sociologists like Robert Nisbet in the US and then Henri Mendras in France, in the wake of Tocqueville's theses. Other theorists would assert the disappearance of the working class, like Alain Touraine, Serge Mallet and André Gorz, in the wake of the 'second left', before the theme of classes resurfaced at the turn of the 2000s. See Roland Pfefferkorn, *Inégalités et rapports sociaux. Rapports de classes, rapports de sexe*, Paris: La Dispute, 2007.

16 Hardt and Negri, *Empire*, 302.

simplistic, teleological philosophy of history, is replaced by pure affirmation, formerly ranged against Hegel by Nietzsche, and by 'an antagonistic and creative positivity',[17] which is rebellious in essence. What is immediately deduced is the prospect of a simple reorientation of the capitalist dynamic, best ally of the communist project, which involves embracing the tendencies at work rather than fighting them in vain.

In embracing the idealized tendencies of the present, what is straightforwardly adopted is liberal and managerial discourse, from its glorification of flexibility to its appeal to the creativity of wage earners, on to the denunciation of the rigidities of the welfare state and the archaisms of class struggle. If Negri has the merit of registering the subversion of work collectives and the decline of a past culture of working-class solidarity, if he clearly perceives the rise of the desire for autonomy and individualization, his critique of Empire always verges on adhesion to liberalism. While conceding this contradiction, Negri carefully euphemizes it, stating it in peremptory philosophical terms at a remove from any detailed inquiry into the real conditions of production or the contemporary situation of wage labour: 'a new sense of being is imposed on the constitution of Empire by the creative movement of the multitude',[18] even foreshadowing an indiscernible 'global citizenship'[19] that prompts the re-emergence of a highly improbable system of planetary law, independent of states and contrary to the tendencies everywhere operative in this regard. But while Negri and Hardt's political theses lack plausibility, they are supported by the development of a new critique of political economy – the theory of cognitive capitalism – which reconnects with a tradition partially deserted by the Marxism of recent decades, while, at the same time, breaking with its most central categories.

A Revolution of Autonomy

The originality of Negri and Hardt's analyses consists in the intellectually seductive and stylistically virtuoso combination of a resolutely

17 Ibid., 61.
18 Ibid., 62.
19 Ibid., 400.

ontological argument, a terminology of conflict and an innovative presentation of the changes at work in the mode of production and labour,
which are often ignored by philosophy. The authors seek, skilfully, to
occupy the terrain of Marxist research and of alternatives to capitalism
while radically redefining the economic and political issues – of value,
labour, the state, party or strategy – as well as the analysis of their articulation. Their argument rests entirely on the idea that immaterial labour,
which is becoming generalized, 'immediately involves social interaction
and cooperation',[20] unlike earlier forms of labour, organized and disciplined from without. The political deduction is all the more direct in
that it provides the premises for the analysis: 'In the expression of its
own creative energies, immaterial labor thus seems to provide the
potential for a kind of spontaneous and elementary communism.'[21] The
claim is bound to seduce readers foreign to the experience of activism
and the widespread success of such books may be interpreted as the
direct result of the extension of an advanced form of depoliticization
that remains shot through with fundamentally political concerns.

    For their own purposes, Negri and Hardt adopt the idea that postmo-
dernity has really arrived and is an actual stage of capitalism, not simply
a partisan reading of the contemporary world conveyed by the notion
despite its strictly descriptive ambition. In this context, the fusion of the
economic and the political, which renders any organization and
programmatic transition superfluous, leads the authors to render
'common' and 'communism' synonymous. The new critique of political
economy is thus centred on the hypothesis of a radical mutation in
contemporary capitalism, which it would suffice to push and accompany to a conclusion for alienation to turn into autonomy and for living
labour to exceed the capitalist framework enfolding it. At the end of
Empire, Negri and Hardt affirm that 'labour is the productive activity of
a general intellect and a general body outside measure'.[22] Directed
against the Marxist theory of value, this redefinition of labour metamor-
phoses it into pure subversive energy. It is no longer conceived as the
contradictory site of capitalist exploitation and resistance to alienation
that must construct its political path; it is instead a vital, gushing,

---

20 Ibid., 294.
21 Ibid.
22 Ibid., 358.

fundamentally inalienable power: 'We can thus define the virtual power of labor as a power of self-valorization that exceeds itself, flows over onto the other, and, through this investment, constitutes an expansive commonality.'[23] Production is obviously under the control of capital but, at the same time, is already wholly autonomous, defined by cooperation and a collaborative network of intelligences and affects, beyond any measurement in terms of value. Their argument distorts concepts taken from Marx, and as they extend the notion of production to social existence itself, its precise meaning evaporates and the notion of value undergoes similar generalization, detaching it from the Marxian dialectic between its three dimensions – use-value, value and exchange-value. Consequently, instead of an analysis of capitalism as a mode of production and exchange of commodities, which makes value not a substance but the form of a social relation, the theory of value in general imputed to Marxism is reduced to a simple problem of measurement and demoted to the rank of accomplice in the accounting logic of capitalism.

This transformation is accompanied by a radical mutation in labour, which dispels traditional class conflicts in favour of the emergence of a new power. Localized struggles, deemed by Negri and Hardt as by Laclau to be 'incommunicable', secrete their necessary transcendence as 'constituent struggles', requiring recourse to no rhetorical construction: 'precisely because all these struggles are incommunicable and thus blocked from travelling horizontally in the form of a cycle, they are forced instead to leap vertically and touch immediately on the global level.'[24] The 'multitude' is the glorious name for this collective power, an immanent subject, needing neither mediation nor representation, a factor of radical autonomy, whose 'scientific, affective, and linguistic forces . . . aggressively transform the conditions of social production.'[25] Ultimately, this aggressiveness projects itself as a call for new rights, without any way to achieve them being defined: 'reappropriation means having free access to and control over knowledge, information, communication, and affects – because these are some of the primary means of

---

23 Ibid.
24 Ibid., 55.
25 Ibid., 366.

biopolitical production'.[26] These issues, and their legal and political aspects, are developed in particular in *Commonwealth*, as well as in a book of interviews significantly entitled *Goodbye, Mr Socialism*.

These two works revolve around the depreciation of socialism and the promotion of a new generation of communism. The link between the political theses of *Empire* and the legal notion of the common is presented synthetically in an intervention by Negri during a conference in London in 2009 on 'The Idea of Communism'. In it he begins by affirming that to be a communist is to be 'against the State' – a hostility found among many theorists who identify with communism today. Such opposition to the state involves opposition to private forms of property, but likewise equally to its public forms, 'that is, the *state* and *national* configurations of all these operations of alienation of the power of labour'.[27] The common is presented here as common labour, embodying active communism against all its deviations, whether capitalist or socialist. We can conclude that 'therefore communism is the enemy of socialism'.[28] Once socialism has been stripped of any specific strategic and political meaning, only statism and its opposite remain in contention.

Placing public and private back to back in the name of a third property regime – the common – allows Negri to simplify a complex history. Starting with the postwar period, it led to the development of a 'social' state which, under the impact of social and political struggles, enabled a partial redistribution of the social wealth privatized by capital, and it could have provided a fulcrum for challenging capitalist logic as a whole. Faced with the alternative between a radicalized break and a return to liberal logic, a fundamentally political choice was made. In this respect, the failure of Keynesianism to overcome the crisis that began in the late 1960s consisted not in its intrinsic technical inability, as an economic policy in the narrow sense, to stabilize capitalism. It stemmed from its unperceived character as a strategic factor (independently of Keynes's own views) open to being integrated into two possible, divergent, political options: either limited social concessions, risking cancellation at the

---

26 Ibid., 407.

27 Antonio Negri, 'Communism: Some Thoughts on the Concept and Practice', in Costas Douzinas and Slavoj Zizek, eds, *The Idea of Communism*, New York: Verso, 2010, 158.

28 Ibid.

earliest opportunity, or the construction of a fulcrum for social and political mobilization in favour of a radical alternative to capitalism.

This period witnessed the loss of the strategic sense of 'socialism', as it was torn between a social-democratic usage sliding towards liberalism, on the one hand, and employment by the Soviet camp, on the other, paralysing its initial dynamic. Seemingly antithetical, these two options made the path of the alternative illegible and unintelligible. Opening it up would have required fashioning and presenting social reforms as tendential, deliberate challenges, of a fundamentally political kind, to capitalist logic. The inability to build such a strategy on popular mobilization occurred in the aftermath of various episodes of electoral victory by the left in France, the Popular Front representing the primal scene of renunciation of class confrontation taken to a conclusion. Social half-measures in the face of unbridled opposition, the betrayal of anti-colonial hopes and procrastination confronted with Franco's coup d'état in Spain form the enduring framework of a long-term refusal to mobilize the popular classes despite a massive initial strike wave.[29] The conviction that electoral victory is enough to conquer the totality of political and social power advances a political culture that continues to weigh heavily on emancipatory perspectives, all the more so when a transnational framework, such as the highly liberal European Union, makes it possible to disarm any progressive programme in advance when it is not conceived as a weapon of class confrontation and the establishment of a genuine social democracy.[30]

But the history Negri recounts is quite different: the construction of Europe is an opportunity to destroy any national sovereignty, the state for him not being one of the sites of class confrontation at the same time as a tool of the dominant class; instead, Negri sees it as an abstract structure of domination to be overthrown as a matter of priority, with a view to liberating the forces of the multitude and establishing 'supreme authorities whose objective is participation, not control'.[31] Thus, Negri

---

29 See Jean Vigreux, *Le Front populaire*, Paris: Presses Universitaires de France, 2011, Chapter 4.

30 Michel Huson, *Un pur capitalisme*, Lausanne: Page deux, 2008, 146. On this subject, see also Alain Bihr, *La Novlangue néolibérale. La rhétorique du fétichisme capitaliste*, Lausanne: Page deux, 2007.

31 Antonio Negri, *Goodbye, Mr Socialism*, trans. P. Bertilotti, Paris: Éditions du Seuil, 2007, 180.

contrasts the old form of self-management with the direct, effective reappropriation of their instruments of labour by productive subjects forming part of the contemporary 'general intellect'.[32] The notion of the common is directly bound up with this view. Analysed via distinct, incompatible legal forms, the question of property is considerably simplified, relieved of its economic and social contradictions, which have always underpinned its successive historical mutations. All that remains is the opposition between common and property, be it private or public.

Connecting the economic and juridical levels, Negri draws a historical sketch that eliminates the contradictions and detours of real history, taking its conceptual instruments from various theoretical traditions. And if Marxism remains a reference, it is precisely to the extent that it is radically reconfigured, in particular via borrowings from 1970s philosophy, especially Foucault, Deleuze and Guattari, and Italian *operaismo* and post-*operaismo*. In this respect, Negri's works are in the vein of the literary return of communism, alongside the oeuvres of Alain Badiou or the Invisible Committee. Their great seductive power stems from this original combination of the theoretical traditions of the 1960s and '70s still extant in contemporary intellectual life, with the endeavour to assimilate the changes in labour and production in a manner that associates with them a professedly novel political perspective. Unlike Badiou's reprise of the communist idea, Negri and Hardt propose a communist path that is far from subversive in the end, but it manifests its radicalism by denouncing the totality of oppositional options, past and present. This strategic choice, exclusively intellectual, steers an economic analysis that is not truly developed as such, as is demonstrated by the pamphleteering tone of *Goodbye Mr Socialism*, in contrast to various earlier texts by Negri.

Some Concrete Proposals

Nevertheless, the analyses seek to be original, responding to a shared need not to separate economic realities and political perspectives. Here the paradox is at its height – for if Negri and Hardt set about

---

32 Ibid., 173, 209.

reconnecting the communist idea and political economy, they immediately seek to detach the communist perspective from any mass mobilization and, even more so, from any revolutionary process, to the point of depoliticizing it. Rallying unreservedly to the ruling democratic doxa, Negri writes: 'I don't think we need a revolutionary party . . . it would be enough just to have democratic governance and decent administration.'[33] He specifies that the priority seems to him to be the introduction of a citizen's income, accusing the left of relaying 'harmful, destructive myths such as permanent work contracts'.[34]

It should be recalled that the defence of universal income, sometimes associated with the promotion of negative tax, both of which were defended by Foucault, are proposals advanced by part of the neoliberal tradition. For it is true that this option disarms any general opposition and reconnects with a principle of updated charity, covering relations of exploitation with an ethical coating. Given this, we shall not be surprised to find ultra-neoliberal US economist Milton Friedman, French president Giscard d'Estaing, ecological theorist André Gorz and social Catholic Henri Guitton among its many defenders. With his habitual lucidity, Foucault had already noted that 'this negative tax is a way of absolutely avoiding social policy having any kind of effect in the form of a general redistribution of income, that is to say, broadly speaking, anything that could be described as a socialist policy'.[35] A little further on, he added: 'this other way is the assisted population, which is actually assisted in a very liberal and much less bureaucratic and disciplinary way than it is by a system focused on full employment which employs mechanisms like those of social security'.[36] For Foucault, as we can see, liberalism remains the opposite of socialism, the latter being characterized by a disciplinary and bureaucratic logic that liberalism seeks to limit. Negri, however, attempts with define a 'third way', politically unclassifiable, combining hostility to socialism and loans from liberalism, each of these terms being recast in the crucible of a critique of capitalism that is radical in tone, especially towards its corrupt financial

33 Ibid., 140–1.

34 Ibid., 143.

35 Michel Foucault, *The Birth of Biopolitics: Lectures at the Collège de France, 1978–79*, ed. Michel Senellart and trans. Graham Burchell, London: Palgrave Macmillan, 2010, 205.

36 Ibid., 207.

elite. Before discussing the question of the common in greater detail, we must stress the fact that this complex position licenses an especially violent denunciation of the classical left that is not at all particular about the arguments it uses. Under cover of options intended to be more innovative, Negri does not hesitate to characterize the French rejection of the draft European Constitution during the 2005 referendum as 'national-socialist', or to condemn the 'corporatist reflexes' of the great French strike movement of 1995. In his view, the top priority should be to abandon these old-style mobilizations. In their place, 'we must get capital to recognize the influence and importance of the common good and, if it doesn't wish to come to terms with it, force it to'.[37] Negri does not specify how capital is to be successfully 'forced' in these conditions. He makes do with declaring that 'any attempt at external organization only disrupts and corrupts the process of self-organization'.[38] Ultimately, in the name of the autonomy of the multitude, the liberal model of governance is imposed, conceived as new political engineering and enhanced technology, without any treatment of its democratic dimension: 'an open infrastructure of information and culture would have to be constructed to develop fully and put into practice the multitude's abilities to think and cooperate with others'.[39]

Does this approach aim to oppose capitalism? Such is not the main goal of Negri and Hardt, who seek in the first instance to break with the traditional options of the left while constructing a middle way, above all theoretical, between opposition to the changes underway and describing them. Thus, Negri boldly declares that today pension funds embody the 'communism of capital' and that it only remains to convert them into the 'communism of the multitude'.[40] In so doing, he invokes Marx's analysis of joint-stock companies in Volume Three of *Capital*, with Negri attributing to him the phrase 'socialism of capital'. However, Marx's analysis is different. This form of capital, which is composed of an association of individual owners of capital, presents itself as 'social capital' (and not 'socialism of capital'): 'it is the abolition of capital as private property within the framework of the capitalist mode of

37 Negri, *Goodbye Mr Socialism*, 235.
38 Michael Hardt and Antonio Negri, *Commonwealth*, 302.
39 Ibid., 308.
40 Negri, *Goodbye Mr Socialism*, 183.

production', which makes it possible to envisage 'the reconversion of capital into the property of producers, although no longer as the private property of the individual producers, but rather as the property of associated producers, as direct social property'.[41] For Marx, a 'reconversion' of this kind involves not taking the logic of capital to its conclusion, but opposing and destroying it. Negri proposes a quite different road, which consists in detecting within present-day capitalism its already realized abolition, its imminent, inevitable materialization requiring neither class struggle nor organization, nor a project.

The redefinition of communism that follows from this goes hand in hand with the naming of a new subject of history (the multitude, but above all casualized intellectual workers, contrasted with the traditional working class), immediately derived from the purported mutation in the conditions of production, eliminating the moment of political construction as well as the mediation of social struggles. Thus, the political dimension of social change is not abolished, but displaced and subtracted from strategic debate, as well as from the prospect of its radicalization and popular generalization. Rather than being conceived as a process and the aim of a possible transcendence of capitalism, it becomes the presupposition of the analysis, guiding a description of the changes in production far removed from the much more composite and complex reality of the world of labour. Laurent Baronian writes: 'Taylorism should be regarded not as a series of procedures, but as a system of principles for managing labour in common which, in the age of information and communication technologies, finds new domains of application.'[42] In Negri and Hardt, mention of the unprecedented role of information replaces any examination of the new forms of alienation affecting all types of labour, even if they now and then recognize that cognitive labour is not always synonymous with autonomy.

What is, all in all, a wildly optimistic presentation of the new forms of cooperation obscures practices of domination, both traditional and novel, the managerial instrumentalization of competitive relations between wage earners and the unparalleled global expansion of

---

41 *Capital Vol. 3*, in Karl Marx and Friedrich Engels, *Collected Works*, Vol. 37, London: Lawrence & Wishart, 1998, 434.

42 Laurent Baronian, 'L'âge du nouveau taylorisme. Critique des théories sur les nouvelles organisations du travail industriel', *Revue de la Régulation* 14, 2013, 41.

capitalist commodification. But the discrepancy between theory and reality is skilfully reduced thanks to a general philosophical approach, occasionally prophetic in tone, which permits Negri never to enter into the concrete details of the analysis. As if the question of the common, merely by being highlighted, was capable of embodying and enacting an alternative to capitalism.

Biopolitics and Death of Mediations

Of the three books co-written by Negri and Hardt, *Commonwealth* is the one that most clearly develops the theme of the common – a notion they employ in the singular, which they take from a highly composite and dynamic intellectual current. Their definition comprises the economic, social and political dimensions of what is not merely a form of property but aims to apprehend a new modality of production, a new social agent and a new political perspective. This common is rooted in the thesis of a production that has become 'biopolitical', to quote Michel Foucault, who was the first to venture a description of this precipitate of production and politics, connected by him with the emergence of bourgeois power – the latter opting for control procedures directed at free individuals rather than disciplinary procedures constraining subjects. In his 1978–9 lecture course at the Collège de France, Foucault argued that it is necessary to 'study . . . liberalism as the general framework of biopolitics'.[43] According to him, liberalism is concerned with combining individual interests, recognized and liberated, and collective interest, maintained and conceived as the pole of security that offsets and balances the pole of liberty by proceeding to multiply micro-powers. He counterposes this 'liberal governmentality' to the absence of 'socialist governmental rationality',[44] its lack explaining (according to him) why socialism could not be an alternative to liberalism.

While simplifying it, Negri adopts Foucault's idea of a complex relationship between civil society and the state. For Foucault, this relationship is both internal and external,[45] whereas for Negri, it is purely

---

43 Foucault, *The Birth of Biopolitics*, 22.
44 Ibid., 94.
45 Ibid., 308ff.

external. And if the latter renews Foucault's critique of socialism, in passing he also redefines biopower as a logic not of control but of production: 'biopolitical production is becoming hegemonic in the contemporary economy, filling the role that industry played for well over one hundred years'.[46] As a result, the caesura no longer runs between disciplinary societies and societies of control, but between industrial societies and post-Fordist societies, the latter supposedly being born before our eyes. Thus distorted and simplified, the notion of biopolitics becomes the key concept of a resolutely postmodern approach, affirming the irreversible fragmentation of the social world at the same time as the death of ideologies, which heralds the death of socialism and capitalism alike. Negri's biopolitics is the power *of* life, in contrast to the power *over* life that Foucault's biopower also is. The emergence of biopolitics attests to the new productivity of bodies and affects, as well as the crucial role of cooperation in immaterial labour. For Negri, this productivity and cooperation are leeched off by capitalism, while they basically elude its authority and irreversibly subvert its logic.

In place of the Marxist contradiction between labour and capital, we find the much more ambiguous and composite figure of a capital now external to the production of value, on the one hand, and an omnipresence of this same capital, on the other. It 'subsume[s] not just labor but society as a whole or, really, social life itself, since life is both what is put to work in biopolitical production and what is produced'.[47] That is why the suggested scenario is no longer a transcendence of class antagonism, but an autonomization of the multitude within the mode of production that gives rise to it, on the model of the flight theorized by Deleuze: 'class struggle in the biopolitical context takes the form of exodus'.[48] Despite its visionary accents, the argument seeks to be as moderate as it is realistic, discrediting the openly anti-capitalist alternatives, which, in Negri and Hardt's view, are incorrigibly naïve: 'we are not proclaiming the demise of capital but rather identifying the growing incapacity of capital to integrate labor-power within itself'.[49] This

---

46 Hardt and Negri, *Commonwealth*, 286.
47 Ibid., 142.
48 Ibid., 152.
49 Ibid., 293.

claim is based on promoting the common as a legal form of biopolitical production, which makes it possible to absorb the political question into the sphere of production. This dynamic replaces a revolutionary break with an autonomy wrested from institutions, paving the way for a communist ethic that involves regenerating the values of love and poverty: 'our slogan to combine the political and the economic might be "poverty and love" or (for those who consider such terms too senti-mental) "power and the common".'[50] Overall, then, Negri's critique of capitalism is focused not on a fundamental logic of exploitation and domination, but on certain social structures isolated from the analysis of contemporary relations of production: 'the individual must flee the family, the corporation, and the nation but at the same time build on the promises of the common they mobilize'.[51] On the one hand, this option – which reactivates themes with a libertarian resonance of an essentially societal critique, while adopting the Hegelian divisions of the section devoted to 'ethical life' in *Principles of the Philosophy of Right* – bypasses and discredits social struggles deemed archaic. On the other hand, what is radicalized is the refusal of mediations of any kind, along with representation – veritable leitmotif of contemporary propo-nents of the return of communism – in favour of a homogenizing conception of Empire and multitude alike.

The thesis of immanence sustains the idea that any site of interven-tion whatsoever is now central, making it possible to distance oneself once and for all from the demands of a labour movement adjudged incurably identitarian. Negri invokes the model of a 'queer politics',[52] generalized but also edulcorated into an identitarian critique of identity. All in all, the analysis does not take into account the persistence of national states, the maintenance and revival of imperialisms or the proliferation of conflicts and military interventions any more than it does the rise of racisms or ethnicized and 'confessionalized' forms of social contradictions. While Negri and Hardt seek to include certain salient features of contemporary reality in their analysis, they banish so many others that their theses prove to be fragile and ever less convincing as real history departs from their prognoses.

---

50 Ibid., 354–5.
51 Ibid., 164.
52 Ibid., 335.

However that may be, *Commonwealth* focuses on the new revolution underway with a view to hitting upon 'a positive, nondialectical solution, leading toward democracy through democratic means'.[53] With this in mind, adoption of the theme of the common enables Negri and Hardt to retain only such features of the contemporary world as seem to them to foreshadow this solution. At stake is developing an alternative that abolishes not capitalism, but the project of its abolition, replacing it with a new institutionalization that risks being more technocratic than democratic: 'governance ... attempts to create social order without representation'.[54] Negri and Hardt lucidly acknowledge that 'analyses of the crisis of representation generally fit within the project of "the liberal critique of liberalism"'.[55] This is a profoundly ambiguous project inasmuch as the disappearance of the state can either lead to denunciation of the cleavage of politics it embodies, in favour of its genuine democratization, or boil down to the project of its quasi-absorption into civil society as it is – that is to say, structured by class relations and dominated by market logics. But instead of an analysis of the capitalist market, the wage-earning class and the exploitation of labour-power, we find an assertion of an instability constitutive of liberal governance that allegedly paves the way for its immanent subversion. This alternative without alterity, and break without conflict, assumes the highly paradoxical form of a revolution at once promised and yet already accomplished.

Cognitive Capitalism

In these circumstances, why especially promote the common? First of all, what does it consist in? It is not reducible to land, the authors write, without furnishing a precise definition, 'but also [comprises] the languages we create, the social practices we establish, the modes of sociality that define our relationships, and so forth'.[56] Negri and Hardt are exclusively interested in the idea that the common, contrasted with private and public property alike, makes it possible to place liberalism and socialism

---

53 Ibid., 363.
54 Ibid., 347–8.
55 Ibid., 347.
56 Ibid., 139.

back to back, with the latter reduced to a form of statism. Remote from traditional views of the common, here the accent is put on cooperation: 'cognitive labor and affective labor generally produce cooperation autonomously from capitalist command, even in some of the most constrained and exploited circumstances, such as call centers or food services.'[57] Negri and Hardt are not afraid to argue that autonomy can be detected in the most typically capitalist sectors, where wage earners are most exploited and casualized. But nothing is said about working conditions and wages, or about the massive retention of Taylorist forms of production; the argument concentrates on the strictly predatory role of capital, which 'captures and expropriates value through biopolitical exploitation that is produced, in some sense, *externally* to it'.[58]

Relying once again on real tendencies that they generalize and push to the limit, Negri and Hardt maintain that contemporary capitalism develops its logic of accumulation through rent much more than via profit. This licenses abandonment, pure and simple, of the theory of exploitation. In these circumstances, the common already proves to be an essential mutant force, which capitalism can only envelop in its logic with great difficulty. Maintaining the momentum, Negri and Hardt risk taking the paradox to its ultimate conclusions. This involves radicalizing the ambiguity: 'we have no intention of celebrating or condemning finance capital. We propose instead to treat it as a field of investigation for tracking down the specters of the common lurking there.'[59] These statements are aimed squarely at the 'old' left, across its whole spectrum, and consist in ranging against it a euphoric adoption of the postmodern theory of the death of politics, along with any project of radical transformation, of the disappearance of classes, of the spontaneous, joyous emergence of 'altermodernity'.[60] The notion of the common makes it possible to develop an older hypothesis of Negri's: the mutation of contemporary capitalism theorized in particular by Yann Moulier Boutang under the rubric of cognitive capitalism.

According to Moulier Boutang, intellectual activities have become a directly productive force. But by dint of their own characteristics

---

57 Ibid., 140.
58 Ibid., 141.
59 Ibid., 158.
60 Ibid., 106–7.

– cooperation, sharing and networking – they are able to transform the operation of capitalism from within, destroying traditional property relations. Supplanting labour-power, 'invention-power' proves capable of subverting this capitalism, 'as unstable a system as the two types of capitalism that preceded it',[61] already installing communist relations of distribution and exchange at the heart of the mode of production most hostile to them. It is living labour, mobilized as such by cognitive capitalism, which directly resists its commodification and incorporation into capital. Tendentially, therefore, capitalism finds itself confronted from within by an unprecedented oppositional power, which hands the economic and political initiative to living labour. New categories of the exploited, their model temporary workers in the entertainment industry, are in the process of replacing the old industrial proletariat and fundamentally rejuvenating struggles as well as the political perspectives bound up with them. On the one hand, 'the increasingly public character of knowledge-goods calls into question the possibility of their being able to be produced through the market system'.[62] On the other, waged work has gone into irreversible decline and is eventually due to be replaced by a guaranteed income, disconnected from employment and more in tune with the contemporary non-differentiation between working time and free time. Finally, a new mode of production is foreshadowed which must be fully brought into being by struggling against the resistance mounted by capitalism to the egalitarian and emancipatory logics it has itself incubated.

In line with this analysis, for Negri and Hardt it can be said that the new productive model is already centred on knowledge. Without any precise or detailed analysis, they proclaim that 'knowledge is no longer merely a means to the creation of value (in the commodity form), but rather the production of knowledge is itself value production'.[63] This supposedly confronts capitalism with an insurmountable challenge: 'the more it is forced to pursue valorisation through knowledge production, the more that knowledge escapes its control'.[64] Like the theorists of cognitive capitalism, Negri and Hardt re-engage with the critique of the

61 Yann Moulier Boutang, *Cognitive Capitalism*, trans. Ed Emery, Cambridge: Polity Press, 2012, 92.
62 Ibid., 103–4.
63 Hardt and Negri, *Commonwealth*, 267.
64 Ibid., 268.

Marxist labour theory of value – a critique that has advanced various lines of argument since the nineteenth century, from the neo-classical critiques by Carl Menger or Léon Walras to the contemporary current of *Wertkritik* represented by Robert Kurz, Moishe Postone and Anselm Jappe. In the event, the crux of this critique consists in reasserting that capital is now incapable of developing the productive forces. This thesis, initially stated by Trotsky in 1938 and bound up with the circumstances of the time, was to be adopted out of context by certain organizations of the extreme left during the 1960s and hardened into a doctrine.[65] If we accept the claim, capitalism – like the state – no longer has the role of organizing production, because 'in biopolitical production . . . the cooperation and communication necessary for the organization of the production of the multitude of productive subjectivities is generated internally'.[66]

If politics and production have fused, the cooperative character of production is the immediate bearer of a different social model that extends to disqualifying the model of the contract, 'a vertical relation with the figure of authority', suffocating 'horizontal relations with others like them'.[67] We can see how here, too, glorification of autonomy can, on the pretext of criticizing a central legal form of capitalism, coincide with the neoliberal theory and practice of deregulation, while disqualifying social struggles in favour of more protective employment law. Describing the radicalization of tendencies as if it had already occurred, abstracting them from the concrete complexity of economic and social reality, Negri and Hardt's theses derive their power from the fact that they seem to build a new critique of political economy without ever penetrating what Marx called 'the hidden abode of production',[68] while ceaselessly invoking it.

By way of their project, Negri and Hardt make do with appealing to an enigmatic 'progressive accumulation of the common',[69] in a strange echo of Kautsky's thesis of the 'passive accumulation' of forces. The

---

65 Patrick Massa writes: 'In the 1960s, when the effects of prosperity become visible to all, only the "Lambertists" of the OCI remained faithful to the idea' (J.-N. Ducange and A. Burlaud, eds, *Marx, une passion française*, Paris: La Découverte, 2018, 102).

66 Hardt and Negri, *Commonwealth*, 302.

67 Ibid., 303.

68 Marx, *Capital Volume 1*, 279.

69 Hardt and Negri, *Commonwealth*, 311.

promised rupture is predominantly theoretical, even rhetorical, exploiting the effect of symmetry with the accumulation of capital. More generally, the notions of 'common', 'value', 'revolution', 'capital' and so on, all of which are opportunities for complete recasting, are interlinked within a systematic conception whose total ambition is more Hegelian than Marxist. That is why the specifically economic dimension of the analysis is based on an ontology of social existence that fundamentally distorts its principles and concepts. Ontologically, if what is revolutionary is defined by 'the self-abolition of identity',[70] Negri's politics above all consist in turning aside from the contradictions at work in the contemporary world to appeal to singularities and multiplicities. We may doubt whether this strategy is equal to the unprecedented crises looming, in the absence of any construction of a political and social relation of force – a concern that is banished by analysis of this kind.

From Communism to the Common

The promotion of the common by Negri and Hardt does not exhaust the question of the definition and role of what is predominantly a legal form of property, which has been the subject of numerous works in recent years. As we have seen, Negri and Hardt instrumentalize the notion, deforming it, while revealing some of the political potential that explains its success. But we must attend to much more precise analyses of the concept, prioritizing authors who share with Negri and Hardt the desire to treat questions of socialism and communism via this economic and legal notion – something that is not always the case, even if growing interest in the idea echoes an at least partial challenge to neoliberal themes. We must therefore begin by stressing that legal analysis of the common is the occasion for very different approaches, with reference to the triple distinction between collective goods, public goods and common goods.

One of the originators of the modern notion of the common is Léon Duguit, whose thinking developed in the early twentieth century. A French jurist close to Émile Durkheim and interlocutor of Léon

---

70 Ibid., 332.

Bourgeois, Duguit researched public service and the development of a
legal theory of the state, but also a theory of the social function of property law. Identifying with the positivist tradition, Duguit linked his analysis of the socialization of property to a critique of the state. While he
rejected the Marxist route, he was not satisfied with the liberal conception and sought to conceive a form of social intervention by the state
that was not a means of 'increasing the power of the rulers'.[71] An apostle
of decentralization, Duguit argued that the growth of public services
was an irresistible historical trend. While this aligned him with the
'socializing' tendencies of the radical current, his critique of the state
and view of public services as economic activities linked him to a liberal
conception of a strictly regulatory state, ensuring social services with a
view to the smooth functioning of capitalism. It is precisely this composite inspiration that we find again in recent treatments of the notion of
the common.

During the second half of the twentieth century, a theorization by
economists of neo-classical observance, not by jurists, took over. It
focused on the issue of the conditions of production and exchange of
certain goods. Detached from the promotion of public services and affil-
iated with the liberal tradition, it paved the way for state intervention
conceived as an auxiliary of markets, not as the tool of a social vocation
whose scale was increasing irreversibly. Recent reflections draw directly
on this reformulation of the notion of a public good, which explains why
the return of the socialist or socializing thematic within it remains basically apolitical. In other words, placed in a subsidiary position, here
common property does not have a vocation to transform or regulate the
whole of social existence. In this respect, the solidaristic tradition of the
Third Republic now seems remote.

Contributing to this liberal elaboration, US neo-classical economist
Paul Samuelson defined collective goods on two principles: non-rivalry
(several agents can use the same good simultaneously, without its
consumption reducing its usage); and non-exclusion (use of the good
cannot be prevented).[72] The classic example is public lighting. Samuelson

---

71 Léon Duguit, *Les Transformations du droit public*, Paris: Armand Colin, 1913,
55.
72 See Paul Samuelson, 'The Pure Theory of Public Expenditure', *Review of
Economics and Statistics* 36: 4, 1954.

considers that, in this kind of instance, markets are not efficient, since no private agent has an interest in engaging in such production. The state has to intervene, using taxation it alone can raise from the set of economic agents. But such state intervention is conceived as strictly limited, substituting for markets only as and where necessary, with a view to protecting their supremacy. That is why, contrary to the dichotomy proposed by Negri, public goods are not controlled by the state on this view: access to them is free in order to enable their utilization as factors of production – something that is notably the case with certain bodies of knowledge.[73] But this in no way prevents that knowledge from being privatized. Privatization is facilitated by intellectual property rights which, checking the diffusion of knowledge, impair its expansion without thereby infringing on the conception that underlies the theory of collective goods. These initial approaches thus concentrated on the legal dimension of the institutional, clearly circumscribed construction of goods of a particular type, which is not to be extended to others.

In a second phase, starting from the 1980s, the unqualified victory of neoliberal options, hostile to the least regulation of markets, tended to restore the political and social dimensions of the property question over and above its exclusively legal dimension. The reworking of the notions of common good and the common in recent decades may be regarded as the result of increasing anxiety about an unprecedented extension of private rights and patents – an extension that has popularized the expression 'new enclosures', facilitating the private annexation of hitherto collective wealth.[74] As regards its practical application, reflection on the common is notable in the specialist sector of the digital commons and free software. It is accompanied by the development of original licences permitting free access, but above all the collaborative enrichment of the informational and intellectual commons, once freed from the logic of exclusive ownership. The very form of the common has experienced a second youth, having previously concerned old rights of access to natural resources (forests, pasture, water and so on). Even so, promoters of free software are not seeking to oppose the capitalist

---

73 Dominique Foray, *L'économie de la connaissance*, Paris: La Découverte, 2009, 61.

74 See James Boyle, 'The Second Enclosure Movement and the Construction of the Public Domain', *Law and Contemporary Problems* 66: 1–2, 2004.

market: the articulation between non-commodity world and capitalist enterprise devised by some of them proves this.[75]

Benjamin Coriat, in the collective work he has edited on the theme, defines the common as 'a social construct that mingles formal and informal rules, market and non-market relations, norms and conventions'.[76] How are we to define this notion, which public debate tends to render even more confused since it has seized on it? The complexity and multiplicity of possible orientations explain the persistent dynamism of theoretical approaches on this level. As regards fundamental research, the US economist Elinor Ostrom published a major work in 1990 which redefined the idea of 'common good' by considering the role of institutions in their construction, in contrast to an approach centred on their intrinsic nature as goods.[77] Jean-Marie Harribey characterizes this as 'a neo-classical approach refreshed by the neo-institutionalist current'.[78] In institutional analysis, Ostrom is situated in the tradition of public choice theory, which analyses politics and the role of the state in the framework of liberal microeconomics. In this context, Elinor Ostrom's approach remains centred on small communities and does not take on board the general political and social conditions that enable – or frustrate – the construction of common goods.

In addition, at no point does she envisage their expansion as a means of escaping capitalism, but confines herself to defining alternative property forms which she deems capable of blocking the 'new enclosures' and the continuous degradation of global goods (such as the climate, oceans, forests, biodiversity and so on). Faced with these threats, she sticks to recommending local measures, which (she declared on the occasion of the Rio Summit in 2012) are more effective than a global, constraining agreement. The political timorousness of this formulation does not prevent widespread adoption and discussion of these theses, including by those who aim at more substantial legal

---

75 See Pierre-André Mangolte, 'Le logiciel libre comme commun créateur de richesse', in Benjamin Coriat, ed., *Le Retour des communs. La crise de l'idéologie propriétaire*, Paris: Les Liens qui Libèrent, 2015.

76 Coriat, ed., *Le Retour des communs. La crise de l'idéologie propriétaire*, 25.

77 Elinor Ostrom, *Governing the Commons*, Cambridge: Cambridge University Press, 1990.

78 Jean-Marie Harribey, *La Richesse, la valeur et l'inestimable. Fondements d'une critique socio-écologique de l'économie capitaliste*, Paris: Les Liens qui Libèrent, 2013.

and social transformation while often distrusting political action and the perspective, deemed unrealistic, of abolishing capitalist relations. Among the most striking of these approaches is the 2014 book by Pierre Dardot and Christian Laval, *Common*. Like Negri and Hardt, they seek to articulate questions of property with a political perspective, without confining themselves to an economic and/or legal analysis of the common.

The Common According to Pierre Dardot and Christian Laval

Dardot and Laval's book closes with the theme of 'revolution in the 21st century' and nine political proposals, following a scholarly investigation that presents and discusses the authors cited carefully, without ever losing sight of its general political stakes. Their analysis is presented as a critical reading of Negri and Hardt's theses, even if they accord the latter the merit of having proposed the 'first systematic theory of the common'.[79] They challenge their definition of communism as well as their interpretation of a contemporary capitalism whose rentier logic supposedly taps autonomous biopolitical production from without. Out of blindness to the specific character of neoliberalism, Negri and Hardt are said to relapse into Marx's central error: believing that capitalism engenders its own transcendence in and of itself. On this level, *Common* forms a sequel to other works by Dardot and Laval, which bear in particular on contemporary neoliberalism but also on Marx and the issue of his relevance. As regards neoliberalism, from one book to the next the authors emphasize the key role of the state, far removed from misleading anti-statist discourse. Liberalism relies on intervention by a state that is at once partner of private enterprise and reformer of public administration, which it subjects to capitalist criteria via the neoliberal management it deploys therein. As for Marx, he is deemed a contradictory thinker who simultaneously defends the thesis of a necessary political evolution and that of a class struggle open to historical initiative.[80]

---

79 Pierre Dardot and Christian Laval, *Common: On Revolution in the 21st Century*, trans. Matthew MacLellan, London: Bloomsbury Academic, 2019, 5.

80 See Pierre Dardot and Christian Laval, *Marx, prénom: Karl*, Paris: Gallimard, 2012.

Starting from this dual critique, *Common* develops a prospective analysis that rejects socialism and communism alike, proposing a third way via institutional invention and democratic control, at a remove from the state and existing political organizations.

Without pretending to summarize this long and complex book, we must attend to the way it proposes a political alternative, constructed around the traditional question of property and theorized in a framework which is that neither of the market nor of the state. To highlight the difference from many existing theorizations of the commons, the authors differentiate the plural and singular forms of the term, enabling them to separate a legal analysis of common goods and a more general political approach, centred on practices, which ranges democracy itself in the common, whose meaning is thus extended well beyond the issue of property. While drawing inspiration from Foucault's notion of an infra-state micro-politics, this approach is located in the tradition of analyses ventured prior to Marx – Proudhon's federalism, but also the anarcho-syndicalism of Fernand Pelloutier. Also mentioned positively are syndicalist jurist Maxime Leroy, theorist of public law Léon Duguit, mentioned above, and especially sociologists Émile Durkheim and Marcel Mauss, theorists of solidarity and the social republic who claim not to dissolve class society but to rearrange it. The authors go so far as to include on their extensive list of references Alexis de Tocqueville, a decidedly liberal defender of community life as a form of political participation. Dardot and Laval's proposal is to keep a general political perspective open, while distancing themselves from communism and socialism alike on account of their allegedly inveterate statism. Denunciation of state communism forms a pendant to analyse the neoliberal utilization of the state and to disqualify any state solution, including that of a social state. They adduce the very real democratic deficiency of public services in support of this critique.[81]

Such an analysis has several merits. To start, it points to the weakness of strictly defensive strategies on the left, which overshadow the issue of the various functions of the state and are snared by the simplistic anti-statist discourse of neoliberalism, contrary to its actual practices. Second, it mentions what was indeed one of the major impasses of so-called 'real socialism' – paralysing state control, but also the

---

81 Dardot and Laval, *Common*, 355ff.

maintenance of social relations of alienation and exploitation, interdicting any real democratic control over production, as well as any genuine collective reorganization of social life by its protagonists. Finally, it goes hand in hand with a definition of the common as construction, which does not concern certain goods essentially and is not reduced to an economic construct as defined by Samuelson. But nor does it boil down to a construct of a legal kind, involving as it does a collective social activity and practices of pooling, which are productive of law, not their passive outcome.

In other words, Laval and Dardot dwell on the instituent dimension of the common, drawing their references principally from Castoriadis and Foucault. Albeit rarely cited, Foucault is the thinker of a production of norms that are no longer to be grasped on the model of old disciplines, instituted by a sovereign state, but must be linked to practices that stimulate social existence in its entirety. As for Castoriadis, he is the resolutely post-Marxist theorist of instituent power, ranged here against Negri's unduly globalizing conception of a constituent power that involves revolutionary breaks for the purposes of inventing new political frameworks. Castoriadis's instituent power consists in attending to the creativity of human practices. Instituent power 'presupposes both certain pre-existing conditions and the act of "working on" these conditions in order to profoundly transform them'.[82] This approach leads Laval and Dardot to value the inspiration of the young Marx over and against the mature Marx, to re-engage with the socialist tradition prior to Marx – a tradition centred on legal intervention and federalism, steering clear of the state. As we can see, while the approach is not philosophical as such, a consistent and coherent argument is at work, guided, as with all the authors concerned with alternatives, by an initial political conviction. In the event, rather than confronting capitalism as an economic and social formation, this political thinking is as opposed to communism as it is to neoliberalism. If the argument is sometimes contorted, multiplying references to authors who are adduced against one another only to be criticized in their turn, the destination discloses relatively classical initial positions. Hostile to neoliberalism, as well as to any form of planning, which is equated *en bloc* with statism, Dardot and Laval opt for a federalism centred on an expanded notion of the common.

82 Ibid., 298.

Endeavouring to make the common thus redefined a political alternative creates several problems. The first emerges in the presentation of the initial chapters of the book: 'the proceeding chapter . . . re-examines a series of different communist models that have historically functioned as so many ways of repressing the common . . . understood as a form of co-obligation that people adopt for themselves'. The authors immediately add that 'the supposed "realization" of the common through state ownership consistently led to the destruction of the common by the state',[83] implying that an 'authentic' common exists whose essence, to be recovered, is independent of existing legal and social relations. However, the authors insist on the invariably constructed character of the common which, far from being a trans-historical truth, unfolds via the transformations of law and collective practices, such as to restore to the collective full possession of its own power. The idea of construction thus comes into conflict with the idea of a common that is, by definition, combined with certain collective rules, compatible with communalist federalism but not with any planning. Here the Foucauldian option for production of norms, or Castoriadis's thesis of the self-institution of the social, contradicts the promotion of a 'politics of the common', whose meaning is supposedly pre-set and, above all, the bearer of a different social model. If it entails the economy being 're-integrated back into social life and becom[ing] enmeshed in democratic society by introducing a plurality of perspectives into the sphere of production, and . . . construct[ing] a new system for managing these conflicting views through institutional rules',[84] it is difficult to see how the operation could escape abstract formalism, on the model of the 'procedural democracy' theorized by Habermas, which is increasingly out of kilter with the ongoing de-vitalization of 'really existing' democracy.

Federalism against Statism: The Return of Proudhon

The common thus sits at the heart of the social organization and administration of common wealth, while skirting the issues of their production as well as the general coordination of human activities. And,

---

83 Ibid., 31.
84 Ibid., 341.

naturally, it expels as irredeemably statist the perspective of capturing state power associated with the project of abolishing capitalism, as well as the issue of class struggle inseparable from it. In this sense, it must be stressed, the common is here constructed more as an alternative to communism than to capitalism. In the form of a historical diagnosis, the formulation of the problem to be solved envelops rejection of one putatively dated option – whether called socialist or communist – in the name of another, equally dated one, which points to the excesses of the market and a parasitic class: 'disciplinary confinement in the context of universal competition is the principal lever that has transformed our societies into environments designed to (greatly) benefit a small but extremely powerful oligarchy'.[85] Removal of it, even if no route to that end is proposed here, replaces analysis of the social relations of production characteristic of Marxism with a schematic binary logic, excluding reflection on the transitions and mediations of radical social transformation.

In this respect, while *Common* astutely reopens reflection on the unduly neglected question of property and ends appropriately with its political stakes, which are so often ignored, it is a matter for regret that it closes off the complex question of political forms beyond a general, abstract opposition to statism, which is accused of being at once communist and liberal. The centrality accorded the issue of institutions precludes thinking of the state as the political form of a social relation of exploitation and domination, and it leaves hanging the issue of an organization combining federalism and a central perspective capable of ensuring its perpetuation and guaranteeing its principles. Furthermore, it abandons the question of the ownership of the means of production and exchange, melting 'citizens' or 'society' into a single homogenous mass confronted with the oligarchy. Here this conception approximates Laclau's theses, which dissolve the issue of the private appropriation of social wealth. With such an approach, it is difficult to see how a legal kind of intervention could successfully transform social reality, other than by denying the inegalitarian and conflictual dimensions inherent in its character as a mode of production. That is why the problems caused by a capitalism whose threats and devastations are now global cannot be treated exclusively at a federal level, which is incapable of targeting its basic springs,

---

85 Ibid., 398.

despite its pertinence to this level of decision-making. What needs to be thought through is precisely the articulation between federal level and democratic centralization, while avoiding schematically counterposing two ahistorical abstractions that evade real contradictions: the cooperative common and the predatory state.

Dardot and Laval's development of their theses takes the form of a sustained discussion with numerous authors, among whom Marx occupies pride of place. They broach his oeuvre by focusing on the question of the alternative between statism and federalism, reckoning that 'the proletariat's first objective is the conquest of state power. The proletariat must centralize its own power, and for this it needs a unitary and centralized state apparatus.'[86] It might be objected to this interpretation that Marx set out affirming the need for the 'withering away of the state' before radicalizing his viewpoint and invoking the 'smashing of the state'. Dardot and Laval offer the portrait of a Marx belatedly and partially enrolling in the school of Proudhon's federalism on the occasion of the Paris Commune, whereas they ignore those of the Commune's measures that imparted content to the theme of smashing the state, which Marx saluted: elected representatives and revocable officials, abolition of the army and the police, schools 'cleared of all interference of Church and State'.[87] In this sense, the unity of the nation does not signify the maintenance of the state, but the recasting of politics. Marx wrote:

> The unity of the nation was not to be broken, but, on the contrary, to be organized by the Communal constitution, and to become a reality by the destruction of the State power which claimed to be the embodiment of that unity independent of, and superior to, the nation itself, from which it was but a parasitic excrescence.[88]

Here he rediscovers, while making it more precise, a critique of the split between state and social existence developed in his early writings. In the interim, he had discovered the complex class function of the state. For

---

86 Ibid., 389.

87 *The Civil War in France*, in Karl Marx and Friedrich Engels, *Collected Works*, Vol. 22, London: Lawrence & Wishart, 1986, 332.

88 Ibid.

Marx the solution is therefore neither direct democracy nor pure federalism, but a democratic construct, including forms of controlled representation and collective management – a 'political form' embodying 'a working-class government' and enabling 'the economic emancipation of labour'.[89]

Given this, why pigeonhole Marx in a statism he always condemned? To criticize him for an 'a-historical conception of the proletarian revolution'[90] makes it possible to disqualify communism from the outset, equating it with every other form of statism, whether it be modern bourgeois statism or the neoliberal statism that does not speak its name. For Dardot and Laval, the crucial boundary thus no longer runs between emancipation of labour and capitalist exploitation, but between statism and alternatives to the state, the latter having been forged in the nineteenth century by the socialist and anarchist tradition. The common thus functions as a bridge between a contemporary critique of public (or private) property and past versions, setting aside the conquest of state power as a precondition for abolishing capitalism but also the state itself. And indeed the references invoked are those of moderate critical theorists, defenders of a politics of the common that reactivates the tradition of solidaristic economics – Durkheim's 'professional groups', Mauss's 'cooperative socialism', which 'has very little to do with the notion of a perfectly unified and classless society' but 'is about building a society that is much more differentiated than modern nations already are, . . . animated by an incessant peaceful struggle to balance exchanges'.[91] This is not a new thesis: the slogan of the disappearance of classes, caricatured as the defence of a 'perfect' unity and repellent homogeneity, makes it possible to promote positive 'differences' and corporative harmony – even if the historical uses of the doctrine of social harmony were scarcely progressive, starting with the corporatist conception of Pétain.[92]

In *Common* the political alternative boils down to the implausible construction of 'new "civic" market institutions that combine the

---

89 Ibid., 334.
90 Dardot and Laval, *Common*, 301; trans. modified.
91 Ibid., 268–9; trans. modified.
92 Jean-Pierre Le Crom, *Syndicats, nous voilà! Vichy et le corporatisme*, Paris: L'Atelier, 1995, 124.

self-government of workers with the collective sovereignty of consumers',[93] far removed from any radical recasting of production and consumption aimed at challenging capitalist logic. All in all, the politics of the common proposed, which seek to go beyond its narrowly legal construction, does not succeed in grasping questions of property in the framework of the capitalist mode of production that organizes it and of which it is the condition. The focus on neoliberalism, which allows the authors to describe a specific modus operandi, involves a nominalist approach, criticizing Marxism for generalizing excessively in his analysis of capitalism and deducing law from economics. Marx by no means forgets the singularity of historical formations and moments, as is proved by his historical texts on France, and endeavours to think the specificity of political and legal forms while linking them to the basic logic of capitalism. The converse approach, projecting an autonomous logic of production of norms and law, does not account for a totality, obviously differentiated, which articulates law with class relations at the very heart of the process of production.

Consequently, neoliberalism is analysed less as a stage of capitalism than as a specific legal regime, distinguished by the formation of restricted economic-political elites who are both the authors of the ruling norms and their sole beneficiaries. The thesis of an accomplished neoliberal order, consolidated by common mores, leads to overestimating the coherence of a world structured around a 'governmentality' (to use Foucault's term), accompanied by its disciplinary and post-disciplinary techniques, rather than as a mode of production based on the exploitation of wage labour, shot through with persistent economic and social contradictions. To ignore these contradictions is to suppress the cause of crises, the spring of social protests and of theoretical critique. That is why the promotion of a new legal property regime – the common(s) – without any examination of the requisite transitions, the exclusive valorisation of local and subaltern experiments and the call for a new 'subjectivation by counter-conduct' ends up replacing the perspective of a supersession-abolition of capitalism. The proposal of the common is much more opposed to the financial logic of neoliberalism than to its reorganization of production and distribution of wealth in the context of heightened class struggle. The dichotomy between a

---

93 Dardot and Laval, *Common*, 341; trans. modified.

rapacious elite and 'populations' or 'citizens', the interests of the latter supposedly being shared and their unity achieved, abandons analysis of, and political opposition to, this reinforcement of class domination.

The argument is taken up in their 2016 book *Never-Ending Nightmare*. Recalling in detail, and very usefully, the steps in the construction of the European Union and its devastating effects economically and socially but also politically and culturally, Dardot and Laval once again foreground the 'oligarchical enemy'. The upshot, according to them, is that it is necessary to pit an equally general strategy, a 'different way of life', against what is a mode of power. Dardot and Laval purport to analyse the social project of liberalism much more thoroughly and intricately than Marxists, assuring us that Marx, who thought in terms of 'economic "mode of production"', did not include social relations in it.[94] Thus they ignore (or seek to ignore) Marx's canonical definition of the mode of production as a contradictory unity of social relations of production and productive forces. Above all, this criticism makes it possible to cast as more radical than communism an alternative that eludes both capitalist economic logic and states which are ultimately merely its quartermasters. The authors abruptly conclude that no recourse should be sought to political organizations presented as straightforward 'oligarchic machines', once again simplifying a much more complex history: that of class struggles.

Instead of any activist engagement, the authors propose the implausible introduction of 'a transnational democratic citizenship that cannot be the work of anyone but European citizens themselves',[95] appealing to 'the *pooling of experience* by the mass of non-experts'.[96] Aside from the fact that it is hard to see how a form of citizenship could be constructed independently of any state structure, whether national or international, it is ultimately the banality of the alternative advanced that is cause for surprise. For it sticks to the old idea that it is possible to circumvent the reality of a class confrontation that necessarily takes the form of confronting state power. Ultimately, the authors' most concrete proposal is abandoning the party-form,[97] relying on Simone Weil's assertion that

---

94 Pierre Dardot and Christian Laval, *Never-Ending Nightmare: The Neoliberal Assault on Democracy*, trans. Gregory Elliott, London and New York: Verso, 2019, 55.

95 Ibid., 98.

96 Ibid., 158.

97 Ibid., 161.

it is 'totalitarian in germ and aspiration'.[98] Making this a goal in itself, along with abandoning the issue of the state on the strange grounds that raising it entails rallying to it, risks weakening the left rather than paving the way for the revolution that the authors ardently desire, without ever clarifying its content beyond a general demand for the 'institution of the commons, as the concrete bases of an alternative'.[99] In addition to the ambiguity that affects term institutions, sometimes vaunted, sometimes decried, it is hard to see how the disappearance of organizations would facilitate the construction of a 'global oppositional arena'[100] accompanied by the sole imperative of rotation of responsibilities. Given the historical weakness of the radical left, a democratic, offensive recasting of the party-form might be reckoned more urgent than calls for its disappearance.

Constructing the Alternative to Neoliberalism or Capitalism?

To conclude on the set of works presented in this chapter, we must start by emphasizing that despite their considerable divergences, these books, radical in tone and comprehensive in intent, all conclude with minimal, local proposals or immediately global ones, without exploring the political roads and mediations of a transcendence of the exploitation of labour and relations of domination. Essentially, the question of property refers to the private appropriation of socially produced wealth – that is, the extortion of surplus value by the dominant class, in the context of the social antagonism characteristic of capitalism. In tackling these relations of production from the tangent of common property as a third alternative to public property and private property, Dardot and Laval ultimately end up reviving an old proposal – cooperative forms that renounce the issue of the state and the public form to be put in its place. For federalism of Proudhonian inspiration, while it pertains to an option of a political kind, is never constructed as a collective project that could be embodied by identifiable forces, enabling a strategic reflection on the conditions of its diffusion and implementation. As to the issue of the

---

98 Ibid., 162.
99 Ibid., 169; trans. modified.
100 Ibid., 168.

dominion of capital over labour, in its articulation with forms of property and contract, it disappears, giving way to the critique of neoliberal management and the logic of financialization inseparable from it. The upshot is a narrow definition of capitalism, reduced to the logic of 'money' and its colonization of the common from without, in a schema ultimately close to Negri and Hardt's theses: 'the negation of common action in the sphere of worker is the main shackle to burst in order to exit capitalism as a system of domination of money over action'.[101] However, the authors honestly signal the limits of formulas for social and solidaristic economics in the unimpaired, ever more crushing context of contemporary capitalism. Consequently, we might reckon that the common, even if democracy is included in it, cannot as such represent an alternative amid the current deterioration in the political and social balance of power, starting with the ongoing destruction of employment law. By contrast, this examination of property and its many forms signals the welcome return of a problem long forgotten or neglected. Like the issues broached by the authors studied in earlier chapters, these reflections signal a return of crucial questions that were traditionally at the centre of socialism and communism. Paradoxically, their present fragmentation contradicts the need for an alternative that prompted them. To believe that it would be possible to propose a unification of these proposals, which are fundamentally divergent and philosophically developed at a remove from any concrete realization, is an illusion and a dead end. Their fragmentation has profound causes which, although manifested in their theoretical dispersion, are not theoretical in kind. The hypothesis of this book is that it derives from a long history which has seen the re-separation of perspectives worked up as philosophical alternatives and social and political mobilization, this dislocation manifesting itself in a spectacular slump in strategic reflection amid the historical weakness of the labour movement but also growing disquiet about the common future.

How can we repoliticize aspirations that are nurtured by brilliant theoretical constructs but fail to organize a mass movement? For such a movement is the only thing capable of combating a neoliberalism that is widely spurned, but whose critique, far from carving out new paths, is the source of increased conflict among its opponents. The first task is to

---

101 Dardot and Laval, *Common*, 341; trans. modified.

reconstruct a genuine collective debate over the alternative, giving pride of place to its strategic dimension, striving to articulate means and ends. In the authors under discussion, this underlying dimension is rarely formulated as such, or it is severed (as in Laclau) from any definite aim. A fresh strategy implies that theoretical debate is no longer a side affair of political action, with an instrumental or decorative function, but a full-fledged component of the reconstruction of a radical perspective, aiming to exit from capitalism and finally overcoming the division of labour between visionary intellectuals and activist foot soldiers. The gravity of the crisis we face obliges us to re-explore all the crucial questions – property and equality, exploitation and forms of domination. It requires redefining democracy and the relationship to nature, rethinking individuality and emancipation together.

In order to broach a contemporary strategic perspective as a question, open to reassembling clearly defined tasks, a detour is required via the first attempt at it – that of Marx. By dint of his historical posterity, but above all on account of his desire to integrate political, social and theoretical dimensions, his discussion remains (as we have noted) at the centre of all living alternative hypotheses today, even if in the mode of ferocious refutation or haughty disavowal. But rather than making his thought, schematized into a doctrine, a fixed point to distance ourselves from, it seems more productive to approach the Marxian question of the alternative to capitalism on the basis of the criticisms and concerns tackled above. Thus, it is from the standpoint of the missing strategy that a rereading of this unavoidable critique of capitalism can now be initiated, the aim being to discover not ready-made solutions, but questions that need revisiting.

4
Marx, Communism and Emancipation

As the preceding pages have shown, contemporary theoreticians of the alternative have maintained, and renewed, a critical dialogue with Marx, stimulating debate both within the academy and outside it. Thus, they encourage us to reread him, not in search of a definitive truth, but to seed the revival of a history: the history of the radical contestation of capitalism. Broaching the communist question in Marx after examining the political and strategic proposals in previous chapters makes it possible to resituate the contemporary issue of the alternative in a wider historical arc, from the birth of capitalism to its current profound crisis, against a background of enduring exploitation and domination. This chronologically inverted order of reading reveals both the political and specifically the strategic dimensions of the critique of political economy produced by Marx, which sought with one and the same momentum to be theoretical and practical.

The time has doubtless come for a new political reception, which the ensuing pages endeavour to delineate by focusing on the question of communism. While the word *communism* rarely appears in Marx's oeuvre and never yields a detailed description, it refers to a radical historical transformation whose characteristics are, in one sense, clearly defined: the abolition of classes and exploitation, the elimination of private ownership of the means of production, the destruction of the state, democratic self-organization of production and social life, and the free development of individuality. This abolition-supersession of capitalism involves a protracted, antagonistic process, a class struggle fought 'to a conclusion' which sees the working class and the other dominated classes seize hold of the political state in order to destroy it and replace it with a democratic reconstruction of social life as a whole. To say the least, any such horizon seems remote. Classified as another impractical utopia, communism is now invariably identified with the failure of revolutions in the twentieth century and so-called 'real' socialism, demonized and simplified by the dominant anti-totalitarian tradition. Consequently, it has become commonplace to separate an analysis of capitalism from a theory of communism in Marx, which nothing will reconnect. Indeed, this thesis is supported by all the authors studied earlier.

To escape this conventional interpretation, which involves searching Marx's thought for the seeds of the subsequent dislocation of critical thinking and political action, we must instead tackle his theoretical and political approaches from the perspective of their articulation, the term *communism* naming this endeavour. This chapter aims not to present *the* political theory of Marx – something alien to his project – but to dwell on the strategic intertwining of critical knowledge and political intervention that he always effected in context, in accordance with the changing conjunctures of his century. Approached thus, Marx's communist project presents itself, first, as inseparable from reflection on the historical conditions and presuppositions of its construction, underscoring the dimension of it characterized here as 'strategic', which is largely unknown. It manifests itself in the way that Marx never separates ends from means, never separates the project from its mediations: the latter are neither mere means nor predefined stages, but a constant readjustment of the project to conditions of realization that include it. In other words, if no revolution is prescribed in advance, it is because it confronts circumstances to which it is subject and that it initiates: in Marx the word *communism* never refers exclusively to a post-capitalist mode of production, but to a mode of historical supersession and invention born alongside the gigantic contradictions generated by capitalism.

In this sense, communism inseparably links a new historical stage with the forms of organization and action that lead to it, without prejudging the steps of its realization. Linking the goal to the mediations and transitions that construct it is a precondition for keeping fundamentally open, and hence relatively indeterminate, a process which can only exist concretely and singularly, including in the form of its repeated attempts, historical revivals and failures. Marx subordinates the definition of communism to intervening as a communist: such an affirmation is not in the least tautological, but expresses the unprecedented difficulty of a historical transformation that is collectively conceived and organized. Tackling the issue in this way makes it possible to elude the twofold stigmatization of communism as vain utopia or totalitarianism incarnate, instead rethinking it as a strategy in the broad sense, including its mediations and defining itself by them.

Such is the interpretative hypothesis presented in this chapter: political and strategic invention, in conditions that determine its possibility and limits, is in fact the central axis of Marx's communism. Approached in light of the political and strategic issues today, this political rereading of Marx is more indispensable than ever not only in order to understand contemporary capitalism, but also to radically transform those conditions. Such a reading seeks not to find answers, but to help reformulate the questions encountered in previous chapters. Not only the comprehensive character of Marx's approach, but also its silences and hesitations, archaisms and illusions, are to be ranged against the present fragmentation of alternatives. For, like us, Marx was marked by the defeat of the labour movement of his time and the absence of world revolution whose advent he believed to be imminent in 1848.

Marx the Young Hegelian

Contrary to all the approaches that attribute to Marx a fixed conception of communism, defined as some ineluctable end of history, but also against the temptation to make him just another academic author, we need to remember the extent to which his political and activist involvement constantly shaped and revitalized his theoretical work and distinguished it. Abandoning legal studies for philosophy, associating from his early years with oppositional currents, and practising journalism, Marx very soon became an indefatigable, combative critic of the political life of his time, but also of the theories that developed in it, of the alternatives to capitalism generated along with it. Out of these confrontations and this engagement emerged an oeuvre characterized by incompletion and constant reworking. It is therefore important to retrace the initial moments of Marx's itinerary, not only because his thought is rooted in them, but because it would never break completely with this initial elaboration, which conjoined critical German philosophy and the discovery of nascent socialist and communist currents. Rather than combining two traditions alien to one another, Marx very early on sought to initiate a mutual recasting of them by adopting and modifying the programme of the Young Hegelian school to which he belonged from 1837 to 1844.

From the time of his university education in Germany, Marx was associated with the intense theoretical and journalistic activity that characterized this group of young intellectuals, who were the inheritors of Hegelian philosophy and opponents of the Prussian monarchy. The group was the product of successive splits in the Hegelian school, which had been shot through with political and theoretical differences that divided German intellectual circles in a situation of political crisis and impasse when, following the Congress of Vienna, the *ancien régime* of the Prussian state reinforced its prerogatives and responded to burgeoning opposition with censorship and repression. In Prussia more than elsewhere in the German Confederation, created in 1815, royal arbitrariness was combined with bureaucracy, in the absence of any parliamentary representation.[1] Rhenish liberalism, implanted in southern Germany, strove to develop, while on its left democratic currents took shape that were concerned with the national question but also with social, economic, religious, legal and constitutional issues. Despite censorship, Prussian echoes of these German debates found expression in the press, at a time when German society was experiencing gradual but profound changes bound up with the start of its industrialization.

Grouping around analysis of the religious question, particularly from an institutional point of view, in the officially Christian state of Prussia, the Young Hegelians radicalized their critiques and ended up defending atheism in the hope of helping to modernize the German *ancien régime*.[2] The watchword of the 'realization of philosophy' united them, before

---

1 See Sandrine Kott, *L'Allemagne du XIXe siècle*, Paris: Hachette, 1999, 9–10.

2 J.-C. Angaut, J.-M. Buée, P. Clochec and E. Renault, 'De la Jeune Allemagne au Jeune hégélianisme', in Friedrich Engels, *Écrits de jeunesse*, Vol. 1, trans. J.-C. Angaut, J.-M. Buée, P. Clochec, M. L'Homme, J.-B. Morin, E. Renault and D. Wittmann, Paris: GEME-Éditions Sociales, 2015, 21.

they moved towards more defined, and divergent, political positions. For his part, the young Marx would pass in a few years from the political liberalism of the *Rheinische Zeitung* in 1842 to the democratic option of the *Annales franco-allemandes*, and then from socialism, invoked in 1843, to communism, proclaimed in 1844, invariably combining with this political evolution a redefinition of the role of theoretical work as such.

Marx was neither the only one nor even the first to move towards communist positions declared as such. On this road, he was preceded by Friedrich Engels and Moses Hess, who likewise belonged to the Young Hegelian movement. Both deemed liberal demands focused on a representative constitution and press freedom inadequate. Hess worked to extend and politicize the critique of Hegel's philosophy proposed by Feuerbach on the terrain of atheism and sensualism, moving towards an analysis of social activity and commodity exchange. As for Engels, his discovery of industrial England and Chartism in the early 1840s led him to outline an initial critique of political economy, identifying what he judged to be the essential contradictions of capitalism. Both of them applied themselves to diffusing communist theses in Germany, developing a critique of private property and money. Marx's political evolution, which was slower, for a long time remained bound up with the German philosophical tradition, left-Hegelian and then Young Hegelian, which was the locus of a particular kind of politicization. A friend of philosopher Bruno Bauer, Marx, before gravitating towards Arnold Ruge and then Hess and Engels, developed a philosophical approach to the political question that also took the form of a critical rereading of Hegel and then a critique of Bauer himself.

Engaged in critical journalism and animator of the *Rheinische Zeitung*, Marx, convinced of the political impact of ideas and the importance of their diffusion, set about denouncing the Prussian state. Unlike Hess and Engels, however, Marx worked to abolish the cleavage between state and civil society, envisaging an alternative to bureaucratic or corporatist representation. This alternative, which the demand for a free press led him to define as 'true representation', abolished the split to result not in a fusion of society and state, but their rearticulation. While Marx subsequently radicalized this initial critique, encapsulated in the thesis of 'true democracy', he never abandoned the original conviction that the point was to rearticulate social life and political life, reconstructing mediations, not abolishing them. This project, situated on both philosophical and political terrains, demonstrates their unity but to the extent that it derives from their mutual recasting. Rooted in Young Hegelianism, it led Marx to break with a group that was set to disperse. Thus, it is striking that Marx's political trajectory was organized initially not around the construction of an alternative social and political project, but the very definition of 'critical' activity, which led him to explore the different options that emerged in the Germany of the time, arriving at a revolutionary, 'communist' orientation.

The Birth of Socialist and Communist Currents

To understand this theoretico-political evolution, we need to dwell on what was meant by the word *communism* at the point when Engels, Hess and then Marx decided to identify with it. How was it distinguished from socialism? In his standard work on the subject,[3] Jacques Grandjonc points out that the term *communism* made its appearance in the late eighteenth century and was initially employed in the context of debates over property and, more particularly, the community of goods. The term *socialist* was born at the same time, without really being used before socialism emerged in the early 1830s. The terms *socialism* and *communism*, but also *anarchism*, then spread rapidly, in close correlation with rising social and political opposition and with the birth of the first forms of labour movement organization. Naming currents in the process of being formed, the terms were thus part of the emergence of a wide range of social and political alternatives, their meaning remaining unsettled and indiscriminating prior to the institutionalization of parties and establishment of parliamentary democracy.

During the 1830s, socialism was to be defined in particular by Pierre Leroux, who attributed to the people themselves the invention of the word *communism*, the adjectival form of which was employed to characterize the popular banquet in Belleville on 1 July 1840, and 'whose echo grew louder in the following weeks, both in conversation and in

---

3 Jacques Grandjonc, *Communisme/Kommunismus/Communism. Origine et développement international de la terminologie communautaire prémarxiste des utopistes aux néo-babouvistes 1785–1842*, Paris: Éditions des Malassis, 2013.

the press.[4] The word made its written appearance in Étienne Cabet, whose *Voyage en Icarie* appeared in 1840, and then in Richard Lahautière and, above all, in Théodore Dézamy, who would prove its ardent and effective propagandist. The word *socialism* was also propagated in Saint-Simonian circles, at the time the term *collectivism* was coined. Jacques Grandjonc stresses the caesura represented by the 1830 revolution and, above all, the revolt of the Lyonnais silk workers in 1831. Henceforth the political vocabulary associated with these initial terminological innovations would develop and diversify.

This French revolutionary lexicon was immediately translated into German and English, and then into other European languages. From the late 1830s, we may take it that the terms *socialism* and *communism*, as well as the accompanying lexical constellation, were widely diffused in Europe, closely correlated with the first organizations that gradually established themselves as well as in the context of the social unrest of the 1840s. In these years, the nascent labour movement sought to develop and advance radical social and political demands, all of which included a profound transformation of property, combined with democratic demands and sometimes national liberation struggles. Faced with the rapid spread of these combative perspectives, hostile and derogatory use of the words *communism* and *socialism* emerged at once, particularly in France, both from representatives of the state and from various political opponents.[5]

All told, the terms *communism* and *socialism*, born at the same time, were never strictly defined but always associated, being confused, articulated or contrasted as discussion of their content developed. This vocabulary, and the debates it disseminated, are what Hess, Engels and Marx discovered in the 1840s – that is to say, at the time of the initial German diffusion of the words and their own intellectual and political formation. From the outset this discovery was marked by the international dimension of the nascent labour movement and the intense revolutionary effervescence of the period, culminating in 1848. In this context it is logical that Marx was one of those to adopt and help develop this novel vocabulary, in the belief that it helped structure political choices and name possible – perhaps imminent – historical bifurcations, so strong was the

---

4 Ibid., 231.
5 Ibid., 237.

sense of a profound crisis as well as of its revolutionary and international dimension.

Superimposed on these political and terminological innovations were various forms of continuity and survival: the Babouvism[6] and neo-Babouvism of the 1840s spread the idea that the French Revolution remained unfinished, and it must be revived and taken to its conclusion. The communist option would exemplify this demand, which consisted not in commemorating a struggle but making it a reality, in the framework of organizations and clubs strongly influenced by Philippe Buonarotti, organizer of the Conspiracy of Equals. Beyond the Babouvist reference, which still burned bright, it was now a question of resolving the new contradictions, political but also social, bound up with the European expansion of the capitalist mode of production. If the 'social question' and its political challenges remained inseparable from the revolutionary legacy of the eighteenth century, they were remoulded in the crucible of the labour movement, undergoing radical change in the early nineteenth century, when the world of labour was transformed and political life was punctuated by revolutions and insurrections. In this effervescent context, socialist and communist currents soon questioned their alliance with the republican current, broaching the issue of the state but not abandoning their alignment on property and inequalities, the right to work, and the forms of political and social transition. Félicité de Lamennais, Philippe Buchez, Louis Blanc, Pierre-Joseph Proudhon, Auguste Blanqui – these few names give an idea of the diversity of options and the vigour of debates, which would leave a profound mark on the international socialist and communist tradition.

At the time, the communist tendency was mainly distinguished from the socialist tradition by the greater radicalism of its critique and its options. The adjective *communist* made it possible to bring militants together, linking them to a shared revolutionary past, without the noun indicating a precise project distinct from socialism. For those who referred to themselves as communists, the project of an economic and social revolution had class exploitation and social injustice as its

---

6 This tradition originated in the thought and activity of Gracchus Babeuf. In 1796, the Conspiracy of Equals attempted to overthrow the Directory in order to replace it with an egalitarian republic, involving a radical reform of property. Despite the failure of the Conspiracy, Babeuf's ideas, relayed and developed by Philippe Buonarotti, had a lasting influence on revolutionary and communist culture.

fundamental cause, along with conquest of the state, with a view to establishing the community of goods, as its precondition. Étienne Cabet was among those who most clearly stated the proposals that distinguished communists, ensuring them significant popular diffusion. Nevertheless, his analysis remained cursory: violent seizure of power, intermediate phase of dictatorship, community of goods, tax reform, education, abolition of trade and remuneration of everyone according to their needs.[7]

While this communism exhibited various archaic features and its organizational forms remained embryonic, these combined demands outlined a comprehensive, radical option that distinguished communism from the republican current, which was predominantly attached to universal suffrage, and from socialism, which, above all, advocated a fairer distribution of wealth.[8] But the obverse of communism's revolutionary dimension, and its greater doctrinal coherence, was the persistent abstraction of a project lacking any genuine social base. In this respect, the persistently utopian character of early communism derived from its nature not as a self-enclosed literary narrative, in the fashion of the utopian tradition of previous centuries, but as an anticipatory programme and the difficulties in constructing the organizations, mobilization and collective action required to realize it. This effort would characterize its subsequent development on both activist and institutional levels, with tension arising between the latter and a project involving a radical break. At the other end of the historical arc, at a time when traditional parties have become exhausted, it is understandable that these initial options – oppositional, doctrinal or insurrectional – are once again proving attractive, at the risk of reverting to a literary, disarmed communism.

In the intervening years, attempts to actualize communist and socialist options would acquire ballast from essentially local and occasional experiences, even if it was primarily during major revolutionary

---

7 Théodore Dézamy, who was Cabet's secretary, and then August Blanqui would variously explicate these issues. This was also true of less well-known theoreticians, such as Albert Laponneraye, Richard Lahautière and Jean-Jacques Pillot. As for Pierre-Joseph Proudhon, he was one of the first French theoreticians to use the word *communism*, as well as the expression 'scientific socialism'.

8 Jean Bruhat, 'Le socialisme français de 1815 à 1848', in Jacques Droz, ed., *Histoire générale du socialisme*, Vol. 1, Paris: Presses Universitaires de France, 1997, 399.

sequences that they were fashioned into alternatives. In France, Saint-Simon and Saint-Simonism, Fourier and Fourierism were the source of ephemeral but influential alternatives. In a different way, the Society of Seasons led by Blanqui prepared an attempted insurrection in May 1839, which failed but attracted attention. This organization reformed almost immediately after being dissolved and its members described themselves as communists.[9] From 1840 onwards, the term became an integral part of French, German and English political vocabulary, featuring in the major dictionaries of the time.[10] The internationalist organizations founded from 1840 onwards would diffuse this vocabulary. This was particularly true of German immigrant organizations in Paris, which maintained a close relationship with the Parisian labour movement. As it happened, during the 1840s, Marx and Engels stayed in France, Germany and England, immersing themselves in this original, vibrant culture.

Calling Oneself Communist

In Germany, French socialism and communism were diffused during international debates that were already old. In the early nineteenth century, the first militant endorsement of socialist theses by Georg Büchner and Friedrich Weidig was violently repressed. The Enlightenment was the principal source of this critical tradition, in a country dominated by the political structures of the *ancien régime* in the north, while the states in the south, in part annexed by France, were characterized by a certain juridical and political, but also administrative and cultural, modernity inherited from the Napoleonic period. Marx's native town – Trier – lay at the heart of this southern history, with the question of the status of Jewry helping to fuel his father's profound attachment to the French Revolution and its thinkers – the origin of Marx's precocious, enduring interest in this period.[11] In this complex situation, amid rising demands, Lorenz Stein's strange book, *Socialist*

---

9 Grandjonc, *Communisme*, 175.

10 Ibid., 179–80.

11 See Jonathan Sperber, *Karl Marx: A Nineteenth-Century Life*, New York and London: Liveright, 2013, Chapter 1.

and Communist Movements since the Third French Revolution, published in 1842, played an important role. Officially intent on denouncing the theses it expounded, it actually helped spread them. On this breeding ground, a distinctive German communism developed, soon merging into the European revolutionary momentum of 1848.

Prior to leaving Germany and actively participating in the European political ferment, Marx and Engels confronted the terms *socialism* and *communism* as they existed in this context. Engels was the first to iden-tify with communism. A very young autodidactic philosopher, he engaged passionately in German theoretical and political battles, early on undertaking a critique of the Rhenish liberalism to which he was initially close. Sent by his father to his Manchester factories in 1842, impressed by the degree of organization and culture of the principal English labour movement – Chartism – he embarked on the project of a critique of political economy well before Marx, stressing the basic injus-tice of capitalism, but also and above all its essential contradictions. The 'Outline of the Critique of Political Economy' was written in 1844 and in it Engels described the way that 'the system of competition', slaughtering 'millions of men', 'drives us to the abolition of this degradation of mankind through the abolition of private property, competition and the opposing interests'.[12] This approach established the essential coordi-nates of communist commitment as Engels and Marx would continue to view it: combining analysis of political and social contradictions with activist intervention, but without aiming to implement a predefined programme.

After his return to Germany in 1844, Engels began to employ the terms *communism* and *communist*. Together with Moses Hess, he devoted himself to organizing political lectures in the small town of Elberfeld. In a letter to Marx in early October 1844, the word *communist* is repeated incessantly, Engels enthusing that in Elberfeld, 'go where you may, you'll stumble on a communist'.[13] But, he added, 'the Teutons are all still very muddled about the practicality of communism';[14] he thus proposed writing a short text for them on communism as it was being

---

12 Karl Marx and Friedrich Engels, *Collected Works*, Vol. 3, London: Lawrence & Wishart, 1975, 440.

13 Karl Marx and Friedrich Engels, *Collected Works*, Vol. 38, London: Lawrence & Wishart, 1982, 5.

14 Ibid., 6.

'put into practice . . . in England and America'. In this brief text, Engels sought to describe small communities founded on the community of goods, counting on the attraction that these organizations might hold for 'the more intelligent among the rich'.[15] It is not so much the utopian coloration that is remarkable here – since Engels did not advocate generalizing such micro-structures – as the foregrounding of the property question and the community of goods which, in his view, characterized the communist option. And this option seemed to him sufficiently definite for him to adhere to it. In fact, for the young Engels, as for Marx a little later on, the term *communism* primarily signified a radical, deliberate political choice which named and marked a break with their own previous hesitations along with political positions that seemed less consistent – a break also, and especially, with the capitalist order even more so than with the German vestiges of the *ancien régime*.

This use of the word refers not so much to the definition of a different social organization as to the declaration of a commitment whose conclusions remain to be drawn. While the goal is to *construct communism*, the pre-eminent point is *being communist*; this commitment defines the term in its own right more than the as yet vague project to which it refers. The linguistic dimension proves to be constitutive of politics: not naming concepts that pre-exist them, here words have to embody a new regime of thought and action. The communism/communist couplet has subsequently continued to convey this complex duality, which combines a societal project that remains to be constructed and a modality of militant commitment, without conflating them.

The young Marx's path differed from that of Engels. Having remained immersed in the German debate for longer prior to his Parisian encounter with the organizations of the labour movement (rather than the industrial proletariat as such), he gravitated rather more slowly than Engels towards radical political positions. What did Marx's initial approach to the communist question consist in? A curious article in the *Rheinische Zeitung* dated October 1842 is worth recalling. It appeared at a time when the paper was obliged to defend itself against accusations of socialism and communism and Marx did not as yet identify with either

---

15 'Description of Recently Founded Communist Colonies', in Karl Marx and Friedrich Engels, *Collected Works*, Vol. 4, London: Lawrence & Wishart, 1975, 227.

of them. A testimony to his prudence or ambivalence,[16] the article states:

> We are firmly convinced that the real danger lies not in practical attempts, but in the theoretical elaboration of communist ideas, for practical attempts, even mass attempts can be answered by cannon as soon as they become dangerous, whereas ideas, which have conquered our intellect and taken possession of our minds, ideas to which reason has fettered our conscience, are chains from which one cannot free oneself without a broken heart; they are demons which human beings can vanquish only by submitting to them.[17]

It is difficult here to separate out the irony, given the constraints on the writer. However, Marx assigned – and always would assign – historical power to ideas, determined by the circumstances of their formation and expanded, beyond these determinants, by the rebound effect historical power could have on a concrete situation. Such a critical analysis delineates the locus and role of an original strategy, which would subsequently be clarified without ever breaking with this initial intuition.

One of the decisive turning points in Marx's trajectory arose immediately after this ambiguous balance sheet, when the *Rheinische Zeitung* found itself directly threatened by Prussian censorship. The measure of proscription, decided in 1841 but only implemented in 1843, provided Marx with an opportunity to continue his political maturation. On one hand, according to his own statements, he found himself relieved of the need to make concessions. On the other hand, however, this development pertained to a decisive choice in favour of a revolutionary transformation, which he openly proclaimed. It is often recalled that Marx gave the word *radical* its etymological sense: going to the root of things. It is remarkable that he defined it here, first and conversely, by the resolute affirmation of the consequences that follow from a stance – that is, by practice as an extension of theory: the 'radical critique of all that exists' is 'radical . . . in the sense of not being afraid of the results it

---

16 See Michael Löwy, *La Théorie de la révolution chez le jeune Marx*, Paris: Éditions Sociales, 1997, 66.

17 'Communism and the Augsburg *Allgemeine Zeitung*', in Karl Marx and Friedrich Engels, *Collected Works*, Vol. 1, London: Lawrence & Wishart, 1975, 220–1.

arrives at'.[18] Thus, if, in contrast to Engels, the figure of the proletariat featured in the young Marx's texts before he had encountered modern workers and working-class activists, his evolution towards communism was no less decisive; it too was punctuated by real experiences and confrontations that accelerated it.

On the basis of these different starting points, the respective intellectual and political trajectories of Marx and Engels would converge even before they met. The distinctive character of this dual trajectory in the political and intellectual landscape of the time must be stressed. While clearly defined historical causes explain it, this political reorientation, which was neither predetermined nor random but at once conditioned and self-determined, clarifies in return the historical moment of its genesis. It combined the global expansion of capitalism and the emergence of alternatives in search of their political forms and social content. The term *communism* was, first of all, charged with stating this distinctive bifurcation: the choice of revolution. Stathis Kouvélakis stresses this: 'the revolutionary stance, in other words, is not one "option" among other available ones, a choice made by a free will or a rational actor; it is the outcome of alternatives that arise from a refusal – of the dictated solution – and also an impossibility'.[19] Thus, Marx and Engels took account of the meaning of the words *socialism* and *communism* as they existed in their time, in order to endorse and criticize them, combining with them their own concerns as formed during the 1840s. If they ended up 'adhering' to communism, this adhesion was both an affiliation and a simultaneously theoretical and activist reworking which made them major protagonists in this history. In short, if the word *communism* runs through the whole of Marx's oeuvre without ever being strictly defined, it is because its role is to refer not to a 'state of things' or a party, but to a dynamic, a 'real movement' that is also the movement of the thought that seizes hold of it – a cardinal point at the same time as a living idea, then, permanently torn between engagement and project, adhesion and invention, past and future. Here we shall venture the hypothesis that it is precisely this theoretical and practical redefinition, never completed, articulating thought and history, which

---

18 Letter to Ruge, September 1843, in Marx and Engels, *Collected Works*, Vol. 3, 142; trans. modified.

19 Stathis Kouvélakis, *Philosophie et révolution de Kant à Marx*, Paris: La Fabrique, 2017, 348.

preserves the term's validity, not in spite but because of its long, manifold past. It is also this constant revival that differentiates the Marxian term *communism* from other political terms, including socialism. Without disqualifying the latter (even if he criticized socialists ferociously), Marx subordinated it to a more thoroughgoing ambition, but also a more indeterminate one, subject to collective invention in a state of constant readjustment, which sought to re-found politics but also the social role of knowledge and ideas. This differential usage, sometimes polemical and strategic, of the word *communism* is what has to be clarified.

The Critique of Politics

Critical adoption of the term *communism* distinguishes Marx from the other Young Hegelians, including Friedrich Engels and Moses Hess, his engagement in an ambitious theoretical project representing one of the pathways of its redefinition. We may take it that for Marx the point was to go beyond the Young Hegelian slogan of the 'realization of philosophy' in the direction of a mutual recasting of philosophy and politics – a recasting that has culminated in a view of communism that includes the dimension of consciousness and collective choice. The outlines of this project are legible from the Kreuznach manuscript written during the summer of 1843, which focuses on the relations between 'civil society' and 'state' analysed by Hegel in his *Elements of the Philosophy of Right*, while developing a more general critique of Hegelian speculative philosophy and logic.[20]

   In the *Elements*, Hegel presented a critique of liberalism that led him to reject both contractualism and the liberal belief in the capacity of private interests to organize and harmonize social life by themselves, thus rejecting Rousseau and Smith alike, but also Kant.[21] Hegel noted that civil society was the site of the accumulation of individual fortunes, on the one hand, and the sinking of 'a large mass of people . . . below the level of a certain standard of living', on the other.[22] The locus of

   20 See V. Béguin, A. Bouffard, P. Guerpillon and F. Nicodème, Introduction to Karl Marx, *Contribution à la critique de la philosophie du droit de Hegel*, Paris: GEME-Éditions Sociales, 2018, 16.

   21 Kouvélakis, *Philosophie et révolution de Kant à Marx*, 58.

   22 G.W.F. Hegel, *Elements of the Philosophy of Right*, ed. Allen W. Wood and trans. H.B. Nisbet, Cambridge: Cambridge University Press, 1991, §244, 266.

conflict par excellence, civil society required the establishment of the political state as its own 'immanent end'.[23] Its mission was not to regulate the sphere of private interests from without, but to 'realize' the general interest that took shape there. The state must therefore intervene economically and socially, but without damaging private property, Hegel including himself here among the posterity of the French Revolution and the 'right to existence' defined by Robespierre.[24] Marx came across this analysis during his legal and philosophical studies in Berlin, when, after drafting his thesis on ancient Greek philosophy, he decided to take up the study of legal and political issues. Such an orientation did not distinguish him from the other Young Hegelians. In the phase of the *Rheinische Zeitung*, organ of a liberalism not hostile to protectionism which invoked Kant, defence of the principle of publication and a rational constitution came to the fore.[25] The Young Hegelians subsequently ended up defending an alternative autonomy of civil society to the liberal conception, and this also distanced them from Hegel's philosophy of the state.

Marx's critical road was different and took the form of a close reading of Hegel. In the Kreuznach manuscript, Marx concentrated on the section of the *Elements* dealing with the 'Internal Constitution', setting to one side the analysis of social contradictions and inequalities. This choice reveals Marx's liberal political option, which focused on the critique of the separate Hegelian state, applying to it the critique of the cleavages and projections for which the Young Hegelians criticized religion, the latter being conceived by Ludwig Feuerbach as the invention of a separate God onto whom the fantasy of a finally consummated human essence is projected. On the level of political theory, its originality was twofold. On the one hand, it stressed legislative power, key in the view of liberals; on the other, the issue of political representation, which this analysis made it possible to raise, enabled Marx to develop an original conception of political mediation and representation, versions of which would recur throughout his oeuvre. At the same time, Marx definitively distanced himself from Feuerbach's critique of religion, powerless to

---

23 Ibid., §261, 283.

24 Kouvélakis, *Philosophie et révolution de Kant à Marx*, 61.

25 See Pauline Clochec, 'Marx jeune hégélien, 1841–1844', doctoral thesis, University of Lyon, 2018, 382.

conceive concrete and functional mediations and hence incapable of thinking politics.

With this text, the question of mediations therefore proved theoretically and politically decisive. Whereas Hegel proposed that a system of socio-professional groupings – the estates – should mediate between civil society and state, in order to resolve social conflicts, Marx defended the representative constitution inasmuch as it marked 'a great advance since it is the frank, undistorted, consistent expression of the modern condition of the state. It is an unconcealed contradiction.'[26] Hegel's corporatist mediation, according to him, was merely an artificial reconciliation that concealed contradictions and blocked their development. In the process, Marx ranged himself even more against a leitmotif of Young Hegelian thought: the ultimate absorption of any mediation in favour of rediscovered immediacy. This was true of Feuerbach as regards the critique of religion, which he countered with the simple prospect of a reconciliation of the human race with itself through love and the promotion of community.

But this was also true of Moses Hess, as Marx denounced above all the alienating mediation that was money: 'the essence of our modern world of wheelers and dealers – money – is the realized essence of Christianity . . . God is nothing more than capital idealized and heaven is the world of commodities theorized.'[27] Regarding capitalism as the realization of a theological principle authorized partial transposition of the anti-religious critique to the market and the state. In both cases, Marx conceived this mediation as alienating a human essence to be rediscovered beyond the forms masking it. This quest for lost unity assumed mystical tones: 'There will be no more alien essence, no middle term that will enter into us to unite us in appearance and from without, "mediatize" us, when it separates us and divides us in reality and from within.'[28] For Marx, by contrast, the point was not to hunt down mediations, but to rework the theoretical and practical critique of real social divisions, thus passing from the 'critique of heaven' to the 'critique of earth'. This critique aimed at a

---

26 *Contribution to the Critique of Hegel's Philosophy of Law*, in Marx and Engels, *Collected Works*, Vol. 3, 75.

27 Moses Hess, 'L'essence de l'argent', trans. P. Cadiot, in Elisabeth de Fontenay, *Les Figures juives de Marx*, Paris: Éditions Galilée, 1973, 128.

28 Ibid., 146.

collective, democratic reappropriation of social life, outflanking and subverting its capture by the state.

What is the bearing of these reflections on the communist question? In the Kreuznach manuscript, Marx's critique of the state as an abstract entity, and of Hegel's mediatizing solution as a ploy, initially resulted in promoting extended representation via universal suffrage, which was insufficient to absorb the state cleavage. However, through this false window, Marx was to retain and revive the issue of representation and effective mediation, not as conciliatory but revolutionary. Neither the liberal road nor the anarchist road afforded a solution in his view. For the real difficulty of redefining politics in a way that eludes both the reality of the cleavage and the idealist perspective of diluting the political in the social is focused on the issue of mediations. It was precisely this question, which has remained highly topical, that the communist option would take up in an attempt to answer it, while redefining the terms of the debate and broadening them from the perspective of general human emancipation. Formulation of this unresolved problem is the real advance of this text and one of the guiding threads of all of Marx's subsequent reflection on the alternative to capitalism.

It should be added that while this analysis remained philosophical in 1843, it was already rooted in the young Marx's actual social practice – critical journalism – and could thus make its goal 'true democracy' as 'unity of the general and the particular',[29] at a remove from Hegel's solution but in line with his problematic. Once universality had been redefined as the heart of the revolutionary process, it remained to specify the contours of this 'true democracy' insofar as it referred to a social but also political dynamic, while going beyond any institutional construct that would seek to establish a simple expressive relationship between social life and the political sphere. While Marx remained a reformist here, the main elements in his argument conveyed the possibility of a revolutionary road. However that may be, this democracy must be not a form imposed from without, but an immanent structuration, the adequate political form of a social content whose precedent was afforded by the French Revolution: 'The French have recently interpreted this as meaning that in true democracy the state disappears.'[30] This 'disappearance'

---

29 Marx, *Contribution to the Critique of Hegel's Philosophy of Law*, 30.
30 Ibid., 30; trans. modified.

foreshadowed what Marx was to discover on the occasion of the Paris Commune: the invention of a 'form capable of development', which is nothing other than communism itself in the shape of the mobilized people, constituting itself as a permanent political agent of social transformation.

Thus, even before the analysis outlined here was set out more fully, Marx's relationship to Hegel turned out to be distinctive, fundamentally political and a vector of politicization, while leading to a problematization of the very idea of politics. From this point of view, contra Hegel, civil society is not in need of the state that will complete it, but worked by the revolutionary prospect of a comprehensive historical recasting: exclusively political emancipation must give way to human emancipation, proclaims *On the Jewish Question*, an article likewise written in 1843.[31] And this time the extension of the suffrage cannot suffice, since the abolition of the census, which is 'the political annulment of private property[,] not only fails to abolish private property but even presupposes it'.[32]

The line of analysis emerging here is an original dialectical exploration of the social and political alternative to capitalism, innovative in its project as well as its procedures, which redefines certain categories of Hegelian philosophy in accordance with an anti-speculative objective. Marx delineates his dialectic in it, inasmuch as it is destined to become neither a method for nor a doctrine of the latent state, but the grasping of a contradictory becoming whose determinate moments include historical possibilities and presuppose active intervention, Marx not bothering to conceptualize this dimension which was immanent in his thinking. If this approach was constructed on the theoretical terrain, as targeted critique of the Hegelian dialectic, it was nonetheless profoundly bound up with an already existing activist drive, which would ultimately become co-extensive with his life and work. It is also this dynamic critique, first encountered and experienced as political momentum working on theoretical research from within, which Marx would identify when he adhered to communism, demanding a more precise, documented analysis of the economic and social world.

---

31 *On the Jewish Question*, in Marx and Engels, *Collected Works*, Vol. 3, 152.
32 Ibid., 153.

Towards a Communism of Reappropriation

Thus, before endorsing communism, which he initially perceived as an abstract doctrine, Marx progressed from democratic to socialist demands, leading him to reconsider the question of the political and social implications of critique. In his letter of September 1843 to Arnold Ruge, he contrasted communism as 'dogmatic abstraction' with the 'socialist principle', of which it was merely 'a special, one-sided realisation'.[33] This communism was that of 'Cabet, Dézamy, Weitling', a hollow humanism. For its part, however, socialism's defect was that it neglected 'the theoretical existence of man'. This letter to Ruge registered the failure of a certain type of democratic struggle in Germany, where, notwithstanding its moderation, the *Rheinische Zeitung* had just been banned. This observation, and this personal impasse, led Marx to reflect anew on the aims and means of political and social transformation. In continuing the encounter between critique of philosophy, on the one hand, and existing social and communist positions, on the other, Marx would endeavour to articulate the philosophical question of alienation with a clearer condemnation of private property: the thematic of reappropriation – of wealth, but also, and above all, of the self – is what links these dimensions, delineating a new concrete universal located at the heart of social individuals and their activity, prior to taking the form of an alternative political project. This time, the polemic targeted certain French political tendencies, shifting the analysis onto a more directly activist terrain.

The approach was sketched out in the 1844 *Economic and Philosophical Manuscripts*, a collection of rather disparate texts forming an 'unstable set of theoretical orientations that were in the process of being transformed under the impact of external and internal constraints'.[34] Paradoxically, the question of property initially distinguished Marx's road to communism from Engels's, rather than aligning them. In fact, Marx denounced 'crude communism' as a unilateral, obsessive desire to abolish private property, remaining subject to the latter as a result. Such a communism turned out to be much more of a symptom than a

---

33 Marx and Engels, *Collected Works*, Vol. 3, 143.
34 Emmanuel Renault, *Marx et philosophie*, Paris: Presses Universitaires de France, 2014, 110.

solution to the social pathologies whose logic it reproduced, while inverting it. This first-generation communism, which can be assimilated to Babouvism and its sequels, was fundamentally an individualism and an egotism, a 'generalisation and consummation of private property', which 'has not yet grasped the positive essence of private property' or 'the human nature of need'.[35] Taking account of this 'positive essence' made it possible to glimpse a different abolition – not sheer negation, but a negation of the negation. The latter encompassed the totality of humanity's relations to itself as well as nature, offering 'the genuine resolution of the conflict between man and nature and between man and man – the true resolution of the strife between existence and essence, between objectification and self-confirmation, between freedom and necessity, between the individual and the species. Communism is the riddle of history solved, and it knows itself to be this solution.'[36] If humanity's return to itself was not the reappropriation of an already existing essence but involved 'embracing the entire wealth of previous development',[37] communism could not be mere abolition but must correspond to the reworking of a social relation starting from that relation. This applied to private property which, so Marx gave it to be understood, must not simply make way for common property, but be radically redefined. Not until *Capital* would he once again present the communist relationship to private property as 'the negation of the negation',[38] this time specifying that it involved restoring 'individual private property'. The rejection of a communism conceived as communion is conveyed by his choice of vocabulary. Paul Sereni has shown that Marx names political communism using the term *Gemeinwesen* (a scholarly term introduced by philosopher Christian Wolf), in preference to *Gemeinschaft*, utilized by some Young Hegelians but also by counter-revolutionary thought and reactionary political romanticism, precisely because it conveyed a fusional conception of social life.[39]

35 *Economic and Philosophical Manuscripts*, in Marx and Engels, *Collected Works*, Vol. 3, 294, 296.

36 Ibid., 296–7.

37 Ibid., 296.

38 Karl Marx, *Capital Volume 1*, trans. Ben Fowkes, London: Penguin/NLR, 1976, 929.

39 See Paul Sereni, *La Communauté en question I. Chose publique et bien commun chez Marx*, Paris: L'Harmattan, 2010, 61.

In addition, the critique of private property was directly connected by Marx with the sphere of production and labour, as the original locus of self-dispossession. Overcoming this dispossession would require means quite other than equality of income and collective property, simplistic forms of reappropriation precisely because they did not comprehend the true nature of the totality of alienations. At the same time, Marx also demarcated himself from the Hegelian conception of alienation, initiating a reworking of this category by dint of a different conception of the historical contradictions in gestation.[40] A text of rupture with Marx's previous project, and a reconstruction of it, the *Economic and Philosophical Manuscripts* outlined a communist perspective concerned with the anthropological and social, but also political and theoretical, dimensions of human existence: 'The entire movement of history, just as its [communism's] actual act of genesis – the birth act of its empirical existence – is, therefore, also for its thinking consciousness the comprehended and human process of its becoming.'[41] The meaning of these utterances, as poetic as they are philosophical, and containing in germ an intuition that was never renounced, remains to be unpacked.

Significantly, the end of the third manuscript dealt with 'socialist man' as communism's target, if correctly construed. Communism here was no longer a predefined project but a historical movement, a concrete dialectic that 'posits the positive as the negation of the negation' and therefore constitutes 'the actual phase necessary for the next stage of human emancipation and self-restoration.'[42] Far removed from any definite political position, as demonstrated by the uncertain, personalized use of the terms *socialism* and *communism*, Marx concluded with an exceptionally dense sentence: 'Communism is the necessary form and the dynamic principle of the immediate future, but communism as such is not the goal of human development, the form of human society.'[43] In many ways, this is an extraordinary thesis: for this form of the 'immediate future' – a form that is constantly changing in a dynamic fuelled by its constant traversal – is clearly distinguished here from the relatively stable one of the society to come, its 'goal'.

---

40 See Lucien Sève, *Aliénation et émancipation*, Paris: La Dispute, 2012.
41 Marx, *Economic and Philosophical Manuscripts*, 297.
42 Ibid., 306; trans. modified.
43 Ibid.

Thus, communism is predominantly cast as an active principle of transformation, underlying the conscious subjects whom it motivates, but with their conscious action as its condition – a principle rooted in the reality it concretely criticizes and subject to the limits consequent upon that rootedness. It nevertheless triggers the process of a radical transformation of the world. In this sense, communism is the immanent, continuous self-criticism of capitalism, but also of itself, in that it long remains the inheritor of the social order on whose abolition it is intent. Once again, it does not designate the form of the society to be realized in conformity with a predefined model, but the historical labour which, from one moment to the next, attempts to construct it in coordinates that are invariably concrete and always changing, not aiming at some ultimate end of history. It may be said that the definition of this theoretical and practical critique prefigures the subsequent theme of 'permanent revolution',[44] a continuous process of transformation requiring a combination of collective action and decision-making at every point. Consciousness, conceived as external and superior to what it describes, makes way for thought implicated in action, which it alters as it proceeds and which transforms it in return. But so as not to remain declamatory, this conception would have to be deployed in critical knowledge of a new kind, neither an academic discipline severed from its consequences, nor a revolutionary rhetoric with no purchase on reality – a dual pitfall that remains ours today.

At this point in his reflection, well before the elaboration of the new modality of knowledge he was to call 'critique of political economy', Marx had not yet come into contact with the existing labour movement; he stuck to journalistic intervention as the sole means of political struggle. We may add that his initial approach to political economy likewise remained relatively external to its object, based exclusively on second-hand analyses. Marx knew this, and that critical awareness is what fundamentally distinguishes him from other theoreticians of his time, inscribing at the centre of his research the very principle of its pursuit, not preformed conclusions merely awaiting confirmation; the succession of texts left unfinished and unpublished proves it. This research already highlights the general theme of the reappropriation by human beings of their social activity, individual or collective – a question whose

---

44 Marx was to use the term in 1850, in *Class Struggles in France* and *Address of the Central Committee to the Communist League*.

theoretico-political unfolding implies that three problems are to be treated more precisely. These are: the place and nature of critical work; the role and modalities of a political struggle capable of radically subverting politics in the classical sense; and the project of a general recasting of social relations of production and exchange understood as an alternative to capitalism. In other words, while it is incorrect to think that Marx's work in this period contains in germ his whole subsequent oeuvre, it is just as absurd to conceive the phases that punctuate it in terms of clean breaks. Understanding Marx's subsequent trajectory involves searching the early works not for the conclusions but for the springs of a research that was militant from the outset – springs that subordinate the critical agenda to the tensions generated by the analyses produced, but also to the historical imperatives of the hour, these aspirations becoming entangled in inner contradictions. Faced with the approaching revolution, the need for a fundamentally partisan, and concretely oppositional, theorization was more pressing than ever.

The Political Construction of the Proletariat

A major stage in this evolution as steered by circumstances interpreted for their revolutionary potential, the *Introduction* intended to open the Kreuznach manuscript but, written after it, affirmed the major historical role of the proletariat. Its sudden appearance, in a theoretical context still marked by Hegelian and Young Hegelian philosophy,[45] has led a number of commentators to regard it as a still wholly theoretical encounter with the real working class, with Marx deducing the historical vocation he assigns it. However, what is prepared and made possible by this reflection, at the point when Marx registers the subordination of critique to the historical moment that includes it, is an actual encounter with the working class. Marx would note this himself in *The German Ideology*, thus consigning his own experience as an attentive journalist to social conflict: 'The existence of revolutionary ideas in a particular period presupposes the existence of a revolutionary class.'[46] Thus,

---

45 See Renault, *Marx et la philosophie*, 99.

46 Karl Marx and Friedrich Engels, *Collected Works*, Vol. 5, London: Lawrence & Wishart, 1976, 60.

theory's relative capacity for anticipation manifests itself prior to being stated, far removed from any reduction of ideas to some merely mechanical reflection of a social state of affairs.

That is why it is wrong to read this brief text as a sacralization of the proletariat as exclusive historical subject, idealized and invested with a redemptive mission – a reading that continues to fuel the thesis of Marx's incorrigible 'messianism'. On the contrary, marking an opening to real history, Marx's reflection reached a decisive turning point in identifying what, at the heart of this history, represents its effective part, at once adopting and going beyond the Hegelian definition of actuality.[47] The term *proletariat* names the working class in struggle, bearer of a political and social alternative. This distinction between proletariat and working class lost its sharpness in subsequent texts, as Marx further explored the conditions for a politicization whose possibility is immanent in the condition of being exploited. The mysterious 'dynamic principle of the immediate future' mentioned in the *Economic and Philosophical Manuscripts* found its political embodiment here, while paring right down a class analysis that would be considerably clarified thereafter. In the immediate present, the proletariat was the social state that embodied 'the dissolution of all estates', replacing Hegel's false mediation and converting reconciliation into revolution. In effect, Marx's definition of the proletariat seems to be a substitute for the Hegelian 'universal class', precisely inverting its role. According to Hegel, civil servants have the mission of effecting the institutional mediation of the private interests of the other social 'estates' on the basis of the state. Against this representation from above, which led Hegel to denounce the subversive principle of universal suffrage, Marx pitted a representation emanating from society itself, a transformative power and not an expressive duplicate. It was imperative that 'a definite class, proceeding from its particular situation, undertake the general emancipation of society'.

---

47 In his *Science of Logic*, Hegel wrote a long passage on the subject of actuality (*die Wirklichkeit*) that concludes Book Two devoted to the 'Doctrine of Essence'. We shall restrict ourselves to signalling that he defined it as unity of essence and existence and hence superior to simple existence and distinct from 'reality': it is the process of its realization, its necessity resulting from a maturation that nevertheless leaves room for contingency. Against speculative philosophy, but also in and through it, what Marx strives to think is a process of determinate invention.

But it was also necessary for it to be 'perceived and acknowledged as [society's] general representative'.[48]

This original political representation, rich in strategic implications that retain their fertility, was conceived by Marx over and above its institutionalized forms, as what overflows and challenges them. Neither delegation nor simple expression, it became the operator of a structuration of social conflict around the fundamental cleavage between 'the estate of oppression' – the bourgeoisie – and 'the estate of liberation' – the proletariat.[49] As a radical power contesting the established order, the proletariat became the unifying principle for other social categories, an active mediation effecting hegemony. Subsequently, Marx would define the specificity of a revolutionary class by its capacity to unify the other classes around it, by proving capable of imparting, initially at any rate, a universal significance to the defence of its own interests.[50] The last oppressed class in human history, the proletariat was the bearer not of a different political regime in the constitutional sense of the term but, much more profoundly, of a different regime of politics, the latter acquiring an ever broader sense of popular-democratic reappropriation of history, of radical emancipation.

Thus, it is a question not of aspiring to some fusional reconciliation of society with itself, but of thinking of political reappropriation from the perspective of the mediations that make it possible, as well as reconstructing the mediations with a view to reappropriating their social activity by human beings. In line with this approach, Marx pursued his redefinition of theoretical work, against both a philosophy separated from other social activities and the status of intellectual illusorily cut off from class struggles when it is actually the result of them. The point, once again, was to criticize Hegel but also to supersede Feuerbach's critique of religious alienation, while relying on aspects of both. While Marx continued to denounce the cleavage from which the state apparatus and its overarching position derived, he highlighted its specific cause: a class division that is an economic, social and political balance of forces. Henceforth, the fundamentally kindred cleavages of the state,

---

48 *Contribution to the Critique of Hegel's Philosophy of Law: Introduction*, in Marx and Engels, *Collected Works*, Vol. 3, 184.

49 Ibid., 185.

50 *The German Ideology*, in Marx and Engels, *Collected Works*, Vol. 5, 61.

money and philosophy could be related not to the denaturing of a human essence to be restored in its unity, but to the division of the social world itself and the birth of antagonistic class interests at a precise point in its historical development. In other words, the critique of these cleavages no longer pertained to philosophical anthropology, but to revolutionary mobilization.

Against the Young Hegelian school, which 'thought it could make philosophy a reality without superseding it', Marx spelt out that 'it is not enough for thought to strive for realisation, reality must itself strive towards thought'.[51] That a social situation 'strives towards thought' signifies that it is riven by such severe contradictions that their resolution requires the development of a revolutionary project and practice, invariably including the moment of consciousness, for 'theory also becomes a material force as soon as it has gripped the masses'.[52] The abolition of philosophy via its realization, of classes through struggle between them, of politics by recasting it: these are not distinct programmatic elements, but the cardinal, combined axes of communism, aiming at the individual and collective reappropriation of social powers that have been separated and confiscated by class domination. Without being able to go beyond the formulation of this project, the *Introduction* triumphantly proclaims this breakaway to new horizons. Above all, it confirms that Marx's communism, while being a resolute, radical political engagement in an organizational framework that remains to be constructed, is the internal and external motor alike of the analysis, a figure of his own extra-philosophical emancipation in a way, which continually destabilizes its conclusions and calls for its resumption on now consolidated bases.

Communism as Idea and as Organization

Thus, his early writings very soon establish the coordinates of the communist question, even before Marx adopted the term on his own account, borrowing it from the most radical currents in the labour

---

51 Marx, *Contribution to the Critique of Hegel's Philosophy of Law: Introduction*, 181, 183.

52 Ibid., 182.

movement. His encounter with working-class organizations during his stay in Paris in 1844 helped transform his reflection on the communist question by directing him towards in-depth study of its social and economic dimensions, but also closer attention to working-class experience and revolutionary culture. In accordance with the basic axis of his initial analyses, and beyond the declamatory slogans of the 'realization' and 'abolition of philosophy', which Marx borrowed from the Young Hegelian tradition at the very moment he was separating from it, he intended to proceed to an ever closer meshing of theoretical reflection and political intervention. The embryonic status of conceptual labour guided Marx towards a new type of politico-critical intervention, equally attentive to facts and ends, concerned to bring out laws and counter-tendencies evincing the contradictions that nurture revolutions. It involved re-founding the dialectic as an analysis of determinate contradictions – a recasting that rules out treating it separately as a general ontology, and which breaks with the Hegelian idea of logic. The notion of communism encapsulates and names this comprehensive reorientation, while advertising itself as adhering to a political and social camp, which contains new questions and propositions to be developed.

In fact, once the necessity and urgency of the revolution have been proclaimed, it remains to ponder its course, organization and objectives. This question follows directly from earlier analyses and concerns the communist idea construed as an unprecedented alliance of thinking and action, 'the weapon of critique' and the 'critique of arms'.[53] Amid the intellectual and political fermentation of the time, this analysis was developed directly from Marx and Engels's critique of ideology from summer 1844. After the preliminary remarks of *The Holy Family* on the theoretical and practical genesis of socialism and communism, Marx and Engels undertook a refined ideological and political cartography, initially by means of the sometimes pernickety polemics conducted in *The German Ideology* and then in the *Communist Manifesto*, the latter of which situates itself more directly on the terrain of political intervention. As it proceeds, the communist thematic is weighted with additional issues.

In *The German Ideology*, Marx and Engels once again attack German philosophers who offer their own conception of communism, whether

---

53 Ibid., modified.

to identify with it (Ludwig Feuerbach) or to denounce it (Bruno Bauer, Max Stirner). In each instance, in their view, this involves a communism travestied sometimes to the point of caricature as the 'theft of personal property' by Stirner and Antoine Destutt de Tracy. It is not so much a question of refuting these various authors one by one as of analysing their ideas as active representations. Their conditions lie in a determinate historical formation, of which they are neither the mere reflection nor the deceptive mask, constituting the expression of the class position of their producers. Faced with the new role of ideas in the modern age, the critique of religion dear to the Young Hegelian school proves impotent. In search of a new conceptualization, Marx reconstructs the notions of ideology and superstructure to affirm both the determination, and the relative autonomy, of forms of consciousness vis-à-vis their economico-social base. But it is also a question of accounting for the necessary illusion that professional thinkers forge on their own subject, by dint of a division of labour whose product they are and of whose nature they are ignorant.

First and foremost, this approach takes for its object the legitimation of the ruling order, but also all the forms of its contestation, including communism. Their emergence is precisely the index of the historical maturation of class conflict and the advent of unprecedented historical possibilities. The terms *socialism* and *communism* are not subject to any precise distinction from the pens of Marx and Engels here, and still less any counterposition to one another. By contrast, substantive communism and the adjective *communist* tend to be differentiated, the former referring to a post-capitalist societal project, whereas the parties, currents and doctrines dubbed communist define a field and, within the labour movement, its most radical current. In line with this tradition, the question of property emerges as the principle of a deep-rooted class confrontation: 'in reality, the actual property-owners stand on one side and the propertyless communist proletarians on the other'.[54] But two problems make it necessary to complicate this approach, demarcating it from a mere reprise of pre-existing communist themes. On the one hand, the definition of the proletariat as a conscious, mobilized class raises the question of its construction within broader contours, which are those of the working class as a whole. On the other hand, the

---

54 Marx and Engels, *The German Ideology*, 469.

communist societal project cannot be defined prior to its collective invention and the formula that states this was to remain famous: 'communism is for us not a *state of affairs* which is to be established, an *ideal* to which reality [will] have to adjust itself. We call communism the *real* movement which abolishes the present state of things. The conditions of this movement result from the now existing premise.'[55] Obviously, this premise is to be sought in social reality and its evolution. If this formulation is to be credited to a construction of communism conceived as invention, not as the application of a prior doctrine, it also attests to the immense political hope that haunts this text, on the eve of the 1848 revolution. The present sequence, if not history in general, leads to communism, the authors have no doubt; they even forecast a rapid denouement.

In the context of this initial attempt to coordinate communist organization and project, Marx and Engels are led to clarify some of the distinguishing features of a project for abolishing capitalism. Among them, the issue of property is, and will remain, central. But if it does not suffice to define communism as such, it is because it remains to be redefined not as sheer negation, but as a fundamental reappropriation – abolition of the self-dispossession engendered by capitalist social relations: 'with the abolition of the basis, private property, [there is established] the communistic regulation of production (and, implicit in this, the abolition of the alien attitude of men to their own product).'[56] It involves abolishing the alienation visited on the individual in work by capitalist property relations and, therewith, paving the way for planning whose modalities remain vague but whose principle is clearly asserted: the 'overthrow of the existing state of society' and the 'communist revolution', as well as 'the abolition of private property which is identical with it', will have the following consequences:

[T]he liberation of each single individual will be accomplished in the measure in which history becomes wholly transformed into world history . . . *All-round* dependence, this primary natural form of the *world-historical* co-operation of individuals, will be transformed by this communist revolution into the control and conscious mastery of these

55 Ibid., 49.
56 Ibid., 48.

powers, which, born of the action of men on one another, have till now overawed and ruled men as powers completely alien to them.[57]

And Marx specifies that 'empirically, communism is only possible as the act of the dominant peoples "all at once" and simultaneously',[58] raising one of the most complex strategic problems, which has lost none of its relevance. Far from counterposing national and international dimensions, investigating the viability of local options involves conceiving the general impact of points of rupture and reflecting on the conditions of their potential expansive force.

The abolition of classes in and through their struggle taken to its conclusion; individual liberation; collective, conscious control over production; and world revolution – these cruces of communism have the peculiarity that they mutually condition one another and, above all, create the conditions for their own development as they proceed. They define the revolutionary process as Marx conceived it at the time. In initiating and maintaining this process, ideas play a determinant role. Their purpose is not to vouchsafe theoretical and utopian anticipation of the new world; instead, they are one of the components constitutive of mobilized social force, an original form of shared consciousness guiding collective action. Here, Marx completely reworks Bauer's theme of self-consciousness that he initially adopted. The *Communist Manifesto* will formulate, but, above all, endeavour to embody, this alternative to the ruling ideas. It is now a matter of thinking about general historical development, the disappearance of classes and the liberation of individuals conjointly as combined conditions of a general process of emancipation, which is viable if and only if it proves capable of redefining itself and correcting its own course as it proceeds. Communism names this expansive historical dynamic, which is concretely and constantly critical.

Among the constitutive features of the communist project, equality is one of the classical demands, destined to occupy a key role and to ensure this critical persistence once it is redefined as a process and not a status. Marx and Engels write:

---

57 Ibid., 51–2.
58 Ibid., 49.

One of the most vital principles of communism, a principle which distinguishes it from all reactionary socialism, is its empirical view, based on a knowledge of man's nature, that differences of *brain* and of intellectual ability do not imply any differences whatsoever in the nature of the *stomach* and of physical *needs*; therefore the false tenet, based upon existing circumstances, 'to each according to his abilities', must be changed, insofar as it relates to enjoyment in its narrower sense, into the tenet, *'to each according to his need'*; in other words, a *different form of activity*, of labour, does not justify *inequality*, confers no *privileges* in respect of possession and enjoyment.[59]

This first mention of Louis Blanc's famous formula was to be taken up in the *Critique of the Gotha Programme*. Here, it serves to counter the 'true socialism' of Georg Kuhlmann, typical of the speculative German tendencies against which Marx and Engels ranged French political culture.

To this egalitarian demand, Marx and Engels add what (according to them) is its condition: the abolition of classes and relations of exploitation. This requirement was initially accompanied by the project of 'aboli[shing] . . . labour itself',[60] the richness of the German term *aufheben*, the meaning of which combines preservation and destruction, not being in contradiction with the more specific project of abolishing wage labour that Marx would invoke next. This second definition was to enable him to signal the difference between free time and working time, the latter surviving in communist society while being subject to complete redefinition, which includes collective management of the production and distribution of social wealth but also the enhancement of individual free time. We must note that this reduction would go hand in hand with the politicization of work – the central track of a non-statist redefinition of politics that Marx was to explore much later, foreshadowed here. For, along with the dialectical abolition of work, Marx and Engels pronounce themselves in favour of an analogous abolition of state political institutions, the two forms of abolition pertaining to the same fundamental project: collective reappropriation of separated, confiscated social activities, without organizational and productive tasks disappearing. Marx

---

59 Ibid., 537.
60 Ibid., 77.

indeed notes: 'previous revolutions within the framework of the division of labour were bound to lead to new political institutions: it likewise follows that the communist revolution, which removes the division of labour, ultimately abolishes political institutions'.[61] This claim continues and expands the analysis of the modern state in *On the Jewish Question* while adding the dimension of class struggle and exploitation it lacked. It remains today to re-explore this dual track, rearticulating what so many critiques of capitalism persist in separating.

In *The German Ideology*, Marx therefore clarifies the project of the reappropriation by human beings of the results and conditions of their own activity. He adds to the previous coordinates an original condition that roots communism in the capitalist mode of production and its essential contradictions, the development of the productive forces. Marx states that 'this development of productive forces ... is an absolutely necessary practical premise, because without it privation, *want* is merely made general, and with *want* the struggle for necessities would begin again, and all the old filthy business would necessarily be restored'.[62] This thesis is sometimes interpreted by certain Marxists, as well numerous opponents of that tradition, as the definition of a historical course principally steered by technological progress and growth. Against this kind of deterministic reading, we need at least to recall that Marx's definition of the productive forces includes the material means of production and technology, but also labour-power – that is, the workers themselves. Their 'development' refers to the numerical growth of the working class, but also the expansion of social forms of cooperation which, for Marx, are major factors in the development of communist awareness. In other words, Marx separates objective and subjective factors only in the context of his analytical study of the labour process and not historically where these dimensions intermesh,[63] unlike some subsequent Marxism with its tendency to restrict the construction of a collective subject to the terrain of established politics. Marx would later say that 'material labour' must become 'not the exertion of the worker as a natural force drilled in a particular way, but as a subject',[64] describing

---

61 Ibid., 380.
62 Ibid., 49.
63 Marx, *Capital Volume 1*, 285.
64 *Economic Manuscripts of 1857–58*, trans. Ernst Wangermann, in Karl Marx and Friedrich Engels, *Collected Works*, Vol. 28, London: Lawrence & Wishart, 1986, 530.

the subjective factor in the labour process as 'labour-power in action',[65] at the antipodes of a purely technological and economistic conception of the productive forces.

In every respect, *The German Ideology* therefore attempts to draw the conclusions of the earlier works while shifting them onto economic and historical terrain – a shift as fertile as it is destabilizing, forcing Marx as it did into a substantial reworking of his initial theses. Embodied in the endless operation of transcending philosophy, Hegelian as well as Young Hegelian, this critical and self-critical endeavour pointed Marx in the direction of an analysis of political economy at once scholarly and militant, which he viewed as one of the weapons of communism, the latter also being rethought as a contradictory process punctuated by radical breaks. Because these latter are the regime of thought as well as its object, the question of revolution is broached from the angle of a clean break with the old order. Against the timorousness of speculative German socialism on this score, Marx and Engels encapsulate in a formula the concrete radicalism of the struggle against the old world and the scale of what is at stake in it: 'the revolution is necessary, therefore, not only because the *ruling* class cannot be overthrown in any other way, but also because the class *overthrowing* it can only in a revolution succeed in ridding itself of all the muck of ages and become fitted to found society anew'.[66] All told, during this period, Marx's definition of communism was clarified and politicized, while evading the snare of a complete description of an ideal world. Its originality consists in the fact that its specific programmatic elements (equality, abolition of exploitation, disappearance of wage labour and the state, free development of individuals, revolutionary mobilization) are also the means of transition, mediations as much as ends. They do not represent separate stages in the framework of a pre-written scenario but 'real premises' developing along the way. Basically, it is in this dialectic that the specificity of communism à la Marx consists. And the small number of occurrences of the term in subsequent texts indicates that it is not so much its definition as a mode of production that concerns Marx as the construction of a political dynamic conveying an alternative to capitalism. It is this concern, involving first the construction of popular mobilization around

---

65 Marx, *Capital Volume 1*, 283.
66 Marx and Engels, *The German Ideology*, 53.

its objectives, immediate but also general, that is named here by the term *strategy*, over and above the classical definition of the word.

A Communism Manifest

On the eve of the European revolution of 1848, this conception of theoretical and political intervention was finally about to meet with its practical moment. The *Manifesto of the Communist Party* encapsulates this new perspective in its title, which once again alters the theses of *The German Ideology*. This textual intervention, which was to become canonical, is, in fact, profoundly bound up with its context, with the forms of organization of the labour movement and with the immense hope generated by the emergent revolution. Thus, the term *communist party* was to be a source of misinterpretations on account of its subsequent usage – for here Marx sticks to affirming that the communists do not form a distinct party or a class, but that they are 'the most . . . resolute section of the working-class parties of every country'.[67]

Neither isolated doctrinaires nor disciplined members of licensed organizations, communists are those who tirelessly militate to win individuals and social strata to their cause, beyond and sometimes despite the structures, transient in essence, of the labour movement. This explains both why Marx continues to fundamentally associate the party with class engaged in struggle and why he believed that organizations are merely ephemeral instruments of propaganda, in an age when the issue of their institutional structuration in a parliamentary framework did not arise. In the course of their activist careers, Engels and he had no hesitation in leaving, but also dissolving, organizations they reckoned useless or detrimental, particularly when unitary policies seemed to them to be on the agenda. The emergence of German social democracy from the 1870s radically transformed the meaning of the word *party*, starting a strategic debate unknown in 1848.

Following an initial version offered by Engels under the title *The Principles of Communism*, the *Manifesto*, which took over a number of its elements, was written and published in February 1848 at the request

---

67 *Manifesto of the Communist Party*, in Karl Marx and Friedrich Engels, *Collected Works*, Vol. 6, London: Lawrence & Wishart, 1976, 497.

of the Communist League – a small working-class organization that descended directly from the League of the Just, founded in 1836 as the German section of the Blanquist Société des saisons. The League developed in Paris, but also in London and Switzerland, and it was shot through with lively debates, particularly over the dichotomy between reformism and revolution. The English delegates, close to Chartism, opted for moderate positions. But the debate also focused on the role of knowledge and 'scholars'. Marx and Engels seemed to the London leaders to be representatives of that social category, which was suspect in their eyes. Following an internal battle, and even though Marx and Engels were far from convinced of the strategic importance of the organization, they proved to be the only ones capable of writing this text in anticipation of the impending political and social explosion. However, Marx never succeeded in completely imposing his own viewpoint within the League, added to which was the very small diffusion and feeble impact of the *Manifesto* at the time it was published.

While one of Marx and Engels's first requirements was that the cult of authorities should be eliminated from the statutes,[68] the latter becoming elected and revocable, they predominantly envisaged the role of the League from the standpoint of diffusing revolutionary ideas. The *Manifesto* is not primarily a political programme but a pedagogical, militant opuscule which opens with a famous passage presenting human history as the history of class struggles. Capitalism is defined in it as a mode of production realizing the domination of the bourgeois class, which 'cannot exist without constantly revolutionising the instrument of production, and thereby the relations of production'.[69] This bourgeoisie has given birth to gigantic productive forces, whose growth, and the contradictions they generate, it cannot control. These forces have thus become 'the weapons that bring death to [the bourgeoisie]', to which must be added 'the men who are to wield those weapons – the modern working class – the proletarians'.[70]

Despite its affirmative tone and militant optimism, the text does not conflate historical and political logic: it notes in passing that the

68 Fernando Claudin, *Marx, Engels et la révolution de 1848*, trans. A. Valier, Paris: François Maspero, 1980, 104.
69 Marx and Engels, *Manifesto of the Communist Party*, 487.
70 Ibid., 490.

'organisation of the proletarians into a class, and consequently into a political party, is continually being upset again by the competition between the workers themselves'[71] these tendencies and countertendencies being destined to become the quintessential terrain for militant intervention. In these conditions, being communist is the task of the moment and consists in working for the unity of the labour movement, nationally and internationally, with a view to the imminent revolution:

> The Communists are distinguished from the other working-class parties by this only: 1. In the national struggles of the proletarians of the different countries, they point out and bring to the front the common interests of the entire proletariat, independently of all nationality. 2. In the various stages of development which the struggle of the working class against the bourgeoisie has to pass through, they always and everywhere represent the interests of the movement as a whole.[72]

In this regard, the text mentions three series of propositions, sketching a specifically strategic reflection on the subject of property, labour and the state.

Marx and Engels reiterate that it is not a question of 'abolishing the right of personally acquiring property as the fruit of a man's own labour', but only 'bourgeois property'.[73] A series of measures – tax reform, abolition of inheritance, expropriation of large landowners and nationalization[74] – should make possible a rapid transition from capitalism to communism. As for the state, defined as 'the organised power of one class for oppressing another',[75] it is destined to be abolished in the course of a process that will see the proletariat initially seize hold of it and organize itself as the dominant class, the better to work towards the abolition of classes in general and the destruction of any state apparatus separated from social existence, with a view to 'win[ning] the battle of democracy'.[76] Nationalizations, the centralization of credit and transport, and the 'coordination' of agricultural and industrial activity are to be placed under the

71 Ibid., 493.
72 Ibid., 497.
73 Ibid., 498.
74 Ibid., 505.
75 Ibid.
76 Ibid., 504.

responsibility of a 'public power' that has lost its political character – that is, its class character. As to labour, the watchword of its abolition is abandoned in favour of the perspective of reversing the subjection of living labour to accumulated dead labour – which in reality comes down to the same thing: 'in Communist society, accumulated labour is but a means to widen, to enrich, to promote the existence of the labourer'.[77] Consequently, 'we shall have an association in which the free development of each is the condition for the free development of all'.[78]

To these demands must be added internationalism – a key dimension of the proletariat's social and political struggles, which is likewise to be counted among the political goals that are also mediations. Marx endeavours to counter utopian currents, which preach love and fraternity. But he also strives to combat voluntarism and adventurism, particularly that of Wilhelm Weitling, an enthusiastic communist preacher who envisaged raising a popular army, swearing exclusively by the immediate seizure of power. Without uncoupling it from the subjective dimension – political decision-making and the rhythms specific to it – Marx stresses the weight of an objective causality rooted in economic and social reality and its contradictions. If the *Manifesto* stands in sharp contrast to the utopian tradition in its class analysis and the anchorage of its project in real conditions, it also deepens Marx's already old reflection on transitions and mediations, bound up with historical analysis of the transition from feudalism to capitalism, even if it tends to avoid questions of collective mobilization, the shape of social alliances (the end of the text broaching only political alliances), as well as the precise conditions of the projected changes.

The rigidly programmatic character of the text in places is attributable to it being commissioned and corresponds to the desire to transform 'professions of faith' and other working-class 'catechisms' into concretely defined proposals. Even so, Marx and Engels's strategic contributions are very real: exposition of the massive economic and social contradictions characteristic of capitalism aims to make the space now available to the political initiative of the proletariat visible and expand it at an exceptional revolutionary moment. Conceived by its drafters as an opportunity to realize the project of combining knowledge and action

---

77 Ibid., 499.
78 Ibid., 506.

politically, the *Manifesto* sets about affirming this unity while delegating to the revolution itself the mission of reinventing politics, as well as the task of reviving theoretical critique. Read from this angle, the polemic with existing oppositional currents at the text's close embodies this determined politicization of critique, its conversion into effective ideological struggle intended to accompany the other dimensions of class confrontation. Inaugurating a protracted, complex debate on organization and its ends, the *Manifesto* tends to extend the earlier reflection to the political forms of social reappropriation – forms whose task is to link the conditions of struggle to the objectives of democratic reorganization and planning, while ensuring emancipation of the individual.

If the explosion of 1848 represented the high point of the ardently desired encounter between theory and action, it soon gave way to what Marx would call the 'descending line' of the revolution:[79] defeat, the collapse of the hoped-for social alliances, Europe-wide repression and reaction – the latter forcing political reflection to redeploy to critical terrain for a time, but with the ballast of an experience as exceptional as it was traumatizing. On the one hand, the pursuit of the critique of political economy leading to the composition of *Capital* would refine exploration of the contradictions of capitalism and clarify the way that the alternative can, and must, be engendered by their evolution, beyond the brief description of 'communist society' sketched in the *Manifesto*.[80] On the other hand, subsequent episodes in a revolutionary sequence in France lasting until 1871 allowed Marx to continue to learn from actual insurrections. His historical analyses in the heat of the moment, but also the declarations written in the name of the International Working Men's Association and other militant texts, led Marx to confront anew problems of organization, class alliances, programme and project.

The effective articulation of critical intervention with revolutionary project may be regarded as the major innovation that the *Manifesto* attempts not to theorize, but to embody. It helps to enrich the meaning of the term *communism*, which now comprises five principal features that must be concretely interlinked and, above all, mutually activated: revolutionary hopes as old as class struggle; a political and social break

---

79 *The Eighteenth Brumaire of Louis Bonaparte*, in Karl Marx and Friedrich Engels, *Collected Works*, Vol. 11, London: Lawrence & Wishart, 1979, 124.

80 Marx and Engels, *Manifesto of the Communist Party*, 498–9.

with capitalism; a political camp organized around the working class; an emancipatory strategy conjoining mediations and transitions; and a post-capitalist mode of production. This constitutive complexity highlights the fundamentally political nature of a coherence that is always to be established circumstantially and collectively. In the conditions of the moment – the 1848 revolution, its defeat, its revivals (thwarted in their turn), the subsequent crises of capitalism, independence struggles and wars, changes in the labour movement – the protracted sequence that extends to the deaths of Marx in 1883 and Engels in 1895 was to be occasion for resumptions, modifications and occasionally substantial corrections of earlier analyses. For Marx was never a spectator of revolution. By dint of his militant involvement in various organizations and in the First International, with his active support for national liberation struggles and rejection of colonialism and slavery, but also through his own exile and way of life, which were as much endured as chosen, he experienced and lived the bond between theory and practical engagement even as he strove to think it.

Repeated Failures and Permanent Revolution

The 1848 revolution was to play a decisive role for the whole generation to which Marx and Engels belonged, definitively making them 'forty-eighters'. The *Neue Rheinische Zeitung*, published in Cologne from 1 June 1848 until 19 May 1849, furnished one of the contexts for active combat during the revolutionary sequence. Associated with the democratic party, the paper defended the unity of Germany and an anti-Prussian line, as well as Polish independence. It analysed the confrontation with Russia and criticized the attitude of the German bourgeoisie, with whom joint action became daily ever more difficult. While it did not directly discuss communism, Marx openly supported the Parisian insurgents of June 1848 and their demand for a 'democratic and social Republic'. The paper's increasing distribution and his title of editor-in-chief guaranteed Marx a relatively stable position for a while. At the same time, even if he remained 'a revolutionary leader of the second rank',[81] he and Engels actively participated in revolutionary

---

81 Sperber, *Karl Marx: A Nineteenth-Century Life*, 223.

agitation in Germany. The point was to apply and develop the theses of the *Manifesto*: intervening actively, and opportunely, in class struggles; encouraging alliances yet subordinating them to ultimate goals; envisaging the subsequent phases of the revolutionary process while adjusting to real episodes as they fell into place. Marx's disagreement with Andreas Gottschalk, the League's representative in Cologne, but also, through him, with Moses Hess, specifically concerned the transitions necessary to establish communism. For Marx, it involved a protracted process, punctuated certainly, but which had to run its course and which would not be realized all of a sudden. Affirming its immediate possibility, without struggle or confrontation, was to deceive those engaged in it.

However, the hope did not last. The political horizon narrowed and repression got underway. If, in February 1849, Marx had managed to transform his trial into a tribune for the theses of the *Manifesto*,[82] the newspaper now found itself abandoned by some of its shareholders and sank into financial difficulties. German democrats broke up the alliance with the working class, rallying with the liberals and the monarchy. From mid-1849, the political situation rapidly deteriorated, Marx was expelled by the Prussian authorities and the last number of the *Neue Rheinische Zeitung* appeared on 19 May 1849, printed in red ink. Marx's hopes for a new revolutionary wave survived, with his attention now turning to social and political struggles in France as he opted for Paris as his place of exile. But in France, too, revolutionary prospects diminished inexorably. In August 1849, expelled once again, Marx settled in London and, without ceasing to participate politically, refocused on his long-envisaged research project: 'critique of political economy' was to be the title of his theoretical enterprise and an unremitting commitment. But it did not betoken any abandonment of political analysis and activity, which more than ever demanded readjusted, general reflection.

This orientation is what Marx attempted to theorize, and the endeavour, as well as its hesitations, emerges in the balance-sheet text he wrote in March 1850, *Address of the Central Committee to the League of Communists*. Addressed to members of the reformed Communist League, this clandestine text proposed a re-engagement with an offensive revolutionary strategy in anticipation of the new revolutionary

---

82 Ibid., 232.

wave deemed imminent, breaking with the earlier options of alliance with democratic currents. In it, Marx presented the thesis of 'permanent revolution', fated to enjoy a long afterlife, which indicated the need for a revolutionary transformation encompassing the defeat of the ruling classes, the conquest of the state by the proletariat and the expansion of communism 'in all the dominant countries of the world'.[83] This general strategic thesis mingled with more conjunctural considerations and polemical remarks, in a text not intended for wide distribution, which served to justify Marx's distancing of himself from the League. Thus, organizationally, Marx deplored the turn of sections of the League to local objectives and the loss of contact with the Central Committee. Given the reversal of alliances by the democratic party, Marx also regretted the consequences of his own original option, occasioning the loss of 'the independence of the workers' to the advantage of 'the petty-bourgeois democrats',[84] skilled in exploiting working-class organizations. Noting these political coordinates and their institutional dimension, Marx advocated a popular organization from below, the establishment of working-class councils, clubs and governments to duplicate bourgeois institutions once the bourgeois democrats were in power, while not allowing a premature 'intoxication of victory' to set in among the dominated.[85] Marx added that, faced with a party 'whose treachery to the workers will begin from the first hour of victory', 'the workers must be armed and organised' and 'must not allow themselves to be bribed by such arguments of the democrats as, for example, that by doing so they are splitting the democratic party and giving the reactionaries the possibility of victory'.[86]

Ultimately, is it not here that Marx's true strategic thinking is to be found? The reprises and reworkings, particularly by Lenin and Trotsky, of the notions of permanent revolution and dual power suggest so. However, their intention was not to explore Marx's oeuvre for its own sake but to gain analytical tools, immediately adjusted to a concrete revolutionary conjuncture. By definition, the latter would be different, but in 1917 as in 1848, it allocated a key role to the problem of political

---

83 *Address of the Central Authority to the League*, in Karl Marx and Friedrich Engels, *Collected Works*, Vol. 10, London: Lawrence & Wishart, 1978, 281.
  84 Ibid., 277.
  85 Ibid., 283.
  86 Ibid., 283–4.

alliances and winning state power. Unbeknown to their authors, these circumstantial approaches regrettably became synonymous with general Marxist strategy, which is now widely regarded as outmoded; it has become tempting to counterpose to it either a rudderless pragmatism or circumvention pure and simple of the issue of the state. This is to forget that such texts must be read in conjunction with the circumstances of their composition, not as political treatises. That is why dwelling on Marx's 'writings', taking on board their diversity of forms and goals, rather than on his 'oeuvre' in the academic sense of the term, is the only way of being faithful to his project and restoring its coherence.

In subsequent works, produced at a distance from any revolutionary urgency without ever breaking with a desire for political intervention, Marx's approach would become more complex, integrating a study of the class relations and partisan logics at work, abandoning the idea of their strict correlation as well as the focus on tactical choices that are, by definition, variable. He also tackled the issue of the destruction of the state as well as crises, more accurately assessing colonial domination and the global expansion of capitalism. That is why his strategic thinking is to be sought in the study of these composite, non-linear dynamics, in conjunction with national and international economic and political analysis, carried out for the purposes of conceiving and guiding the various moments of a struggle that far exceeds conquest of the state apparatus. This wider reflection, which encompasses reflection on the mediations of radical emancipation and goes beyond the logics of organization and seizing power while including them, is what is most sorely lacking today. It is a deficiency that makes it difficult to identify the contours and scope of what, in its time, was a broader conception of strategy whose relevance has not so much to be proved as reconstructed.

5

Marx: Communism as Strategy

Following the defeat of the 1848 revolution, Marx's political thinking, addressing all the concrete issues of the time, became all the more analytical and precise as study of the essential logic of capitalism came to dominate his agenda. From this standpoint, even though he remained politically active, we can say that from the 1850s, his thought became ever more immanent in his theoretical activity, while casting its net wider. Critical development become one of the main sites of active engagement in a period of relative decline of the revolutionary movement. This is the sense in which Marx described *Capital* as 'the most terrible missile that has yet been hurled at the heads of the bourgeoisie (landowners included)',[1] after having stated his wish to 'deal the bourgeoisie a theoretical blow from which it will never recover'.[2]

Another feature of the period, inseparable from the preceding one, is that after 1848 Marx was more than ever attentive to world history. Social and political struggles in France, in England, but also popular revolts in China and India, the American Civil War and slavery, national liberation movements in Ireland and Poland, populist mobilizations in Russia – these afforded opportunities to resume his strategic thinking and sometimes to rectify his previous analyses. Meanwhile, the critique

1 Letter to Johann Philipp Becker, 17 April 1867, in Karl Marx and Friedrich Engels, *Collected Works*, Vol. 42, London: Lawrence & Wishart, 1987, 358.
2 Letter to Carl Klings, 4 October 1864, in ibid., 4.

of political economy sought to grasp the contradictions affecting the capitalist mode of production and bourgeois economic science in their complex logic. The profound unity of these two approaches is what all those commentators who stress the incoherence of Marx's argument have not perceived – indeed, have not wished to perceive. According to them, it is torn between a descriptive and determinist approach, on the one hand, and a historical analysis doing justice to the free initiative of individuals on the other. The other obstacle to an understanding of Marx's political and strategic thought is the standard reading of the *Critique of the Gotha Programme*, which purports to find in it the summary and last word of Marx's strategic reflection on the subject of communism, reducing revolution to a scenario of two predefined phases.

We must, therefore, read in tandem the texts pertaining to the critique of political economy (principally *Capital* and the preparatory texts) and texts studying the recent conjuncture, which focus on world affairs, the Paris Commune and revolutionary prospects in Russia, highlighting the intertwining of economic conditions, social processes and political struggles. Marx's texts in this period, different not only in their style but also their concepts and formats, prove to be profoundly united by their object – capitalism – grasped from different angles and viewpoints. They all contribute to one and the same critique in the theory – and in practice – of politics. In them, the term *communism* continues to refer above all to a political struggle and orientation, not to a societal project to be described in its forms and stages. Marx's attention was focused on the contradictions inherent in the capitalist mode of production and the space they opened up for revolutionary intervention, one of its conditions being precise knowledge of this dialectic, which nurtures awareness of the historical possibilities with which it is pregnant. His already old definition of science was refined, allocated the task of identifying laws and tendencies, but also countertendencies, which each open up their own field for collective action.

In short, what Marx now called the 'critique of political economy' renewed the initial project with a more coherent integration, in changed conditions, of the various lines of theoretical analysis, on the one hand, and revolutionary intervention on the other. After 1848, this project was reconstructed around a twofold imperative: in-depth analysis of the capitalist mode of production and an analysis of the political situation and redefinition of political intervention assimilating the defeat of 1848. The issue of reappropriation continued to flexibly unify all the others and invested from within research that sought to be a reflection of its objective. Once again, communism was to be sought in the undertaking itself – something that in no way diminishes its goals but makes their constant reworking constitutive of their very definition. Given this, mediations are not to be sought in the production of a scenario in stages, but are inscribed in the depths of a process of transformation. For such an objective to acquire concrete scope, consciousness must be collective and organized as a social force. Marx would continue to come up against this fluctuating, problematic historical premise, like all those today who in the absence of any imminent revolutionary prospect regard radical social change as indispensable.

What needs to be reopened is the loop of a seemingly circular causality: the diffusion of revolutionary ideas, which is one of the parameters of popular mobilization, is also one of its consequences. Two consequences follow. On the one hand, critical work is always possible and necessary, even though its impact should not be overestimated. On the other, capitalist exploitation is inseparable from all the forms of domination that condition its reproduction, always striving to turn in on itself the logic of expropriation and alienation. *Capital* and the preparatory texts endeavour both to describe this logic and to overturn it, inaugurating a new kind of knowledge, inseparable from its active social and political dimensions, which it is urgent to explore afresh today. Three themes warrant in-depth treatment, having been broached by the theorists of the alternative studied above: the issue of labour and its capitalist appropriation; the question of democracy as conquest; and, finally, the requisite combination of forms of emancipation. These three topics all reveal communism to be an attempt at reappropriation, negation of the negation of a new kind, which remains charged with deploying its mediations in real history.

Labour-Power: A Revolutionary Power

Aiming at the heart of social conflict, the communist project is born out of real contradictions, but it immediately comes up against the dominant ideology and the spontaneous representations emanating from the capitalist mode of production. For Marx, the discovery of the essential logic of capitalism does not dissolve the appearances that result from it, even though it makes it possible to understand them. As a world turned upside down, set on pursuing the valorisation of value and not the satisfaction of social needs, capitalism generates inverted representations. The consequences of this thesis are political as well as epistemological. In the pages of the first chapter of Volume One of *Capital* devoted to commodity fetishism,[3] Marx emphasizes that value 'transforms every product of labour into a social hieroglyph',[4] concealing from human beings the nature of their activity. This concealment goes hand in hand with a social organization of production and existence, which explains why its denunciation is not a sufficient condition for its transformation but why, on the contrary, 'the veil is not removed from the countenance of the social life-process . . . until it becomes production by freely associated men, and stands under their conscious and planned control'.[5] In other words, it is communism as an alternative, actually realized mode of production, rid of the exploitation of labour and capitalist commodity relations, which makes possible an understanding of the social process that is also its precondition. On the one hand, *Capital* represents this endeavour in advance; on the other, the famous description of a 'free association' of human beings that immediately precedes this passage attempts to impart concrete shape to the alternative via fiction.

In the society imagined in *Capital* Volume One, Chapter 1, labour time is what makes it possible to measure individual participation: 'the social relations of the individual producers, both towards their labour and the products of their labour, are here transparent in their simplicity, in production as well as in distribution'.[6] But how to conceive the leap from one world to another? This passage serves as a hypothetical counterpoint, the better to underscore the opacity of the capitalist economic world. Communism here is a thought experiment, the presupposed abolition of the law of value enabling the rationalization of social

---

3 William Clare Roberts stresses that fetishism is to be understood as a form of domination rather than a form of false consciousness: see *Marx's Inferno*, Princeton: Princeton University Press, 2017, 110.

4 Karl Marx, *Capital Volume 1*, trans. Ben Fowkes, London: Penguin/NLR, 1976, 167.

5 Ibid., 173.

6 Ibid., 172.

relations. Thus, it is expressly presented as the outline of a communism severed from its political dimension, whether it be the struggles that precede it or the steps that punctuate it. But Marx immediately signals that the 'material conditions of existence' which make communism possible are 'in their turn the natural and spontaneous product of a long and tormented historical development,'[7] thus recalling the reciprocal causality of conditions and consequences which, by definition, pertains to the political dialectic of real premises. Thus, far from offering the image of an irenic, transparent communist solution, the anticipated extreme difficulty of its establishment is what opens Volume One, at the very point when Marx stresses the inability of classical political economy to explain 'why labour is expressed in value'[8] – in other words, its inability to rationally justify capitalism.

The ensuing chapters transform the theoretical impasse of bourgeois economics into a historical question, focusing on the concrete conditions that made the transition from feudalism to capitalism possible, this historical question also concerning by extrapolation the issue of the transition to communism. Chapter 32, the last chapter of Volume One, devoted to the 'historical tendency of capitalist accumulation', represents the pendant to the Robinsonade of the first chapter, the issue of communism framing in the strict sense Volume One. It takes up and reworks the Hegelian notion of the 'negation of the negation' already employed by Marx in the third of the 1844 *Manuscripts*. Original capital accumulation has as its condition the 'expropriation of the immediate producers,'[9] owners of their means of labour. The previous mode of production combined 'the development . . . of the free individuality of the worker' and 'the fragmentation of holdings', imposing strict limits on production and social existence but furnishing the conditions for its expansion: it 'brings into the world the material means of its own destruction' – in the event, 'the expropriation of the great mass of the people from the soil [that] forms the pre-history of capital'.[10] This negation of private ownership of the means of production establishes, through violence and 'under the stimulus of the most infamous, the

---

7 Ibid., 173.
8 Ibid., 174.
9 Ibid., 927.
10 Ibid., 927–8.

most sordid, the most petty and the most odious of passions,'[11] the social concentration of property and the dispossession of the individual producer, destined to become a proletarian.

His analysis continues with a presentation of the transition from capitalism to communism that seems to credit the thesis of a necessitarian and teleological view of history in Marx, which explains why this passage is generally cited against him. The text does indeed affirm that the increasing centralization of capitalism is accompanied by 'the growth of the co-operative form of the labour process'.[12] According to Marx, 'the centralization of the means of production and the socialization of labour reach a point at which they become incompatible with their capitalist integument. This integument is burst asunder. The knell of capitalist private property sounds.' And, he adds, 'capitalist production begets, with the inexorability of a natural process, its own negation. This is the negation of the negation.'[13] The determinist tonality of these lines prompts their extraction from an analysis that is, in fact, much more complex, interspersed with rarely mentioned considerations, which re-inject class struggle and consciousness into social transformation.

In fact, Marx immediately specifies that the transition from feudalism to capitalism and the passage that is due to lead from capitalism to communism are profoundly different. Communism is foreshadowed predominantly not on the terrain of property relations and their spontaneous transformation under the impact of unforeseen social circumstances, but within relations of exploitation and the collective consciousness they generate among those compelled to sell their labour-power. Whereas on the side of capital the logic of monopoly is progressively and mechanically imposed, on the side of workers, 'the mass of misery, oppression, slavery, degradation and exploitation grows; but with this there also grows the revolt of the working class, a class constantly increasing in numbers, and trained, united and organized by the very mechanism of the capitalist process of production.'[14] Anonymous logics, analysis of them, and conscious class conflicts intermingle and delineate a singular political space; communism once more becomes the

---

11 Ibid., 928.
12 Ibid., 929.
13 Ibid.
14 Ibid.

dynamic of conscious elaboration of its own concrete premises as well as a goal immanent in the restoration of 'individual property on the basis of the achievements of the capitalist era'.[15] And it is precisely the prerequisite of collective consciousness that makes communism the most gigantic effort, without precedent in the course of history, for humanity's conscious control of its own social organization.

Yet this text does tend to present the transition to communism as inevitable, citing in a note an extract from the *Communist Manifesto* declaring that 'what the bourgeoisie, therefore, produces, above all, are its own grave-diggers. Its fall and the victory of the proletariat are equally inevitable.'[16] From the standpoint of our present, any such claim is irredeemably dated, even if it remains to examine the character of such retrospection and the other, invisible determinism that haunts it. For the failure of nineteenth- and twentieth-century revolutions no more erases the reality of their outbreak, or the rise of mass working-class organizations in the course of this sequence, than it does the growing urgency of an exit from capitalism, which calls for a precise analysis of the causes of this failure.

The resurfacing of the strategic question amid the present context of general crisis, including of the ruling ideas, encourages us to attend once more to Marx's analyses of the pathways to workers' possible reappropriation of the process of production and the social process as a whole, as well as the obstacles to it. The definition of this reappropriation is extended by Marx beyond the objective of restoring individual property, conceived as a guaranteed right of access to goods and services, in the direction of the conditions of their production and collective control, but also for the purpose of developing individual capacities. The associated producers have to wrest back what, in reality, they never had, but which they are now manifestly lacking: collective control of their conditions of labour and production, along with the allocation of the wealth produced. For Marx, by their violence capitalist social relations stamp their form on an activity whose outcomes and also exercise are thereby confiscated, this fundamental dispossession striking the human subject with full force.

Going significantly beyond the traditional critique of private property while including it, this allows Marx to inscribe communism in a

---

15 Ibid.
16 Ibid., 93 n.2.

long-term history that it ruptures and consummates in equal measure.
Marker and motif of this rupture, reappropriation also means the
reappropriation by social individuals of themselves, inasmuch as the
human essence 'is no abstraction inherent in each single individual', but
consists in 'the ensemble of social relations'.[17] Once the scope of the
reappropriation has been redefined as being not a reversion to an initial
state but the fulfilment of unprecedented potentialities, the real difficulty consists in making it a credible, mobilizing political objective, to
be placed at the heart of revolutionary strategy. This is precisely the
question tackled by Marx both in *Capital* and in his political texts,
whether interventionist or analytical, interlinking the issue of ends with
that of mediations.

The communist question must therefore be situated at the centre of
the 'laboratory of production'. In the chapters of *Capital* devoted to
surplus value and its extortion, Marx describes the gradual division of
labour that ends up pitting 'mental labour' against 'physical labour'
despite both initially belonging to the same labour process.[18] This transformation results in the formation of a 'combination of workers',[19] of a
collective labourer who brings out the cooperative character of capitalist
production. On the other hand, the activity of labour is subjected to the
production of surplus value. The valorisation of capital is what steers the
whole productive process and subsequently ends up defining productive labour as such: 'the concept of productive labour also becomes
narrower'.[20] This 'narrowing' of the concept goes hand in hand with
work's loss of meaning and the lengthening of the working day beyond
necessary labour time. This logic makes it possible *a contrario* to define
communism as economy of necessary labour time, an egalitarian allocation of the latter and an increase in free time. While not employing the
term *communism*, this is precisely what Marx describes when he affirms
that

the time at society's disposal for the free social and intellectual activity
of the individual is greater, in proportion as work is more and more

17 *Theses on Feuerbach*, in Karl Marx and Friedrich Engels, *Collected Works*, Vol. 5,
London: Lawrence & Wishart, 1976, 7.

18 Marx, *Capital Volume 1*, 643.

19 Ibid.

20 Ibid., 644.

evenly divided among all the able-bodied members of society . . . The
absolute minimum limit to the shortening of the working day is, from
this point of view, the universality of labour.[21]

By contrast, in the capitalist mode of production, the limit concerns
only the tendency to extend the working day, reducing the living time of
the producer to working time, subtracted from the minimum time
required for the reproduction of labour-power. Alienation consists in
the tendency of capitalist domination to subject social activity and living
time wholly to the valorisation of capital. Behind these two modes of
production – capitalism and communism – two definitions of human
time are ranged against one another. We might add that two conceptions of human individuality likewise clash, even if capitalism, despite
all its efforts, cannot reduce labour-power to a commodity and manufacture its own docile, anaesthetized foot soldiers. For the labour-power
captured by the logic of value is, and remains, in all modes of production the means of self-development, the site of the formation of capacities but also aspirations to a different life. While capitalist exploitation
and domination are indeed exercised at the level of labour-power, resistance to a domination that cannot be total is also manifested there. On
condition that it is politically developed into a collective force and a
project, this resistance is forever reviving and nurturing the desire for
radical social change.

At once objective and subjective, this contradiction stems from the
fact that the labour-power purchased by the capitalist 'as' a commodity
is not, and cannot be, such. By definition, a capitalist commodity is
produced through unpaid surplus labour for the purpose of extracting
surplus value. The formation of labour-power does not result from a
capitalist process of production and its reproduction does not yield
surplus value that workers themselves could appropriate as owners of
this labour-power.[22] While the neoliberal ideology of 'self-entrepreneur'
abolishes class relations in purely imaginary fashion, purporting to plug
accumulation into life itself, Foucault's theorization of biopolitics lends
credence to these theses. But the refusal to consider social mediations

---

21 Ibid., 667.
22 Tran Hai Hac, *Relire 'Le Capital'. Marx critique de l'économie politique et objet de
la critique de l'économie politique*, Vol. 1, Lausanne: Page deux, 2003, 222.

makes it impossible to conceive the contradictions lodged at the heart of human individuality by capitalism, which trigger a clash between the principle of wage earning, on the one hand, and the aspiration to free development of oneself and the emancipation of all, on the other. The 1857–8 *Manuscripts* explore this question, emphasizing that real wealth consists in the reappropriation of time and the expansion of human needs of which the individual is the source, a condition of the flourishing of human capacities.

From this viewpoint, the basic spring of resistance to capitalism is not to be found in the anonymous opposition between living labour and accumulated dead labour – Negri's thesis – but in the ever more acute contradiction between the purchase and sale of labour-power, on the one hand, and its formation as concrete individuality, on the other. This contradiction comes to nestle at the very heart of modern subjectivity, for labour-power consists, above all, in the sum total of individual labourers, either coordinated externally by capital, which devours their living power, or consciously collaborating in their own rationally and democratically conducted social existence. The production – or, rather, formation – of this labour-power derives from unproductive labour. It aims to reproduce and maintain, but also to educate and socialize, a set of human capacities and physical, nervous, intellectual or artistic characteristics, vulnerable to their increasing capitalist appropriation but which remain the stake of collective emancipation, especially the emancipation of women, who are primarily allotted the tasks of social reproduction.

Against bourgeois political economy, Marx therefore affirms loud and clear that 'labour is the substance, and the immanent measure of value, but it has no value itself',[23] so that 'what the worker sells to the capitalist is not a commodity, but her personal subjection to the capitalist during the working day'.[24] It is at this precise point that exploitation and domination are bound together and confront the anger they arouse, forming a contradiction which is profoundly economic as well as social and individual: 'it is not labour which directly confronts the possessor of money on the commodity-market, but rather the worker'.[25]

---

23 Marx, *Capital Volume 1*, 677.
24 Tran Hai Hac, *Relire 'Le Capital'*, 235.
25 Marx, *Capital Volume 1*, 677.

It is their capacities, at once created and denied, and their emancipation, glimpsed but confiscated, that induce the producers to struggle for the reduction of the working day and, ultimately, against capitalism as such. In the instructions written by Marx on the occasion of the First International in 1866, he accorded a central place to the issue of labour time, as means and end of an emancipated politics: 'a preliminary condition, without which all further attempts at improvement and emancipation must prove abortive, is the *limitation of the working day*'.[26] Marx specifies that it will secure for the workers 'the possibility of intellectual development, sociable intercourse, social and political action',[27] attesting to the direct connection in his view between individual and collective emancipation.

Nevertheless, the tendency to counter the exploitation at the heart of labour-power comes up against a powerful countertendency, which derives from the wage form itself, in that it creates the illusion of the sale of labour at a fair price, masking the exploitation of labour-power from those who suffer it. Marx stresses that the wage form not only conceals the extortion of surplus labour, giving workers the impression that they sell their labour at its just price, but also introduces relations of domination of a new kind. In the chapter of *Capital* devoted to piece wages, he indicates that 'the very form of the wage [renders] superintendence of labour . . . to a great extent superfluous', introducing a hierarchy among labourers which facilitates 'the exploitation of one worker by another' as a tool of capitalist exploitation.[28] But this type of wage also encourages the extension of the working day, seemingly decided by the wage earner herself: 'the wider scope that piece-wages give to individuality tends to develop both that individuality, and with it the worker's sense of liberty, independence and self-control, and also the competition of workers with each other'.[29] This artificial autonomy leads to a general fall in wages, seemingly in response to the aspirations of wage-earners but actually to the desire of capitalists.

However, this tendency, at once alienating and individualizing, corresponds neither to a mere managerial stratagem nor to subterfuge. It is

---

26 *Instructions for the Delegates of the Provisional General Council*, in Karl Marx and Friedrich Engels, *Collected Works*, Vol. 20, London: Lawrence & Wishart, 1985, 187.

27 Ibid.

28 Marx, *Capital Volume 1*, 695.

29 Ibid., 697.

the promise, never kept but always repeated, of autonomy and self-realization, leading (depending on the circumstances) either to more intense internal competition between the dominated or to rejection of exploitation. The second option requires what Marx in the same passage calls an understanding of 'essential relations', highlighting the fact that 'in their appearance things are often presented in an inverted way'.[30] Critical knowledge and political rebellion form a whole, just as, conversely, ignorance of capitalist laws and contradictions reinforces seemingly ineluctable domination. The originality of Marx's approach attaches to the dialectical nature of his analysis of contradictions, which is no mere juxtaposition of opposed tendencies: the capitalist labour process is not alienating in one respect and emancipatory in another, but it interweaves these two tendencies at the very heart of the labourer's individuality and of social relations. Contrary to analyses affirming the consumerist integration of the working class, in line with the theses of certain Frankfurt School theoreticians, and the relegation of opposition to the margins of the wage-earning class and social existence, the political possibility of its supersession is played out at the very heart of the organization of production and the wage relationship. The problem consists in knowing how to structure this contradiction to enable its transcendence – that is, the transition to another mode of production, or communism, via the destruction of class domination. And if the word is so rarely used in *Capital*, it is no doubt because the designation of the goal would tend to mask the identification of its motor, located at the heart of the immense dialectic of social relations.

This analysis is developed in the pages that examine the historical progress of the division of labour, which should be read as one of Marx's great texts on alienated subjectivity. The division of labour leads to an extreme parcellization of tasks, so that the worker 'who performs the same simple operation for the whole of his life converts his body into the automatic, one-sided implement of that operation'.[31] This deskilling of the individual producer corresponds to a transfer of skill to 'the collective worker, who constitutes the living mechanism of manufacture, [and] is made up solely of such one-sidedly specialized workers'.[32]

---

30 Ibid., 677.
31 Ibid., 458.
32 Ibid.

Dispossession involves not only collectively produced wealth but, more fundamentally, also the activity of the individual labourer, which has become dead labour objectified in accumulated labour: 'what is lost by the specialized workers is concentrated in the capital which confronts them. It is a result of the division of labour in manufacture that the worker is brought face to face with the intellectual potentialities of the material process of production as the property of another and as a power which rules over him.'[33] More than the paradoxical autonomy of the wage earner, it is the alienating dispossession of the labourer that opens up the converse prospect of communist reappropriation, requiring all the mediations and the protracted time of social and political struggle. This analysis completes and extends the denunciation of bourgeois property of early communism in the direction of an extended, radical-ized critique, which makes it possible to define the objectives of an emancipatory mode of production beyond an egalitarian distribution of wealth. For, if one of the stakes is the re-conquest of their own capacities by the individual, it is the transformation of the whole of the economic and social formation that is its condition as well as its aim. In *Capital*, Marx stresses that capitalism itself creates the need for professional versatility: 'the partially developed individual, who is merely the bearer of one specialized function, must be replaced by the totally developed individual, for whom the different social functions are different modes of activity he takes up in turn'.[34] Conceived thus, the condition of reappropriation is shared knowledge of the overall social process and its contradictions, the elaboration of a critique of political economy. While its modalities are multiple and circumstantial, its goal is singular: the recovery of social power, alienated and incorporated into the general machinery under the authoritarian command of capital. But this reappropriation does not consist of a return to individual ownership of the means of production, by dint of a non-dialectical conception of the negation of the negation. Individual emancipation involves and realizes the re-conquest of the whole of the production process, as a mode of social existence whose procedures and objects are to be rationally and democratically redirected. This re-conquest begins with struggles for reductions in the working day and in favour of genuinely protective

---

33 Ibid., 482.
34 Ibid., 618.

employment law, which should be regarded not as a temporary recourse to law prior to its definitive abolition but a form of reappropriation of politics itself, cognizant of its juridical dimension.

Therewith a solution is foreshadowed to the problem of replacement of the state by the democratic reorganization of social existence; the fact that Marx says nothing precise about it is of little moment. For his analysis clearly suggests that it is basically one and the same cleavage that separates capital from the labour process from which it derives, severing the state from the social existence of which it is the coercive, administrative 'machinery'. Their kinship is essential. In capitalism, on account of its class logic, the products of human activity congeal, separate and rebound against the latter and against the labourers. It is therefore a single reappropriation that is to be set in train, comprising both the labour process and the state institution; substituting for the economic, social and political alienation, they organize a mode of production finally embodying the emancipation of labour by the workers themselves.

Even so, this reunification is not the restored unity of a society transparent to itself: it involves the construction of permanent collective mediations of decision-making and organization, capable of coordinating the separated tasks of conception and execution. Reconciling individual and collective dimensions, this objective defines communism proper not as a 'state' – this is neither a state nor a market – but as a 'real movement',[35] social existence returned to itself and creating its own premises as it goes. This rereading of Marx can be encapsulated in a hypothesis: if the term *communism* is rarely used in *Capital*, it is because the emancipatory project outlined there is subject to future political intervention, which will have to give concrete shape to a distinctive project fundamentally bound up with its historical premises and determinate mediations. Even so, in *Capital*, Marx develops an orientation that is sharply and constantly polemical as regards republican socialism, advocating forms of separate working-class organization and insisting on the necessity of expropriation.[36] In other words, before thinking

---

35 *The German Ideology*, in Marx and Engels, *Collected Works*, Vol. 5, 49.

36 On this point, see the original and powerful reading offered by William Clare Roberts, analysing *Capital* as a political intervention taking aim at the socialist theorists of the time, whether they were Saint-Simonian, Owenite or Proudhonian (*Marx's Inferno*, Chapter 6).

about communism qua emancipated politics as a theoretician, Marx thinks emancipatory strategy as a communist.

A 'Very Possible Communism'

The Paris Commune sprang up in March 1871 as a brief but potent embodiment of this approach to communism, subjecting its definition to actual revolutionary invention. The Parisian insurrection and its rapid unfolding confirmed for Marx that reappropriation of social exist-ence took the form of a redefinition of politics, subverting its statist forms and reinventing it as the genuinely democratic mediation of collective life. This exceptional insurrection must be analysed in the light of a longer sequence, chronicled by Marx in *Class Struggles in France* and *The Eighteenth Brumaire of Louis Bonaparte*. *The Civil War in France*, which completes the trilogy, attests to Marx's passionate atten-tion to the French labour movement, his analysis concerning in particu-lar Bonapartism and the transformation of the state.

However, Marx had initially conceived France's defeat at the hands of Prussia as an opportunity, assuming it would facilitate the unity of the German proletariat even as Bonapartism was paralysing the French labour movement. But once Prussian dynastic interests converted a defensive war into a war of conquest, aiming to annex Alsace and Lorraine, Marx and Engels deemed the siege of Paris reactionary and saluted the daring initiative of the people of Paris, which continued and radicalized the aspirations of 1848. Shortly before the 'Bloody Week', Marx declared in a letter: 'the present rising in Paris – even if it is crushed by the wolves, swine and vile curs of the old society – is the most glori-ous deed of our Party since the June Insurrection in Paris'.[37] Once convinced of its importance, Marx proposed to the IWA that he write an address to the workers of Paris in the name of the International, which was profoundly divided. Given what was at stake in the event, he trans-formed it into a document intended for the global working class.

It opens with an anti-nationalist sally taken from the *Inaugural Address* of 1864: 'if the emancipation of the working classes requires

---

37 Letter to Kugelmann, 12 April 1871, in Karl Marx and Friedrich Engels, *Collected Works*, Vol. 44, London: Lawrence & Wishart, 1989, 132.

their fraternal concurrence, how are they to fulfil that great mission
with a foreign policy in pursuit of criminal designs, playing upon
national prejudices, and squandering in piratical wars the people's
blood and treasure?'[38] Published in June 1871, *The Civil War in France*
was immediately distributed in numerous languages, highlighting the
importance that Marx attributed to an off-the-cuff analysis of events in
Paris. They afforded him an opportunity to develop more general
political and strategic considerations, which were never separated
from this specific historical context. The main lesson of the work is
precisely the reiterated assertion of the dependence of strategy on
concrete circumstances. Thus, while presented as a compressed analysis of the conjuncture, which even sketches portraits of the political
leaders of the moment, the text can be read as a pendant to the
Manifesto, refreshing its political objective and revolutionary ardour,
as indicated by the preface written by Marx for its republication in
1872. If *The Civil War in France* entirely alters its literary and analytical form, a comparison of the two texts, suggested by Marx himself,
brings out the crucial importance he attributed to recasting two inseparable matters: the perspective of the destruction of the state and the
role of a revolutionary programme.

As regards the programme, Marx affirmed the need to abandon
advance presentation of the measures to be adopted, as in the *Manifesto*,
whose second section listed the expropriation of landed property, the
abolition of the right of inheritance, the centralization of credit and free
education. In the 1872 preface, he made it clear that in view of 'the
gigantic strides of Modern Industry', but also 'the party organization of
the working class', and 'the practical experience gained, first in the
February Revolution, and then, still more, in the Paris Commune, it was
to be revised or, rather, relegated to a secondary level, given that 'the
practical application of the principles will depend . . . everywhere and at
all times[,] on the obtaining historical conditions'.[39] In light of this
analytical reorientation, assigning collective invention a more decisive
role than ever, we can understand a claim, at first blush enigmatic, which

38 *Inaugural Address of the Working Men's International Association*, in Marx and
Engels, *Collected Works*, Vol. 20, 12–13.

39 Preface to the Second German Edition of the *Manifesto of the Communist Party*,
in Karl Marx and Friedrich Engels, *Collected Works*, Vol. 23, London: Lawrence &
Wishart, 1988, 174–5.

has remained famous: 'the great social measure of the Commune was its own working existence'.[40] While it is, no doubt, also to be construed as registering an ultimately meagre balance sheet, the formula resounds as a dialectical definition, formulated in Aristotelian terms, of communism. The latter consists in the actualization of a social power that only partially pre-exists it, this endeavour being more effective and decisive than any catalogue of measures announced in advance. Even so, concrete measures have to be taken. In any event, they were decisive: from the start, the Commune legislated on the length of the working day, and night work for women, as well as on public education, politicizing the reorganization of social life while introducing radical reforms that directly threatened the prerogatives of capital.

When it comes to the modern state, the rectification of Marx's analysis was considerable. Bonapartism did not contradict its development but accompanied its metamorphosis into a complex, ramified state apparatus. That is why the initial hypothesis of its tranquil withering away has to cede to the hypothesis of its necessary destruction. Marx is keen to repeat in the 1872 preface what he wrote in *The Civil War in France*: 'the working class cannot simply lay hold of the ready-made State machinery, and wield it for its own purposes'.[41]

This twofold correction on the subjects of state and programme leads Marx to a more than ever political approach to communism, not only as a social alternative in gestation, but above all as revolutionary mobilization and political restructuring of forms of militancy, 'party' as well as 'popular government'. These forms, no longer confiscatory but mediating and structuring, involved both a democratic modus operandi and a new kind of representation, as well as combative decisions responding to those of the class opponent and of unlimited violence. Yet Marx does not engage in any theoretical generalization on these subjects. If communism begins to re-engage with its etymology in Paris, the communal form is not a transhistorical model. It remains the invariably distinct form of a resurgent aspiration to autonomy from the medieval commune, via 1792, to 1848.

Combining democratization of political forms and politicization of cooperative social forms, the communal form must, by the same token,

---

40 *The Civil War in France*, in Karl Marx and Friedrich Engels, *Collected Works*, Vol. 22, London: Lawrence & Wishart, 1986, 339.

41 Ibid., 328.

make possible, first, the reappropriation by workers of their social activity and, second, the tasks of political organization that have been separated and subtracted from it. In this sense, it corresponds above all to the class struggle waged up to the threshold of the future abolition of classes:

> If co-operative production is not to remain a sham and a snare; if it is to supersede the Capitalist system; if united co-operative societies are to regulate national production upon a common plan, thus taking it under their own control, and putting an end to the constant anarchy and periodical convulsions which are the fatality of Capitalist production – what else, gentlemen, would it be but Communism, 'possible' Communism?[42]

Thus, it must be stressed, communism is primarily defined not by the list of social changes it has the task of making, but as a living potential and active political mediation, which gradually constructs the perspective of an integral social reappropriation in the course of a decisive confrontation with bourgeois power in all its dimensions – economic, political, social and cultural.

Despite his initial doubts about the opportuneness of the Paris uprising and his subsequent criticisms of the timidity of the revolutionary government (particularly its refusal to requisition the Banque de France and march on Versailles), the importance of the Commune was therefore unprecedented for Marx. It embodied a non-descriptive definition of communism as a 'real movement', as elaborated by him for some years in line with the formulation in *The German Ideology*, whose terms he adopted here word for word. Among its distinctive features, the palimpsestic nature of this text must be emphasized. Explicitly taking up the *Inaugural Address* of 1864 and *The German Ideology*, and, more implicitly, the *Communist Manifesto*, Marx used the drafting of *The Civil War in France* as an opportunity to rearticulate his past analyses in a new reflection which – by dint of real history and the critical renewal it alone made possible – supersedes them all.

Anxious to single out this moment without idealizing it, Marx wrote:

---

42 Ibid., 335.

The working class did not expect miracles from the Commune. They have no ready-made utopias to introduce *par décret du peuple*. They know that in order to work out their own emancipation, and along with it that higher form to which present society is irresistibly tending by its own economical agencies, they will have to pass through long struggles, through a series of historic processes, transforming circumstances and men. They have no ideals to realize, but to see free elements of the new society with which old collapsing bourgeois society itself is pregnant.[43]

In these lines, which represent one of his most extended passages on communism, Marx stresses the fact that only real history and its 'long struggles' can construct an emancipatory project – in other words, a different 'form of existence' finally satisfying the individual and collective aspirations that are the very motor of those struggles. But we must also highlight the assertion that 'elements of the new society' are contained in the old, for this idea seems to advocate an already present communism whose pre-existing seeds are destined to bloom one day. Yet this interpretation comes up against what these pages describe: not a different mode of production, which the Commune did not have time to establish, but a set of political and legal decisions – in other words, a mode of supersession and emancipation delineated via a new political form paradoxically invented by Jacobins, Blanquists and Proudhonians who proved capable of overcoming their initial ideological affiliations. We may add Marx himself, who finally rallied to the federal idea, Proudhonian in ancestry, that the peculiarity of an effective revolution is that it succeeds in upending even the convictions of those who work for it.

In *The Civil War in France*, it is precisely this unprecedented, combative and inventive democratic organization that Marx salutes: 'when plain working men for the first time dare to infringe upon the Governmental privilege of their "natural superiors" . . . the old world writhes in convulsions of rage at the sight of the Red Flag, the symbol of the Republic of Labour'.[44] An embodiment of permanent revolution, the Paris Commune is placed by Marx in the political tradition of the

---

43 Ibid.
44 Ibid., 336.

defeated revolution of 1848. This leads him to rework his definition of the working class as the universal representative of society formulated in the 1844 *Introduction*, without dismissing a notion that had since been rendered more complex and dialectical. It is now the Commune itself – a political construct, not a social class – that becomes 'the true representative of all the healthy elements of French society, and therefore the truly national Government'.[45] Such a representation is neither metonymic nor delegated, but instituted as 'a government of the people by the people'.[46] On this basis, it becomes possible to take egalitarian tax decisions and intervene concretely in the organization of labour. This expanded political – that is, social and economic – leadership, restored to the historical subject that is the mobilized, self-organized working class, confers on the term *communism* its full meaning, embodying but above all reorienting the young Marx's analyses of the proletariat and democracy.

The Paris Commune is therefore the 'real movement', not fixed but relayed by 'a thoroughly expansive political form', 'the political form at last discovered under which to work out the economical emancipation of Labour'.[47] It involves both preserving the social dynamic and organizing it into the self-government of the producers, which reinvents representation and delegation. The introduction of the binding mandate, given to revocable delegates, aims to maintain 'the unity of the nation' while working for 'the destruction of the State power which claimed to be the embodiment of that unity'.[48] Groping towards their junction are militant forms of organization and the democratic planning of labour (a 'public power').

Surprising on account of its critical accents and pessimistic tone, the letter from Marx to Dutch social-democratic militant Ferdinand Domela Nieuwenhuis in 1881, ten years after the crushing of the Commune, at a time when he had retired from activism, does not say anything different. To his correspondent, who questioned him about the legislative measures to be taken in the event of socialists coming to power, Marx repeated that everything 'depends . . . on the actual historical circumstances' and

---

45 Ibid., 338.
46 Ibid., 339.
47 Ibid., 334.
48 Ibid., 332.

that 'a doctrinaire and of necessity fantastic anticipation of a future revolution's programme of action only serves to distract from the present struggle'. Clearly irritated, he added: '[your] question [is] posed out of the blue'.[49] In passing, adopting the term *socialism* from the social democracy flourishing in his correspondent's country, Marx added that if a socialist victory occurred, the first measures would be political in character, consisting in winning time for autonomous, collective decision-making: 'a socialist government will not come to the helm in a country unless things have reached a stage at which it can, before all else, take such measures as will so intimidate the mass of the bourgeoisie as to achieve the first desideratum – time for effective action'.[50] Time, conceived here as strategic room for manoeuvre, enables Marx to review the Communard experiment to distinguish its political conditions, and the subsequent stages of their alteration, from a positively 'socialist' intervention: 'the majority of the Commune was in no sense socialist, nor could it have been. With a modicum of common sense, it could, however, have obtained the utmost that was obtainable – a compromise with Versailles beneficial to the people as a whole',[51] but on the condition that it 'appropriat[ed] the Banque de France' – something the Communards did not dare do. In light of the preceding lines, this is cast less as a lasting social conquest than as an additional delay secured in the context of a pitiless class struggle, when the Commune had hardly any chance of prevailing. Marx adds: 'the moment a truly proletarian revolution breaks out, the conditions for its immediate initial (if certainly not idyllic) *modus operandi* will also be there'.[52] In other words, the conquest of political power only paves the way for an ongoing class struggle, more bitter than ever, not for a sum of legislative measures to which the bourgeoisie will submit without a fight.

This letter, which confirms Marx's withdrawal from activism and bitterness following the Parisian defeat, and after his support for the Commune had alienated the English trade unionists in the IWA – whereas they had hitherto been his allies in the struggle against

---

49 Letter to Domela Nieuwenhuis, 22 February 1881, in Karl Marx and Friedrich Engels, *Collected Works*, Vol. 46, London: Lawrence & Wishart, 1992, 66–7.
50 Ibid., 66.
51 Ibid.
52 Ibid., 67.

Bakunin[53] – heralded a new period of defeat and retreat for the labour movement, which, for Marx, no 'socialist' programme could succeed in overcoming. He closed as follows:

> My own conviction is that the critical conjuncture for a new international working men's association has not yet arrived; hence I consider all labour congresses and/or socialist congresses, in so far as they do not relate to the immediate, actual conditions obtaining in this or that specific nation, to be not only useless but harmful. They will invariably fizzle out in a host of rehashed generalized banalities.[54]

The distance taken by the late Marx from the ongoing organization of the social-democratic current indicates his doubts as regards strictly institutional victory by means of a party that is certainly the bearer of a programme, but not of an anti-statist revolutionary dynamic. This judgement clarifies Marx's withdrawal from the framework that he had helped to construct: the First International.

We may venture the hypothesis that his increasing pessimism about revolutionary prospects in Europe was one factor in Marx's growing interest in different scenarios and different parts of the world. A few days after the letter to Nieuwenhuis, his response to a letter from Vera Zasulich attests to this concurrent concern in Marx's critical analysis of a different communal form, the Russian *obschchina*. The latter is presented not so much as an immediate instrument for the construction of communism, but as an alternative political path to European social democracy. And, in fact, after Marx's death two years later, the labour movement – social democracy as institution and then as party-state – would verticalize and bureaucratize this structure, concentrating on social gains incorrectly adjudged cumulative and irreversible. Identifying with Marxism, the movement would help erase what for Marx was the dual imperative of a party in the sense, only sketched, he gave the term: anchorage of revolutionary combat in the demands of the working class, but also a specific structuration, organizing and maintaining broad

---

53 Jonathan Sperber, *Karl Marx: A Nineteenth-Century Life*, New York: Liveright, 2013, 382.

54 Marx, Letter to Nieuwenhuis, 67.

popular mobilization beyond the moment of insurrection, as the Paris Commune had tried to do.

All in all, communism is predominantly the political form of a social existence that has finally been restored to itself. This new image of communism is what contemporary theoreticians paradoxically help us rediscover in Marx. For, far from defending the statist relapse of which Badiou accuses him, Marx evinces two worries that correspond very precisely to the defects of subsequent communist strategy: detaching organization from its ends and uncoupling political decisions from reflective strategy, and then separating both from constant democratic control. In this respect, the Paris Commune is the experience that fully chimes with Marx's last, most developed strategic reflection. It is not as a social response but as an open question that communism proves to be an indispensable political instrument: it names the project of a social reappropriation – basing itself on a desire for re-conquest of the self and its time – which implies a struggle waged politically. If the term *communism* also undoubtedly designates the objective of a different mode of production, its strategic pertinence stems mainly from the fact that it outlines a mode of supersession of capitalism, protracted and difficult, in which a new society is foreshadowed.

What to Make of the Gotha Programme?

This analysis of communism as a project for a social existence restored to itself is, however, undermined by an obvious objection. In the *Critique of the Gotha Programme*, written in 1875, does Marx not propose a clearly defined alternative, which takes the form of a distinction between two successive phases in establishing communism? This text is the principal evidence against the thesis of an explicitly strategic Marxian communism, never set down as a programme. Indeed, this phased project seems to assign juridical and institutional transformation a central place, overshadowing the issues of popular mobilization and inventiveness inherent in a revolutionary process, as highlighted elsewhere by Marx. On account of this interpretation in terms of phases, the text, which became canonical in the framework of the Third International, had superimposed on it by Lenin a distinction between socialism and communism that Marx does not formulate therein. However, when read in the context of its composition, a quite different argument emerges.[55] Marx does not in fact posit any distinction between phases, his object being not to define socialism and communism, but to present as essential the problem of the political transition and mediations that lead to the abolition-transcendence of capitalism, in accordance with the analyses that precede and follow this late text.

We must begin by recalling that Marx's text is predominantly an intervention of a strategic and political kind. While he had not been involved in drafting the programme of unification between the General German Workers' Association (ADAV), founded by Ferdinand Lassalle, and the Social Democratic Workers' Party of Germany (SADP) of Wilhelm Liebknecht and August Bebel, Marx reacted with a sense of urgency to the draft programme that had appeared in the German press. He decided to send his correspondent, Wilhelm Bracke, his 'marginal notes on the unity programme', accompanied by a letter explaining his motives. His intervention, conceived from a distance and a position of relative political weakness, aimed to provoke an internal discussion and was never intended as a general theoretical essay on the question of communism. The scale of the disagreement and the unfavourable situation he found himself in led Marx to a textual commentary which, although modest, was intended to be primarily pedagogical, noting Lassalle's ideas as they dominated debates over unification. In the letter to Bracke accompanying his glosses, Marx describes himself as trapped by a situation that weighs on him, prompted to give his opinion from a distance and against his will, but compelled to do so precisely because he found himself in complete disagreement with the proposed programme, which 'is altogether deplorable as well as demoralising for the party'.[56] On this basis, his riposte seeks to adapt itself to the circumstances and views of the authors.

Above all, the juridical axis of the programme is what Marx deems inept, because it precludes thinking relations of exploitation as such. If Marx briefly seems to adopt its perspective, it is to highlight more clearly the aberrations to which it leads. Thus, assuming that 'the individual

---

55 For a developed version of this analysis, see Isabelle Garo, *Marx et l'invention historique*, Paris: Syllepse, 2012, 97–132.

56 Letter to Wilhelm Bracke, 5 May 1875, in Karl Marx and Friedrich Engels, *Collected Works*, Vol. 24, London: Lawrence & Wishart, 1989, 78.

producer receives back from society ... his individual quantum of
labour', the principle of allocation remains fundamentally that of market
exchange between property-owning individuals, an exchange of 'equal
values', whether measured by labour time or market prices. Marx
concludes that 'equal right here is still in principle – bourgeois right',[57]
the demand for fairness in no way impairing the principles of capitalism, but serving to mask them that little bit more. This is precisely what,
as early as 1846, he had objected to Proudhon's proposal to replace
money by labour vouchers. For Marx, 'money is not a thing, it is a social
relation':[58] it is not the cause of a social injustice deriving from a perversion of exchange, which production could easily be rid of thanks to a
system of labour vouchers. It is hard to see how a proposal deemed a
complete dead end by Marx in 1846 could suddenly become the first
phase of communism in 1875.

It must be added that Marx always condemned detailed program-
ming in advance of a political movement which, by definition, had to
make its way in its own complex, unpredictable historical conditions.
From the young Marx to the old, Marxian communism is not so much
a project as a practice. That is why it seems necessary to overturn the
usual interpretation. The first phase broached in the Critique corresponds to an initial, immature politico-theoretical stage of the analysis,
to the bungling of the German socialists, to which Marx thought it judicious to concede a relative pertinence as a first phase not in the history
of emancipation itself, but in socialists' understanding of it. We must
conclude that the 'first phase' designates neither 'socialism' nor even
some 'socialization of the means of production' (mention of which is
singularly absent from Marx's text and the Gotha Programme alike), but
an illusion to be corrected – a just law as spearhead of an overthrow of
capitalism, or even as a means of its improvement for the sake of social
justice (the Gotha Programme demanding 'the abolition of the wage
system' and 'the elimination of all social and political inequality').[59]

An initial conclusion imposes itself: not referring to any socialism,
past or future, the expression 'first phase' plays three combined roles,

57 *Critique of the Gotha Programme*, in ibid., 86.
58 *The Poverty of Philosophy*, in Karl Marx and Friedrich Engels, *Collected Works*, Vol. 6, London: Lawrence & Wishart, 1976, 145.
59 Quoted in Marx, *Critique of the Gotha Programme*, 91.

which make reading this text particularly awkward. Firstly, it characterizes a moment of political analysis, anachronistic in 1875, which
leads to socialist solutions that have already been tried and condemned
to failure. Second, it preserves the possibility of a dialogue with the
leaders of German social democracy at the time of the unification
congress, but also after it. Finally, it raises an issue that is very real in
Marx's view – transitions – about which he thinks politically and
which is only partially targeted in the remainder of the text, devoted as
it is to this aspect and the dictatorship of the proletariat. Contrary to
the usual reading of the *Critique* as a breviary of revolution, for Marx
communism is not the result of a linear process of radical transformation. As to the 'higher phase', the anonymity of the process evoked
should suffice to alert any informed reader 'after the enslaving subordination of the individual to the division of labour, and thereby also
the antithesis between mental and physical labour, has vanished' and
so forth.[60] When did they 'vanish'? And by what miracle? No struggle,
no political moment here, which an economistic reading of Marx
prompts us to accept without question. Following the Paris Commune
and its repression, can it seriously be thought that Marx believed in
the automatic effects that would be induced by reform of a legal kind,
which is moreover unfeasible and whose constitutively 'bourgeois'
character he affirms a few lines earlier? In addition, how can it be
thought that Marx has suddenly forgotten the communist challenge to
capitalist property, particularly ownership of the means of production,
which is absent here, when for Marx it is the site of the junction
between the juridical, the political and the economic? Equitable distribution and its confused perspectives as the only source of a radical
transformation? One might as well erase with a stroke of the pen all
the earlier texts, including the *Communist Manifesto*, which is most
marked by historical optimism about an imminent victorious revolution but, even so, imputes no simple linearity to the latter. What is
striking here is the telescoping of the individual and political levels, so
lacking is the mediation of social struggles, including those leading to
the simple Magna Carta mentioned by *Capital*[61] – a metaphorical
designation for a hard-won employment law.

---

60 Ibid., 87.
61 Marx, *Capital Volume 1*, 416.

In short, if we adopt the orthodox reading, the *Critique of the Gotha Programme* would be Marx's most apolitical text, even though it was intended as an eminently partisan intervention in the context of the construction of one of the first European labour parties. Given this – and granted the interpretative hypothesis that renders description of the first phase a rhetorical concession making it possible to develop a violent condemnation of vulgar socialism – once again, it is the paragraph on communism proper that poses a considerable problem: simple continuation of the process, bifurcation between socialism and communism, or a more complex operation? We must read the following passage carefully:

> In a higher phase of communist society, after the enslaving subordination of the individual to the division of labour, and thereby also the antithesis between mental and physical labour, has vanished; after labour has become not only a means of life, but life's prime want; after the productive forces have also increased with the all-round development of the individual, and all the springs of common wealth flow more abundantly – only then can the narrow horizon of bourgeois right be crossed in its entirety and society inscribe on its banners: From each according to his abilities, to each according to his needs![62]

While these formulations correspond more closely than others to Marx's actual theses, we might be struck by the incomplete, succinct character of this description, which concludes with the sole requirement of transcending bourgeois right, regardless of whether one agrees that its maintenance characterizes the first phase. Everything leads us to believe that Marx's line of argument here retains its simultaneously polemical and pedagogical objective, addressed to those – foremost, the programme's drafters – who think primarily in terms of law and labour, both of them abstractly conceived. Marx seems to be endeavouring to adjust to their categories and prejudices a reasonable suggestion for correction of the incriminated articles. By the same token, in rectifying the abstraction of 'useful labour' by introducing the capitalist division of labour and the productive forces, including concrete individuals, he stresses what would represent analytical progress rather than concrete historical progress, a logical phase rather than a real phase.

---

62 Marx, *Critique of the Gotha Programme*, 87.

Given the insufficiencies, catastrophic in his view, of the programme he is criticizing, Marx's goal could not be to induce the leaders of the German party to refine a two-stage process, which was as foreign to their thinking as to his own options. We may venture the hypothesis that the point was to insist, in relatively diplomatic and pedagogical fashion, on what as a minimum this programme should contain by way of a political perspective: a project for abolishing capitalist relations of production, the division of labour inseparable from them and a radical democratic supersession of the juridical viewpoint, which contaminates even the most political socialist traditions. In addition to the tacit reference to Proudhon encountered earlier, the paragraph includes with a formula borrowed from Louis Blanc and already cited in the *Manifesto*: 'from each according to his abilities, to each according to his needs' – a formula that once again refers to a simple principle of individual distribution of wealth. While French socialism is not named, it is precisely this tradition that Marx is thinking about here, from the angle of its constitutive limits and crying inadequacies, even if (and precisely because) he acknowledges its historical role. For Blanc's key political proposal was the creation of national workshops funded by the state – a conception inherited by the Gotha Programme.

With Louis Blanc's conception probably seeming rather more advanced and flexible than Lassalle's, Marx borrowed a slogan at once in tune with the spirit of the programme's drafters and capable of expressing a more authentically revolutionary project: his own. Already employed in the *Manifesto*, Blanc's formula lends itself to this fresh annexation. It seems impossible to read this paragraph as the most fully developed expression of Marx's views, when he was someone who conceived communism from the standpoint of the abolition of capitalist relations and as the result of a non-state political process of revolutionary popular mobilization that must, where appropriate, utilize universal suffrage. That this complex process is absent from the *Critique* is scarcely surprising: for Marx, the definition of communist society can only be an active definition, a movement of revolutionary, expansive democratization, without a preconceived model, which for this reason cannot be described programmatically, although its general objectives are clearly defined.

Reread thus, the nature of Marx's text changes radically. Far from being the manual he always refused to provide, it was a circumstantial intervention intended not for publication but to get various corrections accepted by the German socialist leaders, attempting to undo the worst blunders that the programme was full of in Marx's view. Thus, 'first phase' is the euphemistic term for a socialist tradition that remains immature and statist, whereas the second aims to induce the drafters to agree to take a further step in the direction of what Marx presents to them as being nothing other, basically, than their own theses, with the prudent and scarcely compromising endorsement of a Louis Blanc. Yet the second formulation remains radically discrepant with Marx's conception of communism, developed elsewhere and, above all, incompatible with its definition of a political process that must create its premises as it proceeds, constantly rectifying and reorienting itself.

If this interpretation is correct, it consigns the 'classical' reading, which attributes a two-stage strategy to Marx, to sheer misinterpretation. Certainly, the abolition of capitalism will take the pathway of a progressive exit, necessarily singular and complex, but its moments cannot be predefined. Above all, they cannot be initiated by a reform from above of a legal kind – a project that characterizes the socialist tradition from which Marx was intent on demarcating himself. Placing socialism and communism in a chronological order, it is not their bifurcation that is illustrated by the *Critique*. But these 'marginal notes' are now covered over by the accumulated layers of an interpretation that has hallowed its theses, to the point of diffusing the well-nigh hallucinatory belief that therein Marx defined 'socialism' – a term that is absent – as the 'socialization of the means of production' – a phrase that is absent. In the ultimate paradox, Lenin was the initiator of this reading in *The State and Revolution* – a text written on the eve of the October Revolution, which, in turn, was to be read as a definitive treatise of political theory rather than as a circumstantial intervention. Concealment of the strategic dimension of certain texts, which become canonical against the grain, has in its turn helped to banish any preoccupation of this kind from Marxism.

In truth, it is the Gotha Programme itself which, when dealing with labour and law, transforms a complex, changing historical reality into an abstraction. The treatment of the key political question of the fate of the state in a communist society demonstrates this. Marx ferociously criticizes any idea of appealing to the state to support the construction of workers' associations. But he remains averse to an anti-statism suppressing the apparatus of domination without envisaging the construction of an alternative instance of cooperation and decision-making, tasked with adjusting production to the satisfaction of social needs:

> The question then arises: what transformation will the state undergo in communist society? In other words, what social functions will remain in existence there that are analogous to present state functions? This question can only be answered scientifically, and one does not get a flea-hop nearer to the problem by a thousandfold combination of the word people with the word state.
>
> Between capitalist and communist society lies the period of the revolutionary transformation of the one into the other. Corresponding to this is also a political transition period in which the state can be nothing but *the revolutionary dictatorship of the proletariat*.[63]

This approach to the issue of transition proves that Marx did indeed conceive the passage to communism as a protracted process. But this transition is not the one formulated by the two phases described earlier. A continuous political process, revolution is punctuated by moments that are themselves political, with the capture of state power making way for its radical transformation. It is no longer a question here of the legal transformation of distribution and simple monetary reform of the conditions of exchange. The establishment of communism must be conceived not as a process operated within state forms as they are, but as a movement recasting politics itself, which Marx had already dubbed 'permanent revolution' and which requires popular mobilization and the invention of original institutional forms. In the text of 1875, here and only here do we find the true definition according to Marx of the process of reconstruction of social existence. We can understand why he is concerned to add that the Gotha Programme 'deals neither with this nor with the future state of communist society'.[64]

Without prejudging future institutional forms, Marx affirms the need for a seizure of power that must in principle coincide with the onset of destruction of the bourgeois state apparatus. It is indeed a radical, abrupt

---

63 Ibid., 95.
64 Ibid.

revolutionary process – the condition for a transformation of social relations, including property and distribution relations. This political transition seems to be Marx's proposed alternative to the dubious transition of the Gotha Programme, whose impasse he has previously signalled. We must then grant that the last part of the text tries to correct its opening, relying on what it should have enabled its addressees, alerted to the disagreement, to spot but also to concede. The pedagogy employed would prove highly ineffective, judging from the abiding misinterpretations prompted by these unduly wily marginal notes, once the context that conferred their meaning on them had disappeared. More generally, in this way, antithetical receptions of Marx's strategic reflection, first neutralized by orthodoxy and then by a certain kind of academic approach, have helped to displace a number of his texts onto a terrain alien to them – abstract political theory, long concealing one of the most fertile dimensions of his analysis.

This is particularly true of the treatment of the state in the notes, which combines theoretical analysis and programmatic position. Marx opposes the new party's economic and social statism as well as its political incoherence, the latter of which derives from its complete misunderstanding of the bourgeois state structure. The stakes of this approach are directly strategic. Just as it is important in Marx's view to demand a 'democratic republic', with a view to establishing genuine popular sovereignty, so this democratic republic must be thought of as 'the last form of state of bourgeois society' in which 'the class struggle has to be fought out to a conclusion'.[65] For Marx, who since the 1850s, in the context of his study of the French situation, had analysed the state as a 'governmental machine', the Gotha Programme erred completely as regards what was to be expected of it in the way of social advances. Given this, the strategic approach to the bourgeois state must be as dialectical as its essence, taking on board the limited but very real role of parliamentary democracy in the process of outflanking it. The strategic dimension of the analysis resolves the aporias of the strictly theoretical approach characteristic of the Kreuznach manuscript.

The dictatorship of the proletariat forms part of this concrete democratic perspective. Very rare from Marx's pen, the expression figures as a hypothesis inseparable from the historical circumstances that render it

---

65 Ibid., 96.

a possible response to the question of the conquest of the state, drawing on a long tradition. Daniel Bensaïd once noted that 'in the nineteenth century the word "dictatorship" still evoked the virtuous Roman institution of an exceptional power, duly mandated and limited in time, to confront an emergency'.[66] Dictatorship is conceived here not as the abolition of bourgeois democracy but as its radicalization, the latest episode in a class struggle fought to its conclusion; it will have to deal with the fierce resistance of the dominant classes but it also serves as a prelude to the disappearance of any class division. This political conception of transition stands out against the proposals of the Gotha Programme (education, freedom of science, restricting the working day to a length naïvely characterized as 'normal'), which are too partial to be vectors of a revolutionary dynamic. As for basic economic and social reforms, no mention is made here of any stage concerning them, because exclusive focus on distribution-production, which skips over the conquest of power, has been dismissed.

In this regard, the end of the notes is firmer and more in line with Marx's own ideas, after the opening has supposedly paved the way for their reception by the leaders of German social democracy. What is crucial is the political question, at the antipodes of the themes of equity and individual right. What matters to Marx is not the determination of phases defined, or even prescribed, in advance, but a process of transition, combining political mobilization, democratic functioning, economic and social transformation, and egalitarian redistribution. Nevertheless, the process has two aspects. On one side, political mobilization defines its goals as it proceeds and eludes any prior sequencing. On the other, it aims at an alternative modus operandi, whose conditions of coherence and viability remain to be defined. The text therefore leaves hanging the question of the correlation between political moments and social transformation – a correlation left to the real historical movement that a working-class party programme must not pre-empt.

---

66 Daniel Bensaïd, 'Politiques de Marx', in Karl Marx and Friedrich Engels, *Inventer l'inconnu. Textes et correspondance autour de la Commune*, Paris: Éditions de la Fabrique, 2011, 49.

Workers of the World . . .

Added to this question is the international dimension of the anti-capitalist struggle. One of Marx's great militant texts in this regard is the *Inaugural Address of the International Working Men's Association*, written in 1864 following a meeting organized in London. Intervening on the subject of industrial struggles in England and in favour of the Ten Hour Bill, Marx describes its conquest as the result of 'the great contest between the blind rule of the supply and demand laws which form the political economy of the middle class, and social production controlled by social foresight, which forms the political economy of the working class'.[67] This clash can be backed up by the creation of 'co-operative factories', whose importance (so Marx declares) 'cannot be over-rated':

> By deed, instead of by argument, they have shown that production on a large scale, and in accord with the behests of modern science, may be carried on without the existence of a class of masters employing a class of hands; that to bear fruit, the means of labour need not be monopolised as a means of dominion over, and of extortion against, the labouring man himself.

They have also shown that wage labour 'is but a transitory and inferior form, destined to disappear'.[68]

But Marx also stresses their limits: 'co-operative labour, if kept within the narrow circle of the casual efforts of private workmen, will never be able to arrest the growth in geometrical progression of monopoly, to free the masses, nor even to perceptibly lighten the burden of their miseries'. He specifies: 'to save the industrious masses, co-operative labour ought to be developed to national dimensions, and, consequently, to be fostered by national means . . . To conquer political power has therefore become the great duty of the working classes.' The pre-condition of this conquest is not only the advantage of numbers, for 'numbers weigh only in the balance, if united by combination and led by

---

67 Marx, *Inaugural Address*, 11.
68 Ibid.

knowledge'[69] – a point on which Marx, from his youth to this last period, is patently consistent.

In addition to the greater precision of this strategic reflection, its innovations are to be underscored. In this intervention, Marx sets about very directly linking working-class emancipation and internationalism. During this period, his attention continuously increased to the international construction of the working-class movement, over and above principled displays of solidarity. The meeting at St Martin's Hall, when Marx delivered a spoken version of the text, founded the International Working Men's Association, later dubbed the 'First International', and supported Polish demands for national liberation. The Polish people were 'the cosmopolitan soldier of the revolution', Marx would say in 1875,[70] highlighting the support they had provided for Hungarian, German and Italian struggles and for the Paris Commune. Marx referred to it in the written version: 'if the emancipation of the working classes requires their fraternal concurrence, how are they to fulfil that great mission with a foreign policy in pursuit of criminal designs, playing upon national prejudices, and squandering in piratical wars the people's blood and treasure?'[71] This concrete internationalist commitment confers its real meaning on the famous formula with which the text concludes: 'the fight for such a foreign policy forms part of the general struggle for the emancipation of the working classes. Proletarians of all countries, Unite!'[72] Here, too, the communist objective is inseparable from a strategy that foreshadows its social and cultural lineaments in the present.

Marx's awareness of the crucially and concretely internationalist dimension of communist politics developed during the 1850s, when he interested himself in the global expansion of capitalism and his analysis of colonialism. His work as a journalist for the *New York Daily Tribune* led him to study various national and regional trajectories, particularly those of India, China, Ireland and Poland, as well as the United States. His analyses of colonial domination and what was at stake in anti-colonial struggles brought out the full significance of the phrase 'domination-subordination'

69 Ibid.
70 Quoted in Kevin B. Anderson, *Marx at the Margins: On Nationalism, Ethnicity, and Non-western Societies*, Chicago: University of Chicago Press, 2016, 76.
71 Marx, *Inaugural Address*, 12–13.
72 Ibid., 13.

used in Chapter 6 of *Capital*.[73] Kevin Anderson, who has tracked Marx's evolution towards increasingly clear anti-colonial positions, has shown that he thus broke with his initial idea of a partially positive role of British colonialism, traces of which are to be found in some earlier texts. At the same time, Marx developed a multilinear conception of history, increasingly integrating the dimensions of race and sex, but without systematizing his approach. His strategic thinking here forms a pendant to, and continuation of, the analysis of the development of individuality in *Capital*, leading him to politicize the latter beyond the ethical considerations traditionally associated with it. The angle of this politicization was twofold. The crushing of human potential and capacities first and foremost concerned the colonized, whose will to emancipation was a major revolutionary source. Second, non-Western societies that had undergone colonization evinced, and to a certain extent retained, communal social forms capable of nurturing alternatives to capitalism.

Marx's attention to colonization was not a recent phenomenon, but it belatedly assumed decisive importance. Within the First International, Marx highlighted the revolutionary dimension of the American Civil War and the abolition of slavery. The Address to Abraham Lincoln that he wrote in the name of the IWA proclaimed:

> While the working men, the true political power of the North, allowed slavery to defile their own republic; while before the Negro, mastered and sold without his concurrence, they boasted it the highest prerogative of the white-skinned labourer to sell himself and choose his own master; they were unable to attain the true freedom of labour or to support their European brethren in their struggle for emancipation.[74]

Marx advocated not only unity, but realization of the essential intertwinement of the dimensions of race and class.

In his letter of 9 April 1870 to Sigfrid Meyer and August Vogt, taking up elements of a confidential circular written shortly before, Marx made the Irish agrarian revolution 'the prerequisite for the proletarian

---

73 Marx, *Capital Volume 1*, 1023.

74 'To Abraham Lincoln, President of the United States of America', 29 November 1864, in Marx and Engels, *Collected Works*, Vol. 20, 19.

revolution in England'[75] rather than its potential outlet. He spelt out his reasons:

> All industrial and commercial centres in England now have a working class *divided* into two *hostile* camps, English proletarians and Irish proletarians. The ordinary English worker hates the Irish worker as a competitor who forces down the standard of life. In relation to the Irish worker, he feels himself to be a member of the *ruling nation* and, therefore, makes himself a tool of his aristocrats and capitalists *against Ireland*, thus strengthening their domination *over himself*.[76]

In these circumstances, the priority was the achievement of unity through the struggle against racism, both 'religious, social and national' prejudices and institutional racism, as long as they divided the British and Irish labourers. For Marx, this did not mean struggling against religion in general or against national demands in general but taking on board the articulation of representations and practices that impeded the political unity of wage earners. Without creating a hierarchy of forms of domination, and without disconnecting them from the essential logic of capitalism, strategic priority must be given to the struggle against forms of discrimination internal to the struggle of the dominated. Here, Marx was violently opposed in the IWA to Bakunin, for whom the Irish cause was merely a diversion that obstructed the proletarian cause.[77]

This needs stressing, so unfamiliar are the analyses that contradict the reputation of a fanatically anti-religious Marx, predominantly concerned as they are with the lot of the white proletariat in the Western countries. During these years, he showed himself more than ever attentive to what blighted the unity of the dominated, deploring the fact that the English worker's attitude to the Irish 'is roughly that of the poor whites to the n[. . .]s in the former slave states of the American Union'.[78] To highlight the importance of ideological questions (and this at a time

---

75 Karl Marx and Friedrich Engels, *Collected Works*, Vol. 43, London: Lawrence & Wishart, 1988, 474.

76 Ibid.; emphasis in original.

77 Anderson, *Marx at the Margins*, 146.

78 Marx, letter to Sigfrid Meyer and August Vogt, 9 April 1870, 474–5.

when the word *ideology* was no longer used)[79] and the active role of representations once they adhere to social practices, Marx pointed out in the case of Ireland that 'this antagonism is kept artificially alive and intensified by the press, the pulpit, the comic papers, in short by all the means at the disposal of the ruling class'.[80] Far from being exclusively descriptive, this observation enabled Marx to call for action within the framework of the International: 'the special task of the Central Council in London is to awaken the consciousness of the English working class that, *for them, the national emancipation of Ireland* is not a question of abstract justice or humanitarian sentiment, but *the first condition of their own social emancipation*'.[81]

But were the internal colonization of Ireland by England and slavery in the US comparable? Not in Marx's view. For him the principal issue in the American Civil War was not the division of the proletariat and it could not be described as a clash between cultures or nations, even if these dimensions existed.[82] Not to be compared with the crushing of national aspirations, the South, according to Marx, was waging a veritable 'war of conquest for the extension and perpetuation of slavery'.[83] 'This would be in full accord with the loudly proclaimed principle that only certain races are capable of freedom'[84] – a principle extended to certain white immigrants, giving rise to a racist variant of capitalism. According to Marx, this perspective led the North to concede the emancipation of the slaves as a condition of maintaining its own social relations of exploitation. The scale and the stakes of slave domination were unique and in no way was it an anachronistic vestige. That is why Marx campaigned for the levying of black troops, whereas Lincoln backed off from this, on the grounds that he might be accused of fomenting a racial war. Marx's declarations in the name of the IWA were to have a real political impact in the US: they led to the formation of American

79 On the history of the concept in Marx, see Isabelle Garo, *L'idéologie ou la pensée embarquée*, Paris: La Fabrique, 2009.

80 Marx, letter to Meyer and Vogt, 475.

81 Ibid.

82 Robin Blackburn, Introduction to *An Unfinished Revolution: Karl Marx and Abraham Lincoln*, London and New York: Verso, 2011, 7ff.

83 Karl Marx, 'The Civil War in the United States', *Die Presse*, 7 November 1861, quoted in Blackburn, *An Unfinished Revolution*, 157.

84 Ibid., 158.

sections struggling for racial and sexual equality,[85] sparking an internal debate that ultimately resulted in the victory of the current dominated by trade unionists hostile to women's rights as well as the struggle for racial equality. In short, over and above the issue of secession, and despite Lincoln's faint-heartedness, the North's victory, without ceasing to concern the emancipation of individuals, had global political implications.

These concerns, increasing in Marx's later texts, went hand in hand with greater attention to the diversity of historical trajectories and the resources they afforded from a global revolutionary perspective. Once again, the identification of the goal (construction of a classless society on a planetary scale) must not lead to underestimating the distinctive mediations and divergent paths. From 1879 until his death, Marx filled dozens of notebooks on the subject of non-Western societies, skimming the anthropological literature of his time, without managing to write a book on these questions, which increasingly preoccupied him.

A Russian Revolution?

Marx's strategic thinking underwent a final development at the start of the 1880s, when he re-explored the transformation of property relations while reflecting on the revolutionary potential of certain traditional social structures, particularly in Russia. Marx's notes and studies of non-Western societies are numerous, many predating this last period, so that we can spot various inconsistencies and variations. As regards the matter of property, traditionally located at the heart of the communist project, Kevin Anderson, following Peter Hudis, stresses that as early as the *Grundrisse*, written in 1857–8, Marx regarded communal forms of production as prior to, and more fundamental than, communal property.[86] In these societies, as in later social forms, the transformation of property rules is not an end in itself and is subordinated to the transformation of the whole mode of production. These issues have been debated, notably in the works of E.P. Thompson, Robert Brenner,

---

85 Blackburn, Introduction, 72ff.

86 Anderson, *Marx at the Margins*, 156–7; and Peter Hudis, 'Marx among the Muslims', *Capitalism Nature Socialism* 15: 4, 2004, 51–67.

Ellen Meiksins Wood and David McNally, with a view to rejecting a mechanical distinction between base and superstructure peculiar to a certain Marxism and foregrounding the role of class struggle in rethinking the historical emergence of capitalism.

Without being able to go into the contributions of these rich debates, decisive for thinking about the transition from one mode of production to another, we may note that Marx, who polemicized with Proudhon and his 'extra-economic origin of property',[87] conceived property as a mediation between the individual and social wealth, which as a result concentrated the features of a given mode of production. At the same time, property is always a mode of appropriation that concerns individuals and helps structure them from top to bottom. The famous text of the *Formen*[88] of this same period contains this exceptional passage on true wealth, which illustrates the issue of reappropriation in which Marx makes the link between pre-capitalist and post-capitalist forms: 'if the narrow bourgeois form is peeled off, what is wealth if not the universality of the individual's needs, capacities, enjoyments, productive forces, etc., produced in universal exchange[?]'[89] This analysis of appropriation highlights the permanent co-determination of social relations and forms of individuality. But how about the conditions and means of transformation of actually existing property forms and the social relations associated with them? What role do individuals play in the course of a transformation that first and foremost concerns them?

Amid his ethnographic reading, work on colonialism and political role in the IWA, at a time when he was abandoning any linear conception of the course of history, Marx ended up reflecting on the social and political resources furnished by pre-capitalist modes of production still extant in some parts of the world alongside, or underneath, the capitalist forms that were seizing hold of them. The point was not to reactivate their original features but to activate their political potential. This is demonstrated by the correspondence with Vera Zasulich in 1881 about Russian communal agrarian traditions. It is because common property

87 *Economic Manuscripts of 1857–58*, trans. Ernst Wangermann, in Karl Marx and Friedrich Engels, *Collected Works*, Vol. 28, London: Lawrence & Wishart, 1986, 412.

88 It is customary to refer by this title to the chapter of the 1857–8 manuscripts devoted to 'Forms Preceding Capitalist Production': ibid., 399–439.

89 Ibid., 411.

forms concern the totality of social relations, and the forms of individuality engendered in them, that they have political potential, facilitating a type of strategic intervention capable of reconciling revolutionary politics and its ultimate goal – communism – without recourse to the slightest philosophy of history, and far removed from any assertion of the exclusive historical mission of the white, male working class – theses often attributed to Marx.

The interest of this correspondence stems from its immediate stakes in a turbulent political context. In February 1881, when debate was raging within the populist movement, Vera Zasulich sought Marx's opinion on the subject of Russian rural communism. In search of a Russian road to revolution without a transition via capitalism, the populists redirected their activity towards the peasantry and banked on the assets of the Russian rural commune, the *obschchina* (or *mir*), for transforming social relations. Its main features were an assembly of household heads and periodic distribution of the land in accordance with a principle of equality in proportion to household size. Despite its archaic, profoundly patriarchal character, the populists believed it could become a revived form of local power in the context of the democratic regime they desired.

Marx wrote four draft responses, which were much longer than the brief letter he ended up sending, where in essence he declared: 'the analysis provided in *Capital* does not adduce reasons either for or against the viability of the rural commune'.[90] But, he added, the commune could be 'the fulcrum of social regeneration in Russia'. The drafts are more eloquent. In them Marx seems to reflect for his own sake, independently of the delicate task of advising a political organization that seemed to expect the gospel truth from him. Refraining from any prediction, he envisaged that the Russian commune could, on certain conditions, 'detach itself from its primitive features and develop directly as an element collective production on a nationwide scale'. He straight away clarified: 'it is precisely thanks to its contemporaneity with capitalist production that it may appropriate the latter's *positive acquisitions* without experiencing all its frightful misfortunes. Russia does not live in isolation from the modern world: neither is it the prey of a foreign

---

90 Letter to Vera Zasulich, 8 March 1881, in Marx and Engels, *Collected Works*, Vol. 24, 371.

invader like the East Indies.'[91] Here, we find elements of the strategic dialectic long explored by Marx. The point is to develop the communal form while conserving it, initiating its transcendence in the complex sense of the German term *Aufhebung* already referred to, which tends here more to 'conservation' and 'elevation' than 'abolition'. But, Marx insists, this hypothesis assumes a developed capitalism elsewhere. Its eventual materialization depends on a unique national or regional trajectory within the framework of a global process of capitalist expansion and the resistance it arouses. In passing, Marx developed the idea of uneven and combined development, adopting it from Russian populist Pyotr Chaadayev. Rather than regarding capitalism as a source of homogenization of social relations throughout the world, as in the *Communist Manifesto*, the perpetuation of locally non-capitalist relations serves its domination. That is why wagering on the emancipatory potentiality of the *obschchina* represents a predominantly political hypothesis, subject to the activation of an effective revolutionary process and its conscious choices. In his 1882 preface to the second Russian edition of the *Communist Manifesto*, Marx added a new condition destined for a protracted controversy – namely, the conjunction between Russian revolution and world proletarian revolution: 'if the Russian Revolution becomes the signal for a proletarian revolution in the West, so that the two complement each other, the present Russian common ownership of land may serve as the starting point for communist development'.[92] Once again Marx's objective here is not to propose a prewritten revolutionary scenario, but to inscribe communism in an extended, global history, at once determined and open-ended, which includes the fact of capitalist expansion without this mode of production being a mandatory stage in human emancipation. Consequently, the persistence of non-capitalist historical conditions, integrated into a strategy mobilizing social groups marked by these traditions, could support a general counter-offensive aimed at the transcendence-abolition of capitalism. Paradoxically, uneven development would likewise be the condition for a revolutionary process capable of being globalized. Such reasoning pertains to the critique of political economy

---

91 'Drafts of the Letter to Vera Zasulich' (first draft), in Marx and Engels, *Collected Works*, Vol. 24, 349.

92 Marx and Engels, *Collected Works*, Vol. 24, 426.

in that it is political. If the underlying logic that engendered capitalism is not the expansion of the market but 'the complete separation of the producer from the means of production' and, more specifically, 'the expropriation of the agricultural producer',[93] and if communism aims at the reappropriation by individuals of their own social powers, then social forms predating this separation, and surviving locally after it, can offer fulcra for a revolution tending to become global while necessarily being initially constructed in national conditions.

This historical reflection by the mature Marx on the causes of capitalism's birth and those of its possible demise thus remains inseparable from the revolutionary project of its abolition and strategic reflection on its concrete conditions, conditions at once historically given and politically developed into premises. In one respect, these conditions are internal to the functioning of capitalism in its essential contradictions, as they are analysed in *Capital*. But they are also external to it or, more precisely, they derive from the contradiction between a capitalism born in the (British) agricultural world and a different social history, which can obstruct and offer an alternative to the installation of such relations of production and exploitation – on condition, however, of becoming the linchpin of a political struggle.

And this is precisely the case in Russia. Marx stresses that as a social form based on sharing and equality, on communal property and individual-personal property, the Russian commune is distinguished from more 'archaic' communities. Marx's communism is not collectivism understood as authoritarian suppression of any private property, but a certain kind of socialization of the means of production. And it is this exclusive particularity of the Russian commune that leads Marx to modify his initially negative judgement while he continues to condemn its patriarchal character. From a strategic standpoint, the property question thus remains crucial in his view, on condition of regarding it not as a strictly legal form, but as both revolutionary political lever and gradient of individual development. By this twofold token, the Russian agrarian commune contains potentialities that can be converted into means of peasant mobilization and, as such, into premises of communism.

---

93 Marx, *Capital Volume 1*, Chapter 32, quoted in Marx, first draft of the letter to Vera Zasulich, 346.

Nevertheless, its possible revolutionary reprise has two conditions, which are highly problematic. The first consists in the introduction of capitalist productive forces and techniques. The second is the intervention of the peasants themselves in the active transformation of the traditional rural commune into the local structure of a general socialization of production. Over and above the circumstantial character of this debate in late-nineteenth-century Russia, the Russian rural commune makes it possible to pose the problem of transition in full, from the angle of its material conditions on the one hand and its political conditions on the other. In passing, the Russian case confirms that the standard reading of the *Critique of the Gotha Programme* is a misinterpretation. In it, communal forms are explicitly viewed as possible fulcra of a political dynamic involving the mobilization of individuals and determinate classes. Here reappropriation is much more than a simple abolition of private ownership of the means of production. Above all, it aims at self-reappropriation, an emancipation synonymous with the individual and social development of human capacities, which are mutilated by all relations of domination. This reappropriation is not defined as reversion to a prior condition, but as an endeavour to abolish alienation and dispossession – an effort rooted in the acute contradictions of the present. Such a will to emancipation is not a utopian aim, but the fuel of the revolutionary flame, resuming an argument already developed in *Capital*. And, in fact, at the start of his draft, Marx refers to the chapter of *Capital* devoted to 'so-called "original accumulation"'. The 1881 notes take up this text and continue it, while modifying it to adapt to the Russian case.

In *Capital*, Marx distinguishes three phases in property forms, extended to the mode of development of individuals and the social conditions of production. The first is 'the private property of the worker in his means of production',[94] highlighting that the condition of 'the development . . . of free individuality' goes hand in hand with slavery, serfdom and 'other situations of dependence', excluding cooperation and 'the free development of the productive forces'.[95] The second phase is the result of a negation generated by the development of the first, which gives birth to 'socially concentrated means of production',

---

94 Marx, *Capital Volume 1*, 927.
95 Ibid.

large-scale property at the price of 'the expropriation of the mass of the people', and the proletarianization of labourers.[96] The third phase has as its spring 'the centralization of the means of production and the socialization of labour', which have become 'incompatible with their capitalist integument'.[97] The productive forces are credited not only with unprecedented productivity, but also with an advanced level of cooperation that directly paves the way for communism. This third phase is that of revolution: 'the knell of capitalist private property sounds. The expropriators are expropriated.'[98]

This hypothesis of several phases is what Marx adjusted in 1881 to the Russian situation. Starting from the Russian communal form, which is more individualizing than archaic forms, two options can be envisaged in the face of capitalist expansion: 'either the element of private property which it implies will gain the upper hand over the collective element, or the latter will gain the upper hand over the former'.[99] The reforms of 1861 had sought to demolish the rural commune and to transform Russian agriculture in a capitalist direction, adulterating personal property. The third, specifically revolutionary, phase presupposed the victory of the Russian collective element, the socialization of large, landed property, but also the 'domains of the state',[100] combined with the advanced socialization of labour inherent in capitalist productive forces. This whole social dynamic, not merely a technical dynamic, was to be imported under the rubric of 'mechanical industry'. The development of the agrarian commune on a national scale, as well as its modernization, then becomes possible: 'the *contemporaneity* of western production, which dominates the world market, allows Russia to incorporate in the commune all the positive acquisitions devised by the capitalist system without passing through its Caudine Forks'.[101] Thus, the traditional commune is to be conceived not as a model to be generalized but as the possible social and, above all, political lever of an alliance between the working class and the exploited peasant class, a lever at once indispensable and extremely difficult to construct, as has been proved by the

96 Ibid., 928.
97 Ibid., 929.
98 Ibid.
99 Marx, first draft of the letter to Vera Zasulich, 352.
100 Ibid., 358.
101 Ibid., 353.

failure of the 1848 and 1871 revolutions. For we must note that, far from essentializing the peasantry, Marx never defined it as comprising a single 'reactionary mass' – a formulation of Ferdinand Lassalle's that he promptly rejected.[102] Although he highlighted the reactionary political role of the French peasantry during the 1851 coup d'état, it was while indicating the reactionary logic of the 'parcel' when not accompanied by any communitarian logic or independent political consciousness. Elsewhere, however, Marx did not stop proclaiming the need for the 'proletarian revolution' to construct 'the choir without which its solo becomes a swan song'.[103] And the Russian situation made it possible to envisage such a choir.[104]

Even so, the Russian peasants who (according to the 1881 text) could become spokesmen for an 'economic need' will not necessarily be the agents of a political project that extends far beyond it. Marx says nothing about the way that the rural commune could progressively transform its own traditional communitarian modus operandi from within, in the direction of the 'self-government of the producers' he saluted in the Paris Commune. Is a process no longer working class and urban, but rural and rooted in tradition, capable of engendering not only its own educated and politicized actors, but also new, democratically organized relations of production? This question contains a conjunctural strategic dimension, but it is at the very heart of the definition of communism. Able neither to treat it nor to omit it, *Capital* seems to reformulate it in condensed fashion and Hegelian terms as the 'negation of the negation', at the risk of exposing itself to the accusation of reverting to the philosophy of history. It may be that the ambiguity of Marx's formulations in this chapter of *Capital* is precisely what motivated Vera Zasulich's letter. And Marx's reply shows that he does not consider the question as settled in advance. On the contrary, it implies a Russian revolution that in 1881 he could only ardently desire.

All in all, this 1881 analysis outlines a strategy in the full sense, coinciding with the redefinition of politics, whose project had been set out

---

102 Marx, *Critique of the Gotha Programme*, 89.

103 *The Eighteenth Brumaire of Louis Bonaparte*, in Karl Marx and Friedrich Engels, *Collected Works*, Vol. 11, London: Lawrence & Wishart, 1979, 193nb.

104 Luca Basso highlights that the expression 'acting in common' that we find in *Capital* clarifies Marx's non-naturalistic conception of the common (*Marx and the Common: From 'Capital' to Late Writings*, Leiden and Boston: Brill, 2012, 106).

by Marx in his earliest texts. Awaiting actual fruition, this strategic communism encompasses all the dimensions of Marx's earlier thought, linking the issue of the democratic reorganization of work to that of the construction of the historical subject of revolutionary transformation. For the time being, Marx stuck to reflecting on the conditions for the peasant masses rallying to revolutionary struggle and socialist transformation. And precisely because the latter was not their main concern, he signalled that forced collectivization would simply result in peasant secession: 'go and seize from the peasants the product of their agricultural labour beyond a certain measure, and despite your gendarmerie and your army you will not succeed in chaining them to their fields!'[105] This advice, given to a Tsarist government hostile to ancestral communitarian forms, would prove premonitory of the failure of the policy of authoritarian collectivization in the USSR.

If the idea of bypassing the capitalist stage has lost all relevance today, it remains the case that logics of uneven development persist and suggest distinctive roads to politicization and subversion of the dominant social relations. It is important to affirm that resistance to capitalist commodification and its social logic remains fundamentally immanent in it. Costas Lapavitsas has shown that non-commodity relations survive which capitalism needs in order to exist. This means thinking not that such non-commodity relations are immediately socialist or that demands for free provision and the right to share suffice to open up a political pathway as such, but instead about 'transform[ing] these non-economic relations by altering the economic foundations of society'[106] in such a way as to redefine the relations between non-economic sphere and economic sphere.

At the heart of this problem, we once again find the issue of labour-power inasmuch as, fundamentally, it is not a commodity, but the preserve of social individuals. Labour-power's multifaceted resistance to attempts at its complete neoliberal submission forms one of the key contradictions of contemporary capitalism, running through the very individuality of wage earners as well as all structures of social existence. However, it is not as such the vector of any definite alternative. If the

---

105 Marx, first draft of the letter to Vera Zasulich, 354.

106 Costas Lapavitsas, *Social Foundations of Markets, Money and Credit*, London: Routledge, 2003, 128.

goal is not to rest content with temporary enclaves or minority utopias, then it is the politicization of these contradictions that specifically defines a communist politics. And among these contradictions must be counted all forms of domination and oppression, which are combined with exploitation without being reducible to it.

In his late texts, Marx develops this original political thinking without being able to resolve any of these problems. Furthermore, far removed from the imagery of the bearded prophet certain of the advent of communism, he highlighted the enormous challenge that would have to be met not by a realized communism, which he did not describe, but by a communist politics – whose most astute thinker he remains – which must at any moment be able to elaborate democratically an unprecedented historical rationality. Impossible task? In our day, it is impossible to defer it any longer. It remains for us to invent modes of cooperation that are also political modes of struggle and the conquest of power, rethinking the political subject of radical transformation, at once multiple and coordinated. This figure of communism as political dynamic, at once goal and transition, project and mediations, is what emerges from a rereading of Marx inspired by contemporary reflections, but which in return confronts them with a strategic dimension they have lost. To conclude this investigation, it remains to develop more precisely, and in the present, the hypothesis of a renewal of strategic communism.

6

Towards a Strategy of Mediations

The objective Possible, to which the dream must hold if it is to be worth anything, holds the dream too, in pre-ordering fashion. The objectively mediated and for this very reason non-renouncing waking dream of perfect life thus overcomes its proneness to being deceived like dreamlessness itself.

Ernst Bloch, *The Principle of Hope*, Vol. 3, trans.
Neville Plaice, Stephen Plaice and Paul Knight,
Oxford: Basil Blackwell, 1986, 1365–6.

A famous formula of Gilles Deleuze's has it that one should 'begin in the middle'.[1] It will be objected that, in politics at least, it is important today to begin again with mediations. The aim of this book is to invoke on the strategic terrain a dialectic that Deleuze repudiated, like most philosophers of his generation. Themselves philosophers but no longer doing battle with the dialectic, and revisiting the question of mediations in their own way, the authors discussed in the first three chapters share a concern to outline an alternative, registering the general crisis of contemporary capitalism, but also the profound crisis of the labour

---

1 The original formulation was rather different: 'Kleist, Lenz, and Büchner have another way of traveling and moving: proceeding from the middle, through the middle, coming and going rather than starting and finishing' (Gilles Deleuze and Félix Guattari, *A Thousand Plateaux*, trans. Brian Massumi, Minneapolis: University of Minnesota Press, 1987, 25).

movement and all the forces of resistance to neoliberal policies. If the alternative cannot be defined on paper, the scale of the present challenge, the dilapidation of left-wing forces and the power of the dominant ideology make critical work more necessary than ever, while requiring that it be redefined.

What, then, is to be done with proposals that are as eruditely elaborated as they are divergent, which have the incontestable merit of relaunching the debate on transcending capitalism? The decision to dwell on a small number of contemporary post-Marxist authors, who are among the most read but also the most innovative, sought to analyse their contributions and their inconsistencies. Their approaches have three essential features in common. First, all of them explore the key classical points of the alternative to capitalism, but isolating them from one another renders their hypotheses incompatible. Second, in confronting the comprehensive anti-capitalist proposals of an earlier epoch while distancing themselves from the inherited forms of the class struggle, they are all constructed as critiques of Marx and Marxism. Finally, they attest to an attempt to repoliticize theory on its own terrain, though this fails to overcome the uncoupling of critical elaboration, political intervention and social reality. While the revival of opposition philosophically is evidently a sign of the weakness of the political opposition to capitalism, it is also an advantage, one way of struggling against neoliberal ideology at the same time as an index of increasing contestation in the search for new political pathways. It renders the confrontation with Marx and Marxism necessary and fertile, helping to reopen the space for an intervention at once critical and militant.

That is why placing a chapter on Marx after these analyses was not intended to refer them back to a pre-existing truth, but to place in contention several views of the alternative. On the one hand, it meant resituating contemporary theories in a long history of social and political opposition to capitalism. On the other, this anti-chronological approach made it possible to compare Marx's thinking with these analyses and their questions, which, in return, clarify its constitutive yet largely unknown strategic dimension. The latter consists in articulating theoretical analysis and political struggle within the capitalist totality, apprehended through the prism of its concrete contradictions and their determinate forms. This strategy of social, political and ideological construction of the alternative is what Marx calls communism, which is not reducible to a post-capitalist mode of production and of which he furnishes no description. Broached on the basis of contemporary questions, the point is to show that this approach retains its fertility beyond elements of a description of capitalism, whose relevance is today readily conceded to the author of *Capital*, but at the cost of persistent ignorance of the political reflection inseparable from it. At a time when the construction of an alternative to capitalism seems more urgent than ever, rediscovery of this lost strategy invites us to rebuild it within the coordinates of the present.

Consequently, at the close of this set of inevitable partial analyses, is it possible to define or at least to clarify the pathways of a contemporary strategy? At a time of political crisis and fragmented struggles, we must aim to outline a mobilizing, majoritarian political road, combining multiple forms of contestation and the construction of a comprehensive alternative, which is radically democratic and resolutely anti-capitalist. In other words, it is a question of reflecting, upstream of any concrete proposal and transitional programme, on the way to effectively connect theoretical critique and political intervention as co-defined social activities, putting this collective task back at the heart of the communist question. Far from tying up ends and means in linear fashion, strategy presents itself as a problem of triangulation, which brings all the weight of historical invention to bear on the construction of political mediations: forms of mobilization and organization, programme and project, but also the reconstruction of a common oppositional culture associated with redesigned forms of social existence that are attractive and capable of expansion.

In this sense, construction of the alternative consists not only in developing concrete proposals, despite their unquestionable usefulness,[2] but also in the ability to conjoin them with a project of radical transformation and with collective mobilizations and individual aspirations as they exist today, for the purposes of creating the political force and unitary momentum they lack. Such an articulation remains to be constructed – Laclau is right about that – but as class struggle

---

2 See, for example, the proposals of GR-PACT, coordinated by Emmanuel Dockès, regarding a reduced, more protective employment law, as opposed to the neoliberal reforms underway: pct.partisanterre.fr; or the proposals on the energy transition synthesized in *Manifeste négaWatt*, Arles: Actes Sud, 2015.

conscious of its conditions and mistress of its goals, equipping itself with organizational forms with the power to unify, a vector as such of an economic, social and political alternative. For at issue is prefiguring and embodying a different way of life, making the prospect of it at once conceivable and desirable, so that the collective, progressive elaboration of its perspective accompanies, and is nurtured by, social mobilizations in all their diversity.

However difficult, the task is possible: it is enough to have participated in a protracted strike to know the rapid and rich shared joy of a genuine social existence, of rethought work, of regained time that flourishes in it. How are such possibilities to be diffused, consolidated, discussed? Active reflections and theorizing interventions are situated at the meeting point of existing structures, parties, trade unions, associations, while it is imperative to go constructively beyond their inherited contours. How to garner this dynamic without suffocating it, combating logics of delegation as well as spontaneisms that have no future? How to construct these possibles while opening them up to their own development – the only way of escaping the twofold pitfall of utopia without struggle and struggle without hope? The perspective of such a strategic revival is what must be explored.

The Paradoxes of Strategy

The difficulty in rendering alternative proposals – whether they concern ecology, public services, wages or transport – politically operative attaches largely to the crisis of credibility that has befallen any project of a break with the capitalist order. Authoritarian neoliberalism, conceding no room for negotiation, destroying any prospect of a Keynesian revival and shattering any fantasy of social dialogue, renders a rupture more necessary than ever at the very moment that it disqualifies it. In France, this prolonged defeat has taken the form of a decline of political and trade union organizations, accompanying the retreat of political forms of Marxism from the 1970s onwards. This decline was initially the occasion for remarkable theoretical effervescence against the backdrop of a multifaceted critique of Marx, which for a time concealed the long-term effects of the strategic eclipse associated with it. Michel Foucault, Gilles Deleuze, Félix Guattari, Jacques Derrida, Jean-François

Lyotard, André Gorz and many others set their minds to confronting Marxism's traditional questions, its class analysis and the communist project, so as to develop a radical critique of it: the deconstruction of the notions of the working class, value, exploitation, ideology and dialectic was at the heart of these oeuvres, whose conceptual and stylistic inventiveness was in inverse proportion to their concern to develop a general alternative.

The political ins and outs of these analyses must be treated in all their complexity, avoiding the pitfalls of perceiving them either as an unavoidable modernization of Marxism or as its liquidation pure and simple – interpretations whose schematic character skirts analysis of what is here called the strategic dimension of theory. Coinciding with the discrediting of communism and the failure of 'real socialism', these options were both an echo and an active catalyst of the crisis of the left and its partial mutation. From this standpoint, their intrinsically political dimension is undeniable, even if – and because – they stand in stark contrast to the views of earlier generations, those of Jean-Paul Sartre and Raymond Aron in particular. Without abandoning social critique, the principal authors in this sequence deserted the ground of classical political commitment, dropped the thesis of the centrality of labour and its clash with capital and abandoned any perspective of transcending capitalism in favour of promoting uncoordinated local strategies of opposition and subversion, invariably disconnected from any critique of political economy.

In some respects, theory, presenting itself as its own practice, could become an end in itself precisely because it sought to be active transformation, full-fledged intervention. The Althusserian notion of 'theoretical practice', coined at this time, made it possible to believe that philosophy had become, and remained, the crux of this conversion, offering academic and media opportunities to intellectuals who were induced to overestimate the impact of ideas and the originality of their thinking. But it is significant that these philosophies, so concerned to rejuvenate thought, omitted an analysis of their own place in a singular historical moment, aside from the Foucauldian thesis of the specific intellectual. For it was at the interface of theory and reality that this complex role was constructed, taking part in political and ideological change while repudiating earlier forms of commitment. In an irony of history, the recent revenge of certain currents of Marxism, from Marx himself to Stuart Hall, via Antonio Gramsci, Louis Althusser, E.P. Thompson or Frantz Fanon, consists in their tools for understanding the particular function of ideas and representations, asserting their nature as social forces without reducing them to passive reflections.

We therefore need to review certain features of the philosophy of the 1970s and '80s, inasmuch as it continues to exercise a profound influence on the contemporary critical landscape, the authors studied in the opening chapters being actors in it or direct inheritors of it. The extreme singularity of their styles masks a fundamental proximity of key themes. In particular, we must highlight the crucial character of a common violent detestation of the dialectic and representation, despite the prima facie secondary importance of concepts that might seem technical, even scholastic. This general denunciation of the dialectic helped to rule out any analysis of the contradictions running through economic and social reality, along with any perspective of the transcendence-abolition of capitalism. It was amplified into a critique of all political mediations – institutions, parties, projects, class struggles – but also of any kind of strategic reflection on the state, and any analysis of the nature and role of critique itself, once the ideas of truth and totality were dismissed in one and the same breath. Rejection of the latter, coinciding with the flourishing of the themes of discourse and deconstruction, problematized a definition of capitalism as a really existing system, along with the prospect of its transcendence.

The paradox must therefore be underscored: how are we to understand the fact that it is precisely in this analytical tradition that reflection on alternatives to capitalism has re-emerged today? How are we to explain that in them, more than elsewhere, we find an opposition once again concerned with strategy, to the point of adopting a vocabulary branded with anathema – that of socialism and communism? It is often said that these theorizations have paid attention to issues not perceived, or downplayed, by forms of Marxism – to social but also cultural inventiveness, to the multiplicity of power relations and forms of resistance, to sexuality and mental illness, to questions of bodies and life. At the same time, analysis of whole swathes of reality disappears: social classes and their conflict, labour and its exploitation. Foucault's powerful theorization of biopolitics, which disseminates power into bodies along with resistance to power, helped make the issue of conquering the state obsolete. The theory of the specific intellectual, the promotion of micro-politics, the assertion of the disappearance of the working class or its rallying to consumer society, its replacement by 'new social movements' or by the plebs, ended up discrediting revolutionary scenarios which were already losing their credibility, what with glaciation in the East, the failure of the Portuguese revolution and the coup d'état in Chile.

With a transformation of capitalism in the offing, political economy and the critique of it found themselves dismantled and marginalized. While destruction of the social gains of the Fordist period had not yet begun, the transition to neoliberalism initially assumed the sunny complexion of joyful protests, rooted in life itself, freeing new spaces for creation. The victory of the Union of the Left, looming and then crumbling, summed up the hopes and the failure of an original perspective, echoed by this critical vitality. But how are we to explain the fact that fifty years later, under assault from neoliberal policies that have since destroyed broad swathes of the social state and defeated even the shared memory of struggles and victories in the first half of the twentieth century, there continues to be an enthusiastic reception for thought so closely bound up with a context that no longer exists? How to explain that its success, albeit marginal and disconnected from any political hope, remains quite unlike the reception of Marx and a Marxism that has gone on renewing itself in these years?

We may venture the hypothesis that if the thinkers of the 1960s, their descendants and commentators remain standard references in critical thinking, it is certainly on account of the mediocrity of the dominant theoretical output, but also because the migration of critique onto philosophical ground has made it adaptable to different historical contexts. Their ability to evoke economic and social reality, but also the social sciences, without ever really confronting them, has endowed their theses with an abiding critical aura and an arresting vision. In the present context of a general crisis of neoliberal capitalism, as well as of the social and political forces opposing it, it is logical that this tradition should continue to offer resources to readers in search of critical tools without satisfying the quest for an alternative once again on the agenda. This defect demands, but also permits, a partial renewal of this philosophical tradition. Without breaking with their past, the authors revisiting the notions of communism and socialism share this preoccupation, whereas the tradition they inherit significantly helped to disqualify them. The revival of a critical dialogue with Marx furnishes them with the means to revisit the issues of the state and social conflict, labour and hegemony, even the alternative to capitalism.

Another paradox then arises. While they are concerned with the political ins and outs of their analyses, these authors do not engage in dialogue with one another. Furthermore, their approaches remain largely incompatible – 'untranslatable', as Laclau would say, adopting a formula from Gramsci. The communist hypothesis as conceived by Badiou has nothing in common with the populist tactics of Laclau; and neither of them is concerned with the changes in labour and the commons studied by Negri. In addition to an absence of public debate on these subjects, a fragmentation of perspectives is evident, condemning these approaches to remain oeuvres all the more powerful and polished for being addressed to readers who, by definition, are isolated and unorganized. We may regard the refinement of these theoretical constructs, equalled only by their dispersion, as the mirror image of the fragmentation of struggles and growing opposition between demands and struggles by the dominated, to the point that the left (notes Jodi Dean from the US) seems to congratulate itself on its own fragmentation and a multitude of singularities.[3]

At this level, too, the sequence that began at the turn of the 2000s is definitely original. It combines a multifaceted crisis of capitalism, an ebbing of the political and trade union forces struggling against it and the rise of a powerful popular rejection, all of which profoundly destabilize the existing political landscape. Critical thinking has seen its role gradually transformed: denunciation of political and social forces organized around the labour movement has progressively lost its currency, while the latter's long-term defeat has struck it on the rebound, depriving it of its own space and some of its themes. That is why, while an interest in explicitly oppositional approaches has re-emerged in a number of readers, some representatives of this intellectual history are seeking to define theory anew as a modality of radical intervention in a social world experienced and conceived as conflict-ridden, though remaining reticent about any concrete active commitment. The permanence, or return, of the confrontation with Marx accompanies this endeavour, helping to revive his contemporaneity at least partially, inadvertently inviting re-exploration of his relevance. In short, as the fertility

---

3 Jodi Dean, *The Communist Horizon*, New York: Verso, 2012, 53.

of post-Marxism is exhausted, the possibility is reborn not of a doctrinaire Marxist politics that is assumed to pre-exist its application, but a
critical, political Marxism, to be reconstructed as a theoretical and strategic culture, overcoming the persistent divorce between reflection and
action of which it was itself a site.

The Neoliberal Moment

Shrewd analysis of the current neoliberal sequence is crucial for intervening within the new terrain of political and ideological combat. We
must begin by noting that the term *neoliberalism* is profoundly ambiguous, referring both to a stage in capitalism and to the discourse that
accompanies it, without it being clear if they coincide, are articulated,
juxtaposed or opposed. According to Marxist geographer David Harvey,
'neo-liberalism is in the first instance a theory of political economic
practices'.[4] Such a theoretical discourse aims to legitimize the policies
of deregulation, privatization and retreat of the welfare state introduced
from the 1970s onwards, in order to respond to 'the double crisis of
capital accumulation and class power'.[5] Neoliberal ideas were not
intended to be an exact representation of the economic and social world;
their mission was to disguise violent class revenge as a concern for the
common good. Subject to the exigencies of changing social circumstances, they were modified considerably during a sequence that began
in the interwar period[6] with promotion of the abstract principle of
individual freedom against all collectivisms and totalitarianisms, and
they continued with the planet-wide implementation of regressive policies, accompanied by assertions of their absolute rationality and
necessity.

Now more a vector of threats than promises, in a context of continuing but weaker hegemony, neoliberal discourse aims, inter alia, to
accompany an attempt to format individuals and remould labour-
power into an automatic, living commodity in a context of more intense

---

4 David Harvey, *A Brief History of Neoliberalism*, Oxford: Oxford University
Press, 2005, 2.

5 Ibid., 44.

6 See François Denord, *Néolibéralisme version française. Histoire d'une idéologie
politique*, Paris: Démopolis, 2007.

exploitation and low growth. But as has been said, this wholesale colonization of social existence represents the major fantasy of capitalism
as prey to its own convulsions, not its reality. While a tendency to its
outright commodification does indeed exist, human labour-power
cannot yield to it, on the one hand because it is not produced as a
commodity but formed as human individuality, living and complex,
within social relations irreducible to their capitalist structuration; and
on the other, and consequently, because wage earners are not simple
cogs in the productive machine, but individuals who persist in resisting
their exploitation. In this sense, contemporary neoliberal ideology is
not a description of what is, but the instrument of a total domination
yet to transpire. It secretes the discursive coating of this attempt at infinite capitalist annexation, refurbishing it as a promise of individual
fulfilment.

That is why the conceptual poverty of neoliberal doctrine is not the
chink in the armour of contemporary capitalism that it would suffice to
pierce for the latter to be overthrown. Its cardboard cut-out anthropology, illusory freedom and dogma of market rationality represent a
doctrinal framework concerned less with the coherence than with the
defence of the policy choices of the moment. It should be added that
this search for consent is accompanied by increasing coercion, made
possible by the current social and political balance of power. The
authoritarian, anti-democratic turn of neoliberalism explains its loans
from reactionary neo-conservatism, even the agenda of neo-fascist
forces, while they help it to consolidate complete class domination and
to quash or divert the protests it prompts. Given this, it seems productive to take up the Marxist notion of ideology understood as a political
and social function, at once distinct from the rest of economic and
social reality and articulated with it.

Yet for reasons attaching to the weakness of forces for social change,
a different critique of neoliberalism has prevailed. Disdaining analysis
of the reception of ruling ideas in group or class terms in connection
with actual neoliberal practices, it rather hastily concedes outright
victory to them, both economically and socially, as well as culturally
and at the level of individuality. Depicted as a consenting adult of
neoliberalism at her profoundest levels, the ordinary individual has
supposedly become an avid consumer, a passive spectator and a fanati-
cal individualist rather than an exploited wage earner, a racialized

individual, a dominated woman or a casualized youth.[7] Compounding
these ambiguities of critical analysis, paving the way for a moralizing
switch of sides against the exploited and dominated, is the weight of an
already old mutation in cultural life, but one that is particularly spectacular in a country like France, once reputed for its intellectual life
and thereby easily led to overestimate its importance: the media conse-
cration of pamphleteers who are ever more reactionary, openly racist
and sexist.[8]

'Media intellectuals' now occupy on the right and extreme right of the
ideological spectrum the place that genuine, creative researchers occu-
pied on its left forty years ago. In conditions of political defeat, social
remoulding and ideological encirclement, it is only logical that intellectuals who persevere with critical thinking are spontaneously led to
experience as the ultimate debacle a situation they broach exclusively
from the angle of ideas, sharing with their opponents the conviction
that their own role is decisive. In these circumstances, it seems impossible to resist representations that have become quasi-autonomous
material forces, which add to their status as ruling ideas that of being
efficacious injunctions. For Christopher Lasch, Zygmunt Bauman and
their very many followers, we are shackled by consumerism and narcissism, the proliferations of screens and the invasion of communication,
the liquefaction of human relations. According to Harmut Rosa, the
acceleration of time is now the key question.[9] Thus, paradoxically, part
of the contemporary critique of neoliberalism seems to have adopted
the neoliberal thesis that there is no alternative.

More fundamentally, this picture of neoliberalism derives from the
description of capitalism in general as an 'iron cage', proposed by Max

7 See Jacques Rancière, *Hatred of Democracy*, trans. Steve Corcoran, London: Verso,
2006; and Daniel Lindenberg, *Le Rappel à l'ordre. Enquête sur les nouveaux réactionnaires*,
Paris: Éditions du Seuil, 2002.

8 See Pascal Durand and Sarah Sindaco, eds, *Le Discours 'néo-réactionnaire'*, Paris:
CNRS, 2015; and Perry Anderson, *The New Old World*, New York: Verso, 2009, Chapter
4.

9 See, in particular, Christopher Lasch, *The Culture of Narcissism: American Life in
an Age of Diminishing Expectations* (1979), New York: W.W. Norton & Co., 2018;
Zygmunt Bauman, *Liquid Life*, Cambridge: Polity Press, 2005; and Harmut Rosa, *Social
Acceleration: A New Theory of Modernity*, trans. Jonathan Trejo-Mathys, New York:
Columbia University Press, 2013.

Weber at the start of the twentieth century, his 'cultural pessimism'[10] having informed the views of the Frankfurt School theoreticians, in particular Adorno and Horkheimer. Ultimately opposed to the Marxist view of class struggle, this view sought to pave the way for a different critique of capitalism – above all, of the technological rationality that is its origin. Reprised today ad nauseam by a fashionable moralism, its simplified version fuels the conviction of a definitive victory by the ruling ideas, which have supposedly succeeded in regimenting the over-whelming majority of individuals without regard to class distinctions. This theory, and the enduring success of its myriad avatars, benefits from being understood as the echo and meeting point of neoliberalism's unperceived contradictions, of its unprecedented kind of hegemony, at once powerful and fragile, amid a general crisis of capitalism and the historical weakness of the labour movement.

It is these contradictions, as much as the inadequacies of analysis of them, that are refracted in the ambivalence of the word *neoliberalism*. It operates a problematic fusion between the characteristics of the present stage of capitalism (stagnant growth, rising inequalities, increased exploi-tation and pressure on wages, destruction of the social state and finan-cialization of the economy) and a much too one-sided assertion of the total integration of social reality into capitalist logic, which has become a mode of production of bodies and souls allowing neither an outside nor an alternative to survive. The return to Foucault as analyst of disciplines and micro-powers leads to reorienting the study of capitalism towards an examination of control and management, at the risk of overestimating the power of supposedly sovereign techniques. In his turn, Spinoza is mobi-lized afresh,[11] following and taking on board his rereading by structuralist Marxism to shed light on the alleged total enrolment of the affects, whose alarmist description replaces study of refreshed and rejuvenated processes of exploitation and the forms of oppression with which they are combined. In reality, the subjective damage of neo-management prompts resignation or anger depending on multiple parameters, including the nature of the political form of their expression and structuration.

---

10 Michael Löwy, *Le Cage d'acier. Max Weber et le marxisme wéberien*, Paris: Stock, 2013, 9.

11 See Frédéric Lordon, *Imperium: Structures and Affects of Political Bodies*, London and New York: Verso, 2022.

In each instance, the focus of critique on neoliberal culture and the mentalities it generates takes the place of a totalizing approach – that is, a critique of political economy, dialecticizing the relationship between ideas and practices and registering the increasing clash between neoliberal discourse and popular rejection provoked by its policy options, as well as the reactionary and neo-conservative counterfire that works this rejection from within. In the absence of such an analysis, neoliberalism is cast as an exemplary existence, overestimating the coherence of a world structured by one and the same 'governmentality' rather than as a mode of production shot through with essential economic and social contradictions which at once fashion and undo its cohesion. To ignore the contradictions peculiar to a mode of production based on the exploitation of wage labour is to suppress, along with the cause of crises, the springs of social protest.

Even so, there is no question that the neoliberal apparatus manages to generate consent and to loop its causes and effects, along with undermining solidarity with the destruction of public services rendered incapable of fulfilling their social mission. But the alliance foreshadowed between neo-conservatism and neoliberalism is an attempt to respond to the secession of the popular classes, threatening the principle of electoral alternation hitherto able to defuse rising anger, while the left struggles to respond to it, and abstention and the extreme right are on the rise. That is why we need to understand the way that neoliberal policies, far from generating a shared imaginary, split classes and groups but also individuals, constructing hegemony by disaggregation rather than adhesion. A more complex approach to the role of ideas and representations, centred on those who diffuse them and those who receive them, is the precondition for a counter-offensive on the terrain not only of theoretical critique but also of active, solidaristic remeshing, a different mediation of reconstructing an alternative to contemporary capitalism as well as a riposte to the subjugating, regressive ideologies it propagates.

An express condition of strategic revival is not to artificially unify the profoundly divergent theses of the authors studied above, but to oblige critique to cede its overarching position. The alternative is to be constructed as a possibility inherent in the conditions of the present, but outlining politically – and not merely in local, cooperative or countercultural fashion – the break with the capitalist mode of production, occupying and thinking on its dialectical breaches. Such was the road explored by Marx in his way, at the dawn of the formation of modern political parties, leaving untreated many questions that were anachronistic. New forms of collective debate remain to be invented, so that reflection is constitutive of a reorganization of economic and social life, capable from the outset of realizing the egalitarian and democratic dimensions firmly expected by all those – youth, women, inhabitants of working-class neighbourhoods, racialized persons – who aspire to engage without losing themselves. Their demands are not to be understood as 'social demands' to be satisfied (in Laclau's expression) but as active ferments and the very means of political reorganization, without which no common project will see the light of day.

That is why Marx's lesson concerning the tendentially politicizing dimension of social struggles remains unmatched, on condition that it is successfully updated. What is to be initiated is precisely a reappropriation, as a key component of communism and as a primer, subjective and shared, of its construction. The abolition of cleavages is more relevant than ever. Targeting everything that severs subjects from their own activity, everything that subjects them to its reified outcome, it is both stake and means of an abolition of capitalism. This thesis concerns knowledge but also the state and labour, as well as all institutional forms as mediations that have turned into instruments of alienation. Their emancipatory potential must be revived when it exists, in order to restructure them and retune them to useful social needs – that is, respectful of human beings and of nature, needs that also must be defined democratically. By dint of this reversal, mediations represent centres of a riposte to their capitalist annexation, sources of contradiction to be reconquered. This is notably the case with public services, whose intrinsically political dimension must be reactivated beyond sheer defence of them.

Yet we must beware of the temptation to overcome splits by simply restoring lost unity or to believe that the death of institutions and the state will de facto liberate social life finally restored to its fundamental spontaneity and autonomy, without any need for institutional forms or delegate representation. The old illusion of reconciliation and restored immediacy – which remains at the centre of various libertarian traditions, left-wing and right-wing – fuels the rejection of all mediations today, propagating a cursory anti-statism as exclusive strategic compass.

Faced with these dreams of reversion to a lost unity, we have to take on board the complexity of institutions and representation, as well as their constitutively dialectical character. We need to rethink the political dimension of consciousness, culture and ideas as determined and determining mediations, condensing all the contradictions of a given historical formation, which makes them the main sites and means of strategic intervention but also of conflict and debate. Here, Antonio Gramsci's contribution, adjusting Marx's analyses to the context of the recession of revolutionary prospects in 1920s Italy, is incomparably rich.

First Counterpoint: Antonio Gramsci, Thinker of Hegemony

It must be noted that Gramsci endeavoured to theorize not cultural hegemony – despite a fashionable misinterpretation which distorts him into a theorist of communication – but the real, circumscribed role of culture in the construction of a fundamentally social and political hegemony – a role determined by the economic and social formation that engenders it. As a result, a communist culture is not characterized by the invention *ex nihilo* of a new content, but above all by a new relationship to existing knowledge, geared to its individual and collective reappropriation. The individual is at the heart of this redefinition of politics. Treating it as a 'focal point' where all dimensions of existence are articulated leads Gramsci to conclude that 'the real philosopher is, and cannot be other than, the politician, the active man who modifies the environment, understanding by environment the ensemble of relations which each of us enters to take part in'.[12] From 1919, Gramsci was involved in organizing training and educational structures, whose mission was to offer not only teaching of the classical kind, but also a 'self-education in personal thought'.[13] This was conceived as a weapon inside the Italian Socialist Party prior to its split, wielded against abstract culture and the diffusion of a fixed, conformist bourgeois subculture. The experience of the Turin factory councils conferred its true

---

12 Antonio Gramsci, *Selections from the Prison Notebooks*, ed. and trans. Quintin Hoare and Geoffrey Nowell Smith, London: Lawrence & Wishart, 1971, 352.

13 André Tosel, *Étudier Gramsci. Pour une critique continue de la révolution passive capitaliste*, Paris: Kimé, 2016, 46.

significance on the project of forming a new historical personality, which is in no way reducible to the acquisition of a pre-existing culture, even if it presupposes knowledge of it.

In this respect, much was at stake in the Turin revolt of 1919. For Gramsci, 'the socialist State already exists potentially in the institutions of the social life characteristic of the exploited working class'.[14] The alternative was above all rooted in the fertile ground of this original, vibrant conciliar culture. A revolutionary strategy, adjusted to it and attentive to the intertwining of individual and social dimensions, must strive to develop this precious, fragile culture, so as to propel a political and trade union revival.[15] Omitting these complex stakes reduces the idea of 'hegemony' to the affirmation of cultural and ideological domination, conceived as the alpha and omega of political and social power – a thesis corresponding not to reality but to the self-representation projected by various political organizations and institutions in general. Gramsci's thesis is quite different.

From 1926 onwards, he reworked this notion of hegemony, borrowed from Lenin, in accordance with his reflection on the United Front strategy. The rise of what he analysed as a 'reactionary Caesarism'[16] had to be confronted with a unifying strategy, the opposite of the 'class against class' strategy imposed in 1928 by the Third International, the consequences of which were disastrous, especially in Germany. This analysis, anchored in the study of concrete social relations, was adjusted to the Italian situation by Gramsci, his goal being to foil a reactionary 'southern agrarian bloc' combining peasant masses and big landowners through the mediation of traditional intellectual factions: priests, teachers, civil servants and so on. The point was to fracture it down the middle, by intervening at the very heart of this intellectual stratum and organizing cultural counter-activity specific to the revolutionary party. Thus conceived, the Gramscian construction of hegemony results from a general analysis of the conjuncture and the project of intervening in it

14 Antonio Gramsci, 'Workers' Democracy', in *Selections from Political Writings 1910–1920*, ed. Quintin Hoare and trans. John Mathews, London: Lawrence & Wishart, 1977, 65.

15 This aimed to renovate the Italian Socialist Party and the CGL (Confederazione Generale del Lavoro). On the history of the working-class movement in Italy in these years, see Gaetano Arfé, *Storia del Socialismo Italiano 1892–1926*, Turin: Einaudi, 1977.

16 Gramsci, *Selections from the Prison Notebooks*, 219.

socially and politically, paying special attention to mediations and representations.

Pursuing this initial analysis, Gramsci developed an original theorization of political transformation, combining intervention in social relations of production and the construction of social alliances cemented by profoundly shared economic and social interests in conjunctures that are always concrete and unique. This strategic approach is located in the tradition of Marx and Lenin, but it also invokes Machiavelli and breaks outright with the determinism and economism of the Second and Third Internationals. Gramsci's attention to crises, historical discontinuities and ruptures of equilibrium connects this hegemonic perspective to the long-term history of capitalism. Here we are far removed from the thesis of an exclusively intellectual hegemony or the construction of social blocs on electoral terrain, which forget the foundational antagonism of labour and capital.

To thwart the censorship that the term 'Marxism' would have alerted, Gramsci uses the expression 'philosophy of praxis' to refer to his project. But beyond this circumstance, the formula adequately expresses Gramsci's political perspective. It involves not producing a pure theory but aiding the development of a new, emancipatory popular common sense, permeated with culture and oriented by a precise political project. Initially, the common sense of subaltern classes comprises various borrowings, which are non-systematic and even profoundly disparate. It is to be reworked and expanded, rendering 'an already existing activity ["critical"]'[17] and then giving it its political import by constructing 'an intellectual-moral bloc which can make politically possible the intellectual progress of the mass'.[18] '[Consciousness] . . . of the solidarity of interests' leads to 'the right [being] claimed to participate in legislation and administration . . . within the existing fundamental structures'.[19]

To transcend this corporative level, the shared conviction has to emerge that the interests of the group 'can and must become the interests of other subordinate groups too'.[20] Thus, against any reduction of theoretico-political work to a mere ideological and rhetorical construct,

---

17 Ibid., 331.
18 Ibid., 332–3.
19 Ibid., 181.
20 Ibid.

as Laclau tends to regard it, Gramsci inserts the cultural moment into what André Tosel calls a 'dialectical social ontology of modernity',[21] which takes on board and articulates three different moments of economic and social formation: the economic structure, the political balance of power and the military level. Their reciprocal relations define situations, whether profoundly organic or simply conjunctural. Bourgeois hegemony derives from the capacity to dominate these three levels while articulating them, leading to the construction of a temporary consensus, reinforced by 'pedagogy'. Faced with this class domination and the instruments of its perpetuation, the subaltern classes find themselves challenged to produce not a similar construct, but a different, unifying and progressive worldview, resulting not from a knowledge that pre-exists its diffusion but from the constant, revolutionary interaction of educators and educated. Here Gramsci pursues and clarifies Marx's intuitions about the reappropriation of knowledge as a component and motor of individual and collective emancipation.

Indeed, during the formation of the popular collective will, it is 'self-praxis' that makes everyone the 'process of [their] actions', leading human beings to become the 'blacksmith' of themselves.[22] For, according to Gramsci, hegemony does not result from the construction by specialist intellectuals of a politically effective ideology, imposed from above on the subaltern, who are destined to remain such. It involves a radical transformation of intellectual and social life, involving a new conception of politics and revolution. Against passivity and conformism, 'the spirit of cleavage – progressive acquisition of an awareness of one's historical identity – is to be developed, a spirit that must aim to extend itself from the protagonist class to the classes that are its potential allies: all of this requires complex ideological work'.[23] Gramsci puts it clearly: the philosophy of praxis, Marxism as he conceives it, is 'the expression of the subaltern classes who want to educate themselves in the art of government and who have an interest in knowing all truths, even the unpleasant ones'.[24]

---

21 Tosel, *Étudier Gramsci*, 154.

22 Gramsci, *Selections from the Prison Notebooks*, 351.

23 Antonio Gramsci, *Prison Notebooks*, Vol. 2, ed. and trans. Joseph Buttigieg, New York: Columbia University Press, 1996, 53; trans. modified.

24 Antonio Gramsci, *Further Selections from the Prison Notebooks*, ed. and trans. Derek Boothman, London: Lawrence & Wishart, 1995, 549.

Thus, far from conceiving counter-ideology as a rhetorical construct or pure knowledge, Gramsci views it as active mediation of communist transformation, which remoulds the intellectual function at the same time as it alters the consciousness of the subaltern classes. It is here that Gramsci fashioned the notion of 'organic intellectual' as distinct from the 'traditional intellectual'. Whereas traditional intellectuals take themselves for representatives of the mind while embodying the social hierarchy of the old world, organic intellectuals are the expression of the subaltern masses, directly linked to the world of production and work. They participate in the elaboration of a new worldview starting from collective praxis and aiding the self-awareness of the subaltern classes and, thereby, revolution. That is why Gramsci affirms that 'all men are intellectuals ... but not all men have in society the function of intellectuals'.[25]

This rereading of the division of labour, the prelude to its transformation, also leads to a reorganization of the revolutionary party, which has to combine 'a style of leadership that articulates voluntary obedience and promotion of creative spontaneity'.[26] Above all, it enables Gramsci to foreground the experience of the Turin councils, in that they transformed human beings: 'they became aware of their reality as producers ... and they began to act and understand themselves as historical creators'.[27] In the long run, in 'regulated society' – the expression from his pen that designates communism – it is a question of overcoming all forms of division between masses and intellectuals, but also between leaders and led, organic intellectuals having nothing in common with 'subaltern party functionaries, bureaucratically zealous and obedient'.[28] The definition of the party as the 'modern prince', with reference to Machiavelli, allows Gramsci to denounce any organizational 'fetishism'. To forget the mediating role of organization results in its degeneration, particularly Stalinist, which reproduces the state cleavage. How are we to transfer the critical rereading of these powerful analyses for the purposes of contemporary strategic renewal? Bruno Amable and Stefano Palombarini, who take up the categories of social bloc and hegemony to

---

25 Gramsci, *Selections from the Prison Notebooks*, 9.

26 Tosel, *Étudier Gramsci*, 171.

27 Ibid., 307.

28 Domenico Losurdo, *Gramsci, du libéralisme au 'communisme critique'*, trans. J.-M. Goux, Paris: Syllepse, 2006, 199.

analyse the French political situation in 2017, end their book with a powerful remark:

> The future of the French economic and social model is being played out in a political conflict whose outcome is bound up with the ability of the competing project to clearly define the social alliances they propose to aggregate, to identify the variables of necessary, effective mediations between the interests that will compose them.[29]

Beyond this model, but starting with it, radical social change requires the construction of an alternative in which classes and individuals recognize themselves precisely because they are its co-authors. Approached in the light of such stakes, Gramsci's strategic thinking remains of the utmost relevance.

A New Critique of Practical Reason

It must be stressed: rereading Marx and Gramsci in light of contemporary critical questions cannot vouchsafe directly transposable solutions. Yet the latter are more indispensable than ever if we are to succeed in breaking with strictly theoretical or narrowly tactical elaboration of the alternative, as well as with the principle of the vertical transmission of a discourse external to those who receive it. A new kind of knowledge has to be invented, which includes, in particular, a historical and critical culture of struggle and resistance but which must also be at the heart of the invention of a different form of existence. Logically but disastrously, historical episodes that attest to this culture of self-government by workers have been forgotten;[30] reflections on the forms and instruments of the transition from capitalism to communism have been excommunicated, as have those on democratic planning of the economy and the redefinition of production and labour accompanying them. Yet democratic economic planning – including collective control over the organization

---

29 Bruno Amable and Stefano Palombarini, *L'illusion du bloc bourgeois. Alliances sociales et avenir du modèle français*, Paris: Raisons d'Agir, 2017, 161.

30 See Catherine Samary, *D'un communisme décolonial à la démocratie des communs*, Paris: Éditions du Croquant, 2017.

of production and the very definition of work and needs – is a crucial condition of the alternative, organizing it as a rational pathway to emancipation. Guillaume Fondu stresses the need for a 'narrative capable of giving shape to collective identities capable of making it live', associated with the 'experienced presence of a horizon of expectation'.[31] It is imperative to revive such reflection, seemingly discredited by the authoritarian planning, and failure, of the so-called socialist countries, but also by the powerful neoliberal campaign that denounces on principle any intervention in an economic sphere deemed to pertain exclusively to private initiative and subtracted from collective decision-making.

The reworking of this political culture, of a new kind compared with what the term *politics* refers to today, assumes constant critical contact with experience – that of cooperatives and self-managed enterprises, peasant communities and solidaristic initiatives. It involves ensuring the constant articulation of these necessarily limited experiences with a societal project that is the vector of a quite different way of life, rational and desirable. Thus, in place of a history of the vanquished, punctuated exclusively by defeats and disasters, it is a debated, comparative critical study of the past and present that is to be revived, to make collective reappropriation of the means of production conceivable and possible once again, to initiate their rational transformation, to recapture a historical narrative that is today completely dictated by the opponent and reduced to the aberrant fable of a finally deregulated market propagating freedom throughout the world. Thus, rearticulated with an ambitious anti-capitalist project, solidaristic experiments can be much more than local, momentary endeavours, on condition of mutualizing reflection on their scope as well as their limits, far beyond the practices of counter-expertise and skill-sharing between specialist activists. For what is at issue is initiating the recasting of the whole of economic and social existence, by reorganizing production and sharing of the necessary knowledge, along with debate on these now urgent perspectives: what is to be produced and how? According to what needs deemed social priorities? How is the division of labour to be rethought? How is the relationship to the environment to be integrated? How are we to organize constant social control over it?

---

31 Guillaume Fondu, 'Une théorie marxiste de la planification est-elle possible?', *Actuel Marx* 65, 2019.

In this regard, we must note and salute the renewal of reflection on democratic planning associated with the term *socialism*, which we find especially in Anglo-American socialist literature, notably in the works of Erik Olin Wright, Pat Devine, Michael Lebowitz and Michael Albert, to mention only them.[32] Yet despite their many merits, starting with the revival of thinking about the alternative from the angle of its social viability and economic rationality, the defect of these projects is that they pertain to expert knowledge constructed independently of any concrete mobilization. This leads them to circumvent the problem of the political conditions of their realization. This new variety of utopianism is in a position, as were the utopians of the nineteenth century, to formulate pertinent questions while deserting the terrain of mediations, devoting themselves to the production of narratives all the more minutely detailed in that they describe a seductive substitute reality, but without a political access route to it. Such proposals for an alternative demonstrate *a contrario* the importance of theoretical reflection directly involved in social transformation, overcoming the schematic, sterilizing opposition between theory and practice, echo of a division of labour that even contaminates contestation of it.

In terms of practice, real self-management experiments have brought out the fertility of a collective, subversive intelligence that knows how to concretely challenge the division of labour and its hierarchies, reunifying execution, conception and administration. The history of the LIP clock enterprise affords a striking example of this. Following the company's 1973 bankruptcy, the wage earners' struggle was organized by an action committee that brought together unionized and non-unionized personnel. This committee called regular assemblies, beginning by imposing a reduction in tempos to allow everyone to participate in the struggle against redundancies and closure; it then worked for the collective reorganization of production. At stake in this episode, which has remained engraved on collective memory, were decisive issues concerning the transformation of the wage relation and overflow onto the terrain of politics, not only politicizing the question of work but also, even more profoundly, helping to

---

32 Erik Olin Wright, *Envisioning Real Utopias*, New York: Verso, 2010; Pat Devine, *Democracy and Economic Planning*, Cambridge: Polity Press, 1988; Michael Lebowitz, *Build It Now: Socialism for the Twenty-First Century*, New York: Monthly Review Press, 2006; Michael Albert, *Parecon: Life after Capitalism*, London: Verso, 2003.

undo the split between politics and economics. Despite the ultimate defeat of LIP in 1977, and granted the significant changes that have occurred since in industrial production, the organization of work and the world of labour, this episode illustrates the power and richness of such mobilization, capable of extending its demands to a popular reappropriation of production and social existence in its entirety.[33]

The revival of a living culture of this kind is a sizeable task. It alone can outline new pathways and illuminate the illegitimate character of the capitalist appropriation of wealth and labour. It summons us to counter it with viable alternatives that will no longer run aground for want of political capacity in isolated cases which are ultimately always devoured from within by the surrounding capitalism. Political development of this question involves thinking through the transformation of objectives into concrete, expansive means of a constantly resurgent struggle, capable of disseminating its sites without giving up targeting the very heart of capitalist logic, while striving to gradually realize different social relations. In other words, such experiences must be seen not as already existing local alternative models, but as forms of mobilization and organization around a new mode of production and existence, a prelude to the development of a more general alternative that is collectively reflected on as it is constructed. At the same time, we have to go beyond a spatial logic of occupation (squares, future development zones, universities, enterprises) with a temporal and historical logic of inventing transitions (measures of social justice, defence and revival of public services, re-conquest of media space and so on) liable to mutually galvanize one another.

If social struggles and the invention of political and institutional forms are to be recombined, we must also reconcile collective engagement and aspirations to individual autonomy. Self-reappropriation is the nucleus of the communist project, but the absence of a veritable active dialectic of the collective and the individual sterilizes any prospect of ambitious transformation. Mobilizations like Occupy and Nuit debout attest to these difficulties. Bursting into the centre of gentrified cities, hostile to all organized forces, fetishizing spontaneity and horizontality, they ended up renewing traditional logics of delegation by

---

33 See Xavier Vigna, *L'insubordination ouvrière dans les années 68. Essai d'histoire politique des usines*, Rennes: Pur, 2007.

disappearing without leaving any trace, having nurtured and diffused hopes of a different world. For their part, the main left-wing parties in crisis have been applying themselves for some decades to embracing what they regard as the growing tendency to engagement that is predominantly ethical and private in kind, prompting them to resort to opinion surveys to determine their line and programme, even to conceive their proposals in market terms of supply and demand. Such approaches persist in uncoupling individual involvement 'à la carte'[34] from the construction of a general offensive, which in return fuels disaffection and the search for quite different ways.

That is why it is also a question of registering, and responding to, the seductive power of autonomous activism, its practices and its writings, among broad sections of youth. The libertarian, insurrectionary themes articulated by Tiqqun and the Invisible Committee in brilliant, combative texts resonate with a collective anger that is as considerable as it is atomized.[35] The focus on enslaved subjectivity,[36] privileging an ethical and cultural refusal of the ruling order, is combined with a culture of deliberately spectacular urban riot. If the powerful and original mobilization of the *gilets jaunes* in 2018 shared some of these forms of intervention, as well as the critique of political and trade union organizations, it conveyed social demands that reasserted a class logic while demanding the introduction of mechanisms of direct democracy into political institutions whose functioning was rightly denounced as confiscatory.

Thus, faced with the growing social violence of neoliberal policies, new forms of mobilization are being sought and are multiplying, whereas from one defeat to the next, the labour movement is weakened by disavowal of it. Yet these protests remain bereft of the perspectives that the socialist and communist traditions were able to create and of the

---

34 This is demonstrated by Julian Mischi in analysing the evolution of the French Communist Party from centralism to the promotion of the individual and 'activism à la carte' (*Le Communisme désarmé. Le PCF et les classes populaires depuis les années 1970*, Marseilles: Agone, 2014), incommensurate with the radical reflection, individual and collective, demanded by the era.

35 For example, Tiqqun, *Theory of the Bloom*, trans. Robert Hurley, Black Cart, 2014; Invisible Committee, *The Coming Insurrection* (2007), Los Angeles: Semiotext(e), 2009; and *To Our Friends* (2014), Pasadena: Semiotext(e), 2015.

36 See Ugo Palheta, 'L'insurrection qui revient. Les influences visibles du Comité invisible', *La Revue du Crieur* 4, 2016, 58–73.

collective power of a solidaristic counter-society. They have to confront the atrophy of an activist culture that remains indispensable, beginning with the strike. They are hit head-on by the fragmentation of alternatives, the fascination with definitive theories, the temptation of individualistic withdrawal. In these circumstances, how can we renew and preserve a legacy that is much more than a memory? How can we get the most out of existing aspirations and mobilizations? And, above all, how can we transcend and transform them, in and through their encounter, into active solidarities, into an activist remeshing of working-class neighbourhoods and workplaces? While this task is certainly practical, it includes contemporary political reflection, individual and collective, at the interface between theory and action.

We must therefore register existing mobilizations and not decree what they should be. We must also participate in them, in order to reconstruct social and political forces that are vectors of an alternative at once radical and capable of rallying the majority formed by today's workers and employees, including immigrants, women, young casual labourers, the unemployed and all those who comprise the new contemporary proletariat.[37] Recombining social confrontation, politicization and democratization means avoiding several pitfalls. Thus, in some respects, enthusiasm for direct democracy conveys the illusion of a potentially reunified people, capable of settling social questions by majorities and referenda while bypassing the basic class confrontation with capitalism. However, it also attests to the search for contemporary forms of self-government that comply with collective decision-making and debate, taking the principle of popular sovereignty literally in the face of measures imposed despite their rejection by a majority, in the context of electoral processes distorted by the blackmail of not wasting one's vote and mass abstention. Renewing democratic forms is not something that can be done in strictly institutional fashion; it involves the intrusion of social struggles onto the terrain of political forms and, conversely, the revitalization of militant political intervention on the social terrain, with a view to recombining delegation, control and direct democracy, but also to rearticulating immediate demands and long-term changes.

While we must note the rejection of institutional politics, it is up to the political and trade union organizations of the radical left to keep

---

37 See Sarah Abdelnour, *Les nouveaux prolétaires*, Paris: Textuel, 2018.

alive, and regalvanize, an irreplaceable culture, which has in the past proved itself a force of social conquests without parallel, as well as the means of expression and political organization of the popular classes. In France, the Communist Party, in particular, was able to play the role of driving force at several points in its history. Today, it is the whole activist culture of the labour movement which, if it is not to wither away, must be reinvented. This involves sketching the transversal axis that links the struggle against one form of oppression with all the others, while not purporting to synthesize them from without, but working to highlight and give new life to their objective, complex links. For it is in starting from existing struggles – especially feminist and anti-racist struggles – and the forms they take that it will be possible to overcome the rejection of existing organizations, which are partly responsible for it.

Here, too, the strategic question proves medial, not final. Escaping the general crushing of individualities involves constructing forms of emancipation that root their dynamic in this initial outline of liberation[38] – forms capable of renovating and reconstructing the party-form, as opposed to calling for its disappearance in favour of mobilizations that are divided and fleeting, or aesthetic and mediatic, or movements encouraging the verticality they denounce. Jodi Dean puts it powerfully as a desire: 'Neither instantiation nor representative of the people, the party formalizes its collective desire for collectivity.'[39] This labour of living formalization must be synonymous with the construction of organizational and institutional mediations which render a radical alternative conceivable and desirable. While foreshadowed, these forms are not already present; they are to be invented in the course of mobilizations that also assign themselves the objective of their construction, drawing on the long, complex history of popular assemblies, neighbourhood and factory committees, and collectives of struggle.

---

38 See Lucien Sève, *Penser avec Marx aujourd'hui*, Vol. 2, *L'homme?*, Paris: La Dispute, 2008, esp. 510ff. Sève clarifies there the potentially emancipatory dimensions of the 'engaged life'.

39 Dean, *The Communist Horizon*, 249.

Second Counterpoint: What Is a Mediation?

Among the most urgent tasks, dialectical theoretical culture must be revitalized as a full-fledged component of a strategic renewal, far removed from any narrow political instrumentalization. This means re-exploring the problem of radical social change and renewing revolutionary culture, avoiding both the fetishism of spontaneous insurrection and 'parliamentary cretinism' and republican idolatry – symmetrical versions of a refusal to envisage the political and social construction of a class relation of force as the condition for inventing an effective alternative to capitalism. If we must transcend purely external alternatives as well as strictly immanent solutions, escape the return of impotent dreams and the old view of transitions in which the revolutions of the twentieth century foundered, and if we must also redefine the cleavages and reaffirm social contradictions, we must explore anew the very notion of mediation, including philosophically, where its dialectical grasp was developed long ago.

What is a mediation? A juridical category often employed today in conflict resolution, the term assumes that conflict is a simple opposition between two entities that are external to one another, between which is inserted an external third party, who is supposed to enable termination of the clash through simple reconciliation. Some philosophers, particularly Aristotle and Hegel, elaborated much more complex conceptions of mediation, which break with this juxtaposition of elements formed independently of their interrelationship, conceptions that Marx inherited. All three authors strove to link theoretical work with a social and political reality that they regarded as both condition and object of their elaboration. As a result, the successive meanings of the notion of mediation accompany the development of philosophy and the transformation of its historical role, culminating in the self-criticism of its status as separate knowledge, severed from social life and thereby disarmed and deprived of critical power.

In Aristotle, mediation is a category without any equivalent because it is defined on the triple terrain of logic, ethics and politics, but it is also deployed in the analysis of market exchange. In the context of his analysis of reasoning and the definition of the three moments of syllogism ('1. Man is an animal / 2. All animals are mortal / 3. Therefore man is mortal'), Aristotle conceives the middle term ('animal') as the attribute that is inserted between the major ('mortal') and minor ('man') terms, thus making it possible to arrive at a conclusion ('man is mortal'). Here, to know is to logically attribute a predicate to a subject by means of its inclusion in the species and genera that actually subsume it, reasoning disclosing a pre-existing, indisputable definition. Nevertheless, the middle term is what makes this inclusion possible, in the context of a formal reflection on valid reasoning. Its definition by Aristotle is not as mere analytical instrument; it corresponds to the identification of an active element of knowledge, like the propositions it links. In this sense, the middle term contains the whole syllogism by cementing its propositions to one another: 'I call that the *middle* which both is itself in another and has another in it – this is also middle in position.'[40] As conceived by Aristotle, logical mediation, far from pertaining to a mere method, opens onto Being itself and its structure, at a time when the strict distinction between knowledge and reality had no meaning.

By virtue of this non-distinction and the systematic architecture of his philosophy, Aristotle developed this analysis of mediations in the case of the practical sciences, with mediation no longer characterizing the form of reasoning but instead certain realities as such. In ethics and analysis of the virtues, the median is defined as the golden mean between two excesses (courage lies between temerity and cowardice). But, once again, the Aristotelian notion is much richer than the summary arithmetic of the passions often attributed to it. The median is not a tepid half-measure, but an excellence, inhabited by the concrete ideal of the 'prudent man' who provides it with its living embodiment. His existence confirms that the fulfilment of a virtue – prudence – pre-exists its potentiality and guides its realization, which leads Aristotle to affirm that what is actual is prior to what is potential. As for monetary mediation, it brings into relation distinct things (shoes, a house) as means of measurement that reveal a profound kinship, a principle of real equivalence. Even so, money can sometimes free itself from its intermediary role and become the purpose of exchange, in the framework of the perverted economics that Aristotle calls 'chrematistics',[41] pathology of exchange

---

40 Aristotle, *Prior Analytics*, trans. Robin Smith, Indianapolis: Hackett Publishing Company, 1989, A4, 3.

41 See Aristotle, *The Politics*, ed. Stephen Everson and trans. Benjamin Jowett, Cambridge: Cambridge University Press, 1988, 1257a–1258a, 12–14.

being a perversion of social existence. Aristotle was the first to think on this ambivalence of real mediation, either a condition of activity or adulterating it by usurping the status of purpose. Marx was to remember this pioneering work and would pay it homage.

After Aristotle, it was in theology – around the figures of Moses and Christ – that the notion of mediation was deployed and enriched, these developments being adopted by later philosophy (including in the critique of religion, as in Feuerbach). Beyond all subsequent reductions of mediation to the rank of mere technical means, an intermediary subject to a purpose that it does not determine but which it can distort (in Kantian philosophy, in particular), the elaboration of the dialectic of mediation was continued by Hegel, in the context of his analysis of contradictions and their development. His speculative reworking of the syllogism took the form of a critique of the separation between thought and thing, of which (according to him) Aristotle had been guilty, Aristotle's logic boiling down to 'the injunction to think correctly'[42] and to an inventory of forms of reasoning on the model of the fixed classifications of natural history.

However, the movement of thought, being that of things themselves, must be known and developed as such. Aristotelian mediation remains an abstract, static relationship between separated elements, a 'logic of the finite',[43] whereas it is necessary to think about real mediation, which overcomes the opposition between the objective and the subjective, a movement of unfolding of the infinite that works the finite from within and guides its development. 'Being is . . . absolutely mediated.'[44] Hegelian mediation is productive and inventive because it subjects the immediate to a wholly internal 'labour of the negative'. Negation is no longer a negation in the sense of ordinary logic – that is, the refutation of a theoretical proposition – but a real process leading what is to separate from itself, to become other than itself, before returning to itself following the stages of an itinerary that is no mere return to the starting point but an expansion and a concretization: 'mediation is nothing beyond

---

42 G.W.F. Hegel, *Leçons sur l'histoire de la philosophie*, Vol. 3, trans. P. Garniron, Paris: J. Vrin, 2000, 603.

43 Ibid., 605.

44 G.W.F. Hegel, Preface to *Phenomenology of Spirit*, trans. A.V. Miller, Oxford: Oxford University Press, 1977, 21.

self-moving self-sameness'.[45] This attention to history and to development, but also to negativity and contradiction, leads Hegel to think
differently about all orders of reality, including political life. And it is
precisely on political terrain that he reworks the notion of mediation, in
the paragraphs of the *Elements of the Philosophy of Right* devoted to the
state, in an analysis of great power that is not discredited by Marx's
subsequent critique of it.

Wholly consistent with the previous analysis, Hegel conceives the
relationship of philosophy to politics not as understanding external, and
subsequent, to its object, but as reflection of the one in the other, developing in the course of a history that must lead to the introduction of a
state which is finally rational. This state has the task of integrating and
overcoming the particularism of private interests reigning in chaotic,
non-egalitarian civil society, first as an 'external state' unifying this
dispersion from without, then as a state of reason and freedom overcoming its initial appearance to become a concrete universal, registering
the exigencies of individual singularity while unfolding its higher political truth. The ascent from singularity to the universal takes the form
here of family and then estates or corporations (*Stand*), 'the second . . .
ethical root of the state',[46] grouping individuals by professional bodies
purportedly effecting the mediation between particular needs and
universal right, between civil society and the state. This mediation is
therefore not a stage destined to disappear into its outcome, but a
constant, lasting process that constructs and maintains unity without
absorbing social diversity into the state instance, but, on the contrary,
causing the state to spring up from its social fertile ground, as demonstrated by its own self-consciousness: 'the state therefore *knows* what it
wills, and knows it in its *universality* as something *thought*'.[47]

The state-corporation presents itself as an instance for managing
private interests under the control of the public power, protecting fami-
lies and enabling individuals to integrate into the universal via professional pride, which raises them to the dignity of 'a conscious activity for
a common end'.[48] Hegel adds that participation in corporative affairs

---

45 Ibid., 11.
46 G.W.F. Hegel, *Elements of the Philosophy of Right*, ed. Allen W. Wood and trans.
H.B. Nisbet, Cambridge: Cambridge University Press, 1991, §255, 272.
47 Ibid., §270, 290–1.
48 Ibid., §254, 272.

compensates the 'limited share in the universal business of the state' allowed individuals in modern states,[49] inasmuch as it contains a pedagogical role of initiation into the universal, on condition that the state ensures it. Such an analysis, powerful and original, also attests to Hegel's registration of British political economy and its critique of the state. At stake is avoiding 'a destructive mass opposed to all organization':[50] it is precisely here that Hegel resorts to the notion of 'mediation', avoiding thinking of the relationship between corporations and the state as opposition – something that would risk nurturing contestation of the latter. He adds that this mediation is inserted not only between civil society and the state, but also between the people and the state, in the absence of which 'the masses will always express themselves in a barbarous manner'.[51] He thus raises this question: does mediation have a pacifying vocation, deactivating popular political creativity and bridling the historical dialectic?

As we have seen, this was the question tackled by Marx in the Kreuznach manuscript, arguing that in the estates are to be found 'all the *contradictions* of Hegel's presentation':[52] Hegel 'makes the *estates element* the expression of the *separation* [between civil society and the state]; but at the same time it is supposed to be the representative of an identity which is not there'.[53] Highlighting the archaic, pre-modern character of Hegel's argument, Marx stresses the non-surmounted dualism of civil society and the state. Contrary to every expectation, it is the Aristotelian syllogism, surreptitiously adopted, that clarifies the limits of Hegel's mediation: 'the middle term is the wooden iron, the concealed opposition between generality and singularity'.[54] Despite his protests, Hegel returns to Aristotle because his mediation is no more than a union of opposites, external to one another and linked solely by the intermediary of a third term that does not overcome their conflict but embodies it, alongside clashing opposites: 'it is the story of the man and his wife who fought, and the doctor who wanted to step between them as mediator,

---

49 Ibid., §255, 273.
50 Ibid., §302, 343.
51 Ibid.
52 *Contribution to the Critique of Hegel's Philosophy of Law*, in Karl Marx and Friedrich Engels, *Collected Works*, Vol. 3, London: Lawrence & Wishart, 1975, 73.
53 Ibid., 74.
54 Ibid., 84.

when in turn the wife had to mediate between the doctor and her husband, and the husband between his wife and the doctor'.[55] If the dialectic is not vaudeville, it is by dint of thinking about real mediations, participating in the definition of purposes they render constructible.

It happens that this first objection to Hegelian mediation, which precedes Marx's commitment to communism, was followed by a lengthy reflection on the intertwining of politics and philosophy, on the one hand, and on the nature and function of mediations under capitalism and beyond, on the other. Inheriting the extended treatment of the issue of mediation through the history of philosophy, Marx develops in original fashion its twofold belonging to the register of consciousness and to the world of objective historical determinations. Hegel's view of an institutional pacification of social conflict, and the prospect of a rational state as the immanent purpose of the course of history, gives way to an analysis of class struggles that are bearers of their own possible abolition. The precondition of the abolition of class domination is mobilization of the proletariat, attaining, as it goes, consciousness of itself and of the alternative of which it is the vector and principal historical subject. Mediations are regalvanized and located at the exact meeting point between historical determinations and collective, conscious human intervention. We may add that class struggles, and the forms of organization they endow themselves with, are bearers of the alternative to capitalism only if they can prefigure an organization of social activity that integrates the reflexive, critical moment of its own democratic planning: soviets and councils, strike committees and communes constantly invent, and reinvent, these expansive forms. The dialectical recasting of mediation secretes a popular, revolutionary reappropriation of knowledge, itself transformed into knowledge of practice in the process of inventing and correcting itself as it proceeds.

That is why, in the course of Marx's reflection, the notions of 'mediation' and 'representation' end up referring to very different realities that nevertheless evince basic similarities of formation and function, at stake in all of which is that reappropriation. Money, the state and institutions, consciousness and knowledge – these are mediations as well as representations which, splitting off to a certain extent from the social totality fractured into classes that generates them, participate in the operation

---

55 Ibid., 87.

and reproduction of the capitalist mode of production. By this token, they can also become factors blocking it as sites where all the contradictions of its essence are concentrated. Mediations then prove to be the privileged sites for the activation of specific crises, which make the social totality visible and afford access to it, giving purchase to specifically strategic intervention.[56]

Aiding reflection on the initiation of a radical transformation starting from present conditions, and its theoretical recovery, the concept of mediation is not systematized by Marx. He uses it to refer not to the means of a transformation, or a step in the latter, but a kind of open-ended evolution, specifying a contradiction amenable to several kinds of development and inflected by a conscious, collective project. Thus, transposed onto the level of a non-teleological historical and political analysis, mediation anchors the revolutionary project in the materiality of the economic and social phenomena that make it possible, without ever inscribing its implacable necessity in it. In this sense, politics redefined aside from any state cleavage and any philosophy of history becomes permanent mediation, enabling social activity to constantly reflect on itself, orient itself and adjust itself. That is why the main interest of the notion, in addition to its transcendence of the simplistic opposition between objectivity and subjectivity, is to encompass the ways and forms of the transition to a disalienated – radically democratic – regime of politics and reason finally harmonized as the two sides of social control.

Being Communist, Reinventing Socialism

Rethinking strategy in the broad sense is the only way of not getting stuck with disjointed alternatives and fragmented mobilizations, without claiming to fuse them by force in a pre-existing unitary framework, theoretical or organizational. On the contrary, it involves rearticulating from within a project with its real social conditions – that is, with

---

56 Analysing the way that buying and selling are separated during crises, Marx writes: 'the crisis manifests the unity of the two phases that have become independent of each', suddenly rendering visible the contradictions that constitute capitalism as such (*Theories of Surplus-Value*, in Karl Marx and Friedrich Engels, *Collected Works*, Vol. 32, London: Lawrence & Wishart, 1989, 131).

multifaceted forms of contestation such as they are, and in which are foreshadowed not communism or socialism, whose germ is allegedly already there, but, more fundamentally, the inseparably objective and subjective coordinates of social transformation. Approached thus, the alternative is not so much in pieces as severed from the social forces of its realization as well as a reconstructed collective culture. There is then a strong temptation to deduce from this a definitive fragmentation of the social world, the disappearance of the working class and the irreversible rise of cultural questions and identities. This one-sided analysis becomes the basis for a strategy developed by experts and communicators. Striving to embrace the reality of a sociology of allegedly immutable convictions, this approach nurtures the fragmentary vision of reality denounced by it, at the expense of a grasp of its contradictions.

In other words, reappropriation must first target the alternative itself, its conditions of elaboration suffering the same abstracting cleavage as the other forms of social mediation: social wealth converted into accumulated capital; collaborative organization perverted into a separate state; collective knowledge segmented into confiscated knowledge. That all these reappropriations are, in fact, conditions of one another can only be a practical truth, slow to transmute into concrete political forms of decision-making and planning but whose possibility and project must be prepared for in the present. For an understanding of real contradictions is inseparable from the transformation already initiated, once one ceases to conceive that understanding as overarching knowledge. It can only be the fruit of shared reflection, involved in real struggles, attentive to existing organizations as well as to their rejection. André Tosel thus calls for thinking 'crucial struggles in the horizontal space of a plurality of kinds of emancipation in analogical resonance'.[57]

Thus, the idea of 'convergence' must not remain a mere abstract horizon, the dream that will suddenly reveal to individuals or groups their fundamental community, without them having to build their congregation against the centrifugal forces at work in all sectors of social reality under capitalist domination, even among individuals themselves. This repoliticization of mobilization, the reverse side of its indispensable theoretical and practical structuration, is what must be

---

57 André Tosel, *Émancipation aujourd'hui? Pour une reprise critique*, Paris: Le Croquant, 2016, 68.

aimed at and organized. Marx's strategic intuitions retain their relevance here: they consist not in identifying the germs of the new society in the old, which would contain its preformed reality, but in offering objective fulcra for political interventions, the only ones capable of realizing revolutionary potentialities. It is striking that the strategic sites of political intervention and social reappropriation correspond to the main perverted mediations of capitalism: money, state, knowledge. Against the social autonomization of capitalism, Marx ventures the thesis of a tendency to socialize financial capital, the prelude to its real socialization.[58] Against the formation of a separate state confiscating social power, he stresses the political resources afforded by traditional communal forms, notably in Russia. Finally, against the specialist knowledge formatted by capitalist logic as a means of oppression, he highlights the industrial worker's tendency to versatility, prefiguring the 'totally developed individual'[59] that distinguishes the communist mode of production. And he describes *Capital* as a 'missile'.

These hypotheses, which Marx did not trouble to harmonize in a coherent scenario, do not form distinct pathways pointing to so many disparate options. They indicate the primary sites of activist, strategic intervention, as well as its major stakes. Their diversity attests to their diffraction throughout the historical formation of the essential contradictions of capitalism, pending their conscious expression and political organization in a comprehensive alternative. Only their activation as mobilizing factors and collectively developed projects can transmute them into active political forces, so true does it remain that 'it is not enough for thought to strive for realisation, reality must itself strive towards thought'.[60] Without a doubt, this dual tendency is operative in contemporary societies, without yielding any outcome predictable in advance.

Such a conception of strategic mediation, including its institutional dimension, is what we must reconstruct to escape both the shams of libertarian immediacy and the lures of electoralism. No insurrection will change the world and the conquest of political power via the ballot

---

58 See *Capital* Vol. 3, in Karl Marx and Freidrich Engels, *Collected Works*, Vol. 37, London: Lawrence & Wishart, 1998, 434.

59 Marx, *Capital*, Vol. 1, 618.

60 *Introduction to the Critique of Hegel's Philosophy of Law: Introduction*, in Marx and Engels, *Collected Works*, Vol. 3, 183.

box will immediately subject any progressive government to the unimpaired social power of the dominant classes, as well as the gigantic pressure of national and supranational institutions, which will set about defusing transformative objectives as quickly as possible. Without mass social mobilization, without awareness of the scale of the class conflict, no elected government will be able on its own to lead to the emancipatory overthrow of the capitalist logics that percolate throughout the mode of production and find myriad relays in it. The real problem is to succeed, in a period that is obviously not revolutionary, in maintaining and consolidating such momentum, which is doomed to exhaust itself and which must be converted into genuinely democratic organizational capacity and enduring social creativity. This takes the form of setting up institutions of a new kind that are never independent of the social life they relay and structure, continually subject to its control. For example, citizens' assemblies, but also elected delegates, organized on the model of the rotation of mandates, will have to be linked to one another, in such a way as to connect the instructions, results and objectives.

Amid the decomposition of the organizations of the labour movement and their forced integration into state structures, we have to face up to the dangers of being torn between ineffective activism and the growing professionalization of trade union and political activities. One of the most urgent challenges is to succeed in inventing a new structuration, combining social offensive and institutional process, rethinking revolutionary culture and militant practices, combining forms of representative delegation and those of direct democracy. Thus, anti-capitalist forces must strive to reconstruct an open, combative class identity, centre of political culture and militant existence, conceding nothing on the radicalism of the changes to be made but devoted to unifying (without annexing) the myriad struggles underway, which are often ignorant of one another and sometimes oppose one another. Reconstructing a culture of solidarity and combining it with a radical alternative involves rebuilding an imaginary, but also being capable of basing it on effective collective practices, initiating an alternative way of life, refusing its imprisonment in social or territorial marginality even if all initiatives of that kind are to be supported. It is to tirelessly endeavour to counter disparate, misleading discourse not with a different rhetoric, attuned to allegedly majority opinion via opinion surveys, but general, precise

critical thinking, arguing step by step in the everyday and reconstructing over the long-term perspectives of political engagement and social
transformation that are at once rational and exciting.

Given these observations, should such a project, which aims to
construct an alternative to capitalism but cannot consist in a programme
defined in advance, be called 'communist'? The term *communism* designates par excellence the transcendence-abolition of capitalism. But it
has the drawback of defining it by its final ends, whose signification
today is torn between poorly defined aspirations, neo-utopian surges
and demonization of past uses. To conceive such a project as being foreshadowed within capitalist social relations sometimes conduces to
attenuating the radicalism of the political rupture and the scale of the
collective construction required for a project of abolishing capitalism.
As we have seen, in Marx's political writings, the substantive *communist*
precisely takes charge of this militant, combative dimension of the alternative, whereas the term *communism* is rare from his pen.

For its part, the term *socialism* has been lacerated by similar tensions
in the course of its history. It ended up foundering in the interminable,
ultimately failed transition of the countries that invoked it in the twentieth century, while continuing to be used by organizations that develop
programmes of transitional demands, in line with the proposals developed by Trotsky in 1938. As regards social-democratic formations,
socialism as a project has disappeared from the concerns of organizations that have rallied to neoliberalism, except when its adoption makes
it possible to reactivate the oppositional dimension of radical sections of
the Democratic Party in the US or the Labour Party in Great Britain. If
we add that the term *communism* is tending to become a thematic more
theoretical and philosophical than political, and that repoliticizing it
consists in thinking not only the transition, but also the durable political
mediations of its construction, then we are obliged to consider that
socialism continues to refer to concrete perspectives of those who think
of themselves as communists.

We must be cognizant of the fact that this whole lexicon, in part
disfigured and widely anathematized, also attests to magnificent battles
and considerable victories. These words are the only ones still able to
name a contemporary radical project, faced with a capitalism whose
name must also be retained, in order to bring out the essential logic that
has been imposed during a protracted sequence and which persists in

and through its diverse variants. This complex history, and the debates these words carry with them, is an integral part of the alternative to be reconstructed. Rather than counterposing socialism and communism, at the risk of rigidifying their meaning and fetishizing their names, it is the reprise and inventive reworking of the two discredited labels that will make it possible to wrest them from the narrative of the victors, as well as the fatality of the defeat they ended up designating.

Unity Is a Multitude of Battles

It remains to conclude with a rapid strategic agenda registering the main dilemmas that paralyse political reconstruction of the alternative today: short-term pragmatism or preservation of an ultimate but inaccessible horizon; circumvention of the issue of the state or institutional integration; dispersion of struggles or unity decreed from above. Recasting a mobilizing perspective and the invention of a desirable possible future, but also of new forms of organization rooted in existing structures and political culture, is a collective task to be placed as such at the centre of imperatives. With a view to outlining its contours, we must first try to rethink a unitary project starting from social and political protests as they exist and are transformed today. The cardinal axes of the alternative defined in previous chapters – state and party, property and labour – must be reinvested, taking account of the fact that they are now traversed and reconstructed by the equally decisive issues of ecology and anti-fascism, race and gender – battles that must be developed not as side issues but as the very forms of class struggle, abandoning any hierarchy or subordination. The peculiarity of strategic reflection is fully disclosed here: it attaches to the autonomy that it grants politics, uncoupling it from the causal or historical order of the dimensions that constitute it. In other words, the reconstruction of an emancipatory, anti-capitalist popular bloc is the condition of the progressive, collective reworking of a viable radical alternative, faced with a social and environmental emergency that no longer brooks any delay.

State and party

The persistent opposition between supporters of bypassing the state and partisans of an exclusively electoral road is one of the major obstacles to the reconstruction of a unitary perspective. This twofold oversimplification must give way to a more developed grasp of the issue of institutions. The conquest of state power, imperative condition of a social transformation that is not reducible to it, must be conceived as a necessarily protracted process, but we must aim from the outset to recast it into an instance of democratic coordination and planning. This is not a secondary transformation: at stake is the very reappropriation of politics, the modern state being constructed through its cleavage as a specialist instance and instrument of confiscation by the dominant classes of the management of social life – in other words, as the antithesis of self-government by workers and citizens. The repressive dimension of this state as well as its social interventions, reactionary and progressive alike, are products of this alienating uncoupling, which class struggles, depending on their intensity, succeed in partially contradicting, but at the risk of being penetrated and captured by a statist logic. On these issues, it is important to revisit the theorizations of Antonio Gramsci, as we have seen, but also those of the late György Lukács, Nicos Poulantzas, István Mészáros and Pierre Bourdieu.

To remedy this situation, it is more important than ever for theoretical exploration to link up with practical intervention and be organized in accordance with original forms of collective intelligence. How to restore to human societies torn apart by the logic of capital conscious, cooperative control over their economic and social options? While there is nothing imminent about such a prospect, we need to try to reconfigure in the present, practically and theoretically, social mobilization but also self-managerial struggles, aspirations of direct democracy, and the defence and redeployment of public services around a general perspective of reappropriating politics. This superior rationality must be rooted in a culture of solidarity articulated with a general offensive project. Thus, from 2011, in Greece, powerful social mobilization established self-administered free clinics, coordinated with one another, working for a concrete redefinition of social medicine and public health at the same time as they offered free care. The capitulation of the Tsipras government in 2015 shattered the possible expansion of this fundamentally political solidaristic logic, stimulating popular initiative and struggle against all forms of discrimination, nurturing feminist, anti-racist and anti-fascist mobilizations.[61] Knowledge and transmission of these experiences, but also their tireless revival, are so many means of combating neoliberalism, which is intent on destroying in rapid succession not only social conquests, but also their culture and their memory, spreading apathy and despair.[62]

Opposition to ever more devastating neoliberal policies cannot make do with a backs-to-the-wall defence of the 'social conquests' (in Bernard Friot's words) of earlier periods. We must both resist the dismantling of public services and reinvent them as means and mediations of a social reappropriation to be taken ever further. Faced with the transformation of the functions of state apparatuses, the reconstruction of an alternative strategy involves a capacity to analyse, and intervene in, them actively. This is particularly the case with the military and police apparatus, whose dependency on arms industries must be brought out at a time of authoritarian stiffening of the so-called *Rechtsstaat*, of bellicose interventions throughout the world, and of anti-terrorist struggle as a tool of continuous restriction of public liberties and social protest.[63]

In addition, the neoliberal transformation of the state is inseparable from its integration into transnational institutions, which it acts to relay and which undo traditional forms of popular sovereignty, however limited, stoking nationalist reaction. We must counter this process with a concrete internationalist perspective, constructed starting from the possibility of breaking with neoliberal domination and the institutions that impose its options with an iron fist, starting with European institutions. That is why the debate on the development of Europe that divides the political scene must be at the heart of contemporary strategic questions, in order to escape the fatal false alternative between nationalist rejection and submission to neoliberal orientations that have become indisputable directions. Having entered into deep crisis, European construction is betraying its political fragility at the same time as its manifest inability to reorient its course from within towards a social

---

61 Alexis Cukier, 'Après la défaite de Syriza', in Cukier and P. Khalfa, eds, *Europe, l'expérience grecque. Le débat stratégique*, Paris: Éditions du Croquant, 2015, 19.

62 See Naomi Klein, *The Shock Doctrine: The Rise of Disaster Capitalism*, London: Allen Lane, 2007. The analysis remains relevant.

63 See Claude Serfati, *Le Militaire. Une histoire française*, Paris: Amsterdam, 2017.

Europe. Constructed around its banking and financial institutions, the European Union as it exists today organizes the destruction of public services, the deregulation and the dominion of markets, while proscribing any divergent political orientation, emptying of any meaning the democratic principles that serve as its banner.

In view of this, it is urgent to open this debate so as not to abandon it to the extreme right, which is burgeoning on the European continent. Only promotion and discussion of prospects for defiance of the treaties, even of exit from the single currency, can make it possible to escape this straitjacket and confer viability on different political orientations, necessarily decided at a national level, while embodying an international project reconstructed around progressive social solidarities and orientations. Cédric Durand clarifies this strategic reflection, in a situation of low social mobilization of the European popular classes but widespread rejection of the choices imposed:

> Such an orientation must be capable, on the one hand, of mobilizing class affects hostile to the institutions of the European Union in as much as they embody a deepening of neoliberalism, while on the other preserving aspirations to the development of political solidarities beyond national frontiers starting from the experience of Europe as it has developed.[64]

In order to reopen political and historical perspectives that have been closed, we need to intervene in a mode at once militant and critical, reconstruct collectives at the heart of the key sectors represented by energy, transport and health, but also education and culture, whose structures and contents must likewise be returned to collective reflection and retuned to radical emancipatory perspectives. Reflection on school curricula, the training and working conditions of teachers and pupils, on school missions but also the functioning of public and private institutions of knowledge and culture – these are at the heart of the political tasks of social reappropriation. Added to them are the construction of innovative forms of collective production of knowledge and expertise, whose scope is directly strategic; the critique of the uses and

---

64 Cédric Durand, 'Les prolétaires n'ont pas d'Europe', *Contretemps*, June 2018, contretemps.eu.

abuses of scientific research, from purportedly green capitalism to the post-humanist delirium of Google, Apple, Facebook, Amazon and Microsoft; and the implementation of ethical and political control over technological and biomedical innovations, highlighting the urgency and feasibility of a reconversion of civil and military nuclear industry.

Thus, while it is impossible to confine ourselves to the slogan of conquering the state apparatus, it is just as inoperative to claim to construct an alternative while bypassing, and thus abandoning, the definition of a 'true democracy' and the questions attached to it, beyond ever more devitalized parliamentary forms. But we must distance ourselves from belief in the immediate, self-sufficient virtues of direct democracy, local spontaneity and the autonomy of the social. 'True democracy' must be constructed around its collaborative reorganization and within the forces calling for it – parties, trade unions, associations – given that statist logic and its train of dominations are necessarily refracted there. In short, it is a question of finally taking seriously the famous assertion that 'the emancipation of the working classes must be conquered by the working classes themselves',[65] extending it to the whole of social existence and building the new institutions of its self-organization in the here and now.

Labour and property

Pertaining to a register at first sight just as classical, the issues of labour and property, property relations and forms of distribution of wealth, are immediately situated on the terrain of class struggle. Profoundly destabilized by recent changes, contemporary analyses of these matters often tend to delegitimize social conflict and the very notion of class. This is true of discussion of property relations from the angle of the commons, which nevertheless has the merit of reviving reflection on the social and juridical dimension of the alternative and a debate lost sight of by left-wing parties, increasingly frightened of themes that are constitutive of socialist and communist traditions. In these organizations, the themes of poverty and exclusion have replaced an analysis of inequalities related to the exploitation of labour and the permanence of a profoundly

---

65 *Provisional Rules of the Association*, in Karl Marx and Friedrich Engels, *Collected Works*, Vol. 20, London: Lawrence & Wishart, 1985, 14.

transformed working class. Julian Mischi has studied these concessions to ideology by the Communist Party since the late 1970s, interpreting them as the 'sign of a weakening of the PCF's capacity for resisting the dominant values'[66] and signalling the tendency to renounce its self-definition as the 'party of the working-class'. That is why re-exploring the question of property today is equivalent to working for a general repoliticization of the issue of production and labour, beyond velleities about a fairer redistribution but also beyond the strictly juridical approach of the commons, separated from the political and social conditions of its realization.

This re-exploration assumes reconnecting the issues of property and labour, but also those of value and wealth,[67] from the standpoint of a common causal logic that specifically defines the capitalist mode of production as a system of class exploitation and extortion of surplus labour and surplus value and which involves legal property relations guaranteeing the legality of this appropriation. At a time of more intense exploitation and casualization of wage labourers, when work collectives and solidarities are the target of a neo-management intent on generalizing competitive logic, the return of these questions is inseparable from the reformulation of the inherently political dimension of the question of work: democracy, far from being confined to representation of a parliamentary kind, also, and in particular, concerns the very definition of work and not only employment, as well as the organization of the production and distribution of socially created wealth. It is therefore a question of restoring all their relevance and political significance to issues of democratic planning, including but going beyond locally existing cooperative forms, which necessarily remain prisoners of the overall capitalist context where they operate and are compelled to embrace some of its criteria.

In the framework of the capitalist mode of production, wealth creation is, in fact, subject to the dual imperative of capital accumulation and increase in the rate of surplus value, disconnected from any estimate of social needs as well as any registration of human and environmental criteria. Proposals for a lifetime wage, extension of free goods

---

66 Mischi, *Le Communisme désarmé*, 75.

67 See Jean-Marie Harribey, *La Richesse, la valeur et l'inestimable. Fondements d'une critique socio-écologique de l'économie capitaliste*, Paris: Les Liens qui Libèrent, 2013.

and degrowth, independently of the divergent social projects they accompany, all come up against the prerequisite of the social and political conditions for genuine challenges to capitalist logic. To affirm the self-sufficient character of these proposals, outside of any confrontation with capital, has as its theoretical correlate abandonment of the law of value, the latter being one of the founding theses of Marxism: the exchange-value of commodities is no longer determined by the quantity of social labour they crystallize, but by their content in knowledge and information. This is what is claimed by Antonio Negri, radically disconnecting this thinking from any active contestation. Faced with these theses and their demobilizing effects, it needs to be reasserted that it is indeed on the terrain of labour, and in conditions of its continued centrality, that we have to construct alternatives and mobilize wage labourers around a project that can articulate local reappropriation with the political expansion of this developing alternative, confronting the logic of capital not as an anonymous power or solely from the financial angle, but as a class logic.

Alexis Cukier emphasizes that a cognizance of richness and the complexity of the notion of labour makes it possible to reaffirm its centrality. Neoliberalism must be analysed as a 'project of "de-democratization" of the economy',[68] seeking to prevent any political intervention by workers and attacking any democratic sovereignty. Consequently, self-management construed as 'workers' control' is what has to be revived, aiming at the establishment of democratic institutions conducive to the creation of 'new democratic rights identifying economic, social and political citizenship'.[69] This ambitious project of a new 'conciliar democracy' is to unlock the anti-political horizon of the themes of the commons or cooperatives remaining isolated in a capitalist logic that ends up absorbing them, reinventing the figure of the 'worker-citizen'. But if this reflection offers precious strategic indications, it is on condition of popularizing and constructing these theses in concrete, interlinked projects, which are thereby vectors of an anti-capitalist perspective capable of beginning to be embodied in the here and now.

---

68 Alexis Cukier, *Le Travail démocratique*, Paris: Presses Universitaires de France, 2018, 60.
69 Ibid., 227.

A strategic option of this kind assumes taking account of labour-power in all its complexity, analysing the potential and limits of contemporary capitalism's attempt at wholesale commodification, which strives to transform individuals into consenting channels of a fantasized, radicalized logic of self-exploitation without an exit. It is by rethinking, conjointly and concretely, social production and reproduction that we can contest the reality of a supposedly total annexation of bodies and souls to the law of capital, extending its theoretical grounds into battles with a veritable power of persuasion and expansion. This perspective, which takes its place in the long history of social conquests inscribed in law and institutions,[70] is in essence inseparable from feminist and anti-racist struggles, which can never be separated from logics of exploitation even though they are irreducible to it.

The resources for this re-conquest are at the very crux of labour-power and individuals who, far from being merely bearers of it, embody it. For Marx, labour-power, not labour, is what the capitalist buys, with a view to extracting a surplus value that derives from the difference between its purchase price (the wage necessary for its maintenance and reproduction) and its productive consumption (its setting to work as a capacity to create wealth). But this labour-power, bought and sold 'like' a commodity, is not one, first because it is not produced as such and second because it is inseparable from the individuality of the labourer. That is why, as we have seen, the tendency to resist exploitation is inherent in labour-power thus conceived, even if this potential resistance still awaits the social and political forms of its expression, beyond merely individual rejection of exploitation and its ambiguities.[71] This dialectic is what is to be rearmed theoretically and concretely, because it is the bearer of immediate demands concerning wages, working conditions, free time, training and challenges to the separation of execution, conception and management of production, while being a condition of collective organization in accordance with an affirmed class logic – and this at the very heart of capitalist relations of production as they are.

---

70 See Claude Didry, *L'institution du travail. Droit et salariat dans l'histoire*, Paris: La Dispute, 2016.

71 Christophe Dejours, *Travail vivant*, Vol. 2, *Travail et emancipation*, Paris: Payot, 2013.

In this sense, rather than waiting for capitalism to vouchsafe the conditions of its own transcendence, the contradictions central to both individuality and social life are to be accentuated as sites of the awareness and conditions of any collective struggle. In this respect, the reappropriation by the exploited classes of their own social potential, as well as the establishment of a true democracy extended to the whole of social existence, continues to play out at work and in the workplace, whether private enterprise or public service, in the detail of concrete situations and at the heart of the general logics they convey. Faced with neoliberal changes in the organization of work conducive to the working class moving from the status of 'mobilized class' to that of 'disarmed' and de-structured group,[72] we should not take literally the managerial ideology too often regarded as victorious by its supporters as well as its opponents. It is not an omnipotent discourse, but a set of practices imposed under duress, which create individual suffering but also collective anger and rejection, whose progressive, emancipatory orientation is not a given but requires a political fight, notably against the extreme right.

That is why strengthening class struggle also takes the form of rehabilitating the notions of class and the proletariat while redefining their pertinence and stakes.[73] Renewal of the debate on their objective contours (a determinate place within social relations) and their subjective dimension (the consciousness of a filiation and forms of solidarity) has nothing scholastic about it. At stake is maintaining the centrality of labour in all the battles that are articulated with it: feminist, anti-racist, anti-fascist and ecological.

Ecology

A more recent and, apparently, broadly unifying theme, the ecological question is one of the most active strategic sites, running through all the preceding themes while being traversed by them. Here, it is important to denounce the fake windows of 'green capitalism' seeking opportunities for profit amid the disasters it engenders – for example, via the

---

72 Stéphane Beaud and Michel Pialoux, *Retour sur la condition ouvrière. Enquête aux usines Peugeot de Sochaux-Montbéliard*, Paris: Fayard, 2004, 431–2.

73 Sophie Beroud, Paul Bouffartigue, Henri Eckert and Denis Merklen, Introduction to *En quête des classes populaires. Un essai politique*, Paris: La Dispute, 2016, See also Abdelmour, *Les nouveaux prolétaires*.

commodification of emission rights – while clearing its name by denouncing misdeeds indiscriminately attributed to human activity in general.[74] We must also stress the absolute climate emergency, as one after another the limits taking us to the verge of irreversibility are crossed, leaving the consequent imperative of superseding the capitalist way of life. Such a task is also political, in that accelerating degradation of the environment does not de facto imply the end of capitalism[75] but exponential growth in inequalities and barbarism. To consider the ecological question as a social question renders obsolete any linear view of technological progress, but also any economistic reduction of social complexity, while opposing the essentialization of a nature diametrically and naïvely opposed to history.

To overcome the low theoretical and political coherence of mainstream ecology, manifested by its radical powerlessness to exercise real influence despite growing worldwide awareness, the current of ecosocialism aligns with the Marxist tradition while developing innovative approaches that combine democratic control, social equality and priority of use-value.[76] To these should be added (following Michael Löwy) collective ownership of the means of production, democratic planning, and a new technological structure of the productive forces – 'in other words, a revolutionary transformation socially and economically',[77] setting in train a veritable change of civilization that has been reflected and decided upon.

The ecological question quintessentially demonstrates the need for an alternative at once radical and comprehensive to counter capitalism, whose threat extends to humanity and the planet as a whole.[78]

---

74 Andreas Malm, *Fossil Capital: The Rise of Steam Power and the Roots of Global Warming*, London: Verso, 2016.

75 See Razmig Keucheyan, Conclusion to *Nature Is a Battlefield*, trans. David Broder, Cambridge: Polity Press, 2016.

76 Marx had begun to register the devastating effects of capitalism upon the environment, conceiving them as a rupture of the metabolism between human societies and nature. But it is largely outside Marxism, and against it, that ecological arguments have been constructed since the 1970s. Today, we are witnessing the rebirth of a Marxist approach to the ecological question. See, in particular, John Bellamy Foster, *Marx's Ecology*, New York: Monthly Review Press, 2000; and Paul Burkett, *Marx and Nature: A Red and Green Perspective*, New York: St. Martin's Press, 1999.

77 Michael Löwy, *Ecosocialism*, Chicago: Haymarket Books, 2015.

78 See Daniel Tanuro, *L'impossible capitalisme vert*, Paris: La Découverte, 2010.

Transformation of lifestyles as well as forms of political intervention, its dominant analysis in terms of a radically depoliticized transition conceals the issue of mediations and its evolution into a collective project, which is to be included on the agenda of a class confrontation. By dint of the scale of the transformation required, political ecology especially lends itself to post-capitalist projections, usefully demonstrating the rational necessity and viability of a quite different mode of production and consumption, realigned with collectively defined priority social needs. The scale of the objective is an incitement to detail the future perspective rather than to link it to a present that seems to depart ever further from it. But the whole problem is to transform this perspective into an active, mobilizing demand, requiring the development of class struggles on the terrain of ecology and vice versa.

This political road can likewise only be constructed at the intersection of all the other axes of mobilization: reconstruction of the labour movement, struggles of indigenous peoples as well as the dominated populations of the South and the North, anti-colonial struggles and feminist struggles – these are now inseparable from a fundamentally transformed relationship to nature.[79] We have to act in such a way that these convergences become veritable axes of mobilization, broad and lasting, articulating local struggles and general stakes around urgent demands, capable of unifying broad swathes of the popular classes. This work presupposes both the diffusion of rigorous data and detailed knowledge, and the sharing of concrete experience as well as the creation of firm international solidarities. From this viewpoint, internationalism and ecology must be rearticulated as common causes with the utmost urgency, pertaining primarily not to ethics but to an anti-capitalist political orientation that has become vital for humanity.

Anti-fascism

Compounding the devastation wreaked by contemporary capitalism is the renewal of the fascist threat: naming and defining its resurgence as such, while registering the changes it has undergone, is one way of countering it.[80] This danger is inseparable from the banalization of the theses

---

79 Löwy, *Ecosocialism*, Chapter 5.
80 See Ugo Palheta, *La Possibilité du fascisme*, Chapter 1, Paris: La Découverte, 2018.

of the extreme right, which now dictates its xenophobic agenda (stigmatization of immigrants, wars on refugees, Islamophobia) to other political forces that reckon it opportune to concede to it, including on the left, out of short-sighted electoral logic. It accompanies the turn towards authoritarianism and policing in the neoliberal state, part of the current decay of representative democracy associated with a new 'regressive Caesarism' – a Gramscian concept that helps us to think about the mutation in the present political and social form of a capitalism that has entered into long-term social and political crisis. Faced with the regular rise in the scores of the extreme right in France, Europe and the world, faced with the multiplication of governments that draw inspiration from it and the international ramification of neo-Nazi currents, the revival of anti-fascism is an absolute strategic priority.

Once again, we have to rethink it not only as a defensive intervention, but as a mobilizing and unifying power, necessarily associated with a broad anti-capitalist perspective. For no humanist pedagogy will suffice in and of itself to contain a phenomenon that has its roots in colonial, neo-colonial and imperialist logics that have never disappeared and which is nurtured both by the general capitalist crisis and the policies meant to remedy it, stoking racist, misogynistic and nationalist regressions.[81] The spectacular comeback of fascism is instrumentalized and reinforced via the blackmail of a 'practical vote' for supporters of policies of social vandalism that cannot acquire a majority social base. This illusion must be made intelligible in order to neutralize it, combating it head-on without seeking to seduce a racist electorate, part of which, today as yesterday, derives from the ranks of the working class, even if it is not the guilty party in this surge. Only a socially combative strategy, registering increasing polarization and resolutely taking its stand in it, will be able to obstruct the resistible rise of racism and xenophobia.

It is therefore necessary to realize the full extent of a threat that is materializing before our very eyes. As Ugo Palheta has shown, we must struggle against the economic, social and political causes of the new fascism in gestation, as well as against its ideas and all its public manifestations, riposting step by step to all its attempts to take root in

---

81 Concerning the colonial history of capitalism and its various analyses, see Jean Batou, 'De la canne à sucre à la machine à vapeur: la traite négrière, precondition de la révolution industrielle?', contretemps.eu.

neighbourhoods, enterprises and places of education.[82] At the same time, it is a question of concretely crossing and conjoining the various dimensions of emancipatory struggles at every point of social contestation and democratically reconstructing the alternative with innovative forms of solidarity. Attempts to construct a white bloc unified by racism must be countered by building a majority popular bloc, white and racialized, bearing the emancipatory values of the class struggle.

Gender and race

These struggles, although quite distinct, are to be taken together by virtue of their objective intersections and their alleged externality to the class struggle. Consideration of questions of race, gender and sexuality by Marxism and the labour movement has always been problematic, being raised and yet marginalized, while sparking especially intense, divisive controversies. It has to be said: part of the labour movement has long had a tendency to consider these themes at best as appendices, at worst as parasitic on, and subversive of, a class struggle narrowly defined and conceived as the principal or exclusive axis of confrontation with capitalism. The cause of this hierarchical ordering attaches basically to the perpetuation, whether conscious or not, of such relations of domination within these organizations, along with the blindness of those whose privileges (white, masculine and/or heterosexual) are not spontaneously conscious and who are offended by the very idea that it is necessary to admit their existence. Thus, it is striking that the authors studied in earlier chapters either do not concern themselves with these dimensions or scarcely do so, whereas they apply themselves to pointing out in detail the deficiencies of existing political organizations at a time when the societies subject to neoliberal policies are experiencing a spectacular resurgence of xenophobia, racism and sexism.

In today's reactionary contemporary context, the risk of fragmentation and isolation is the charge usually levelled against those who deem it legitimate to organize autonomously. Against this are adduced the dangers to which they would expose an idealized republicanism and mythified *laïcité*.[83]

---

82 Palheta, *La Possibilité du fascisme*, 251.
83 See Jean Baubérot, *Les sept laïcités françaises*, Paris: Maison des Sciences de l'Homme, 2015.

This self-proclaimed universal ignores the complexity of its institutional and political history and denies the forms of domination it entails, and conceals or even relays the forms of segregation and oppression that capitalism fuels. Transformed by the dominant media into vectors of anti-feminism and racism, this ideology and the forms of discrimination it accompanies logically reinforce the formation of reactive, closed and exclusive identities, tempted to imprison political struggle in a cultural dead end. But this summary dichotomy of the political and the cultural also needs to be overcome: from this standpoint, no political alternative can desert the terrain of values, today confiscated by conservative currents.

In fact, anti-racist, feminist and LGBTQ+ mobilizations are experiencing a revival today, in conjunction with the reaction underway and the enhanced stakes of social contestation, affording a glimpse of several scenarios: either fratricidal divisions fracturing a political landscape in profound crisis still further, or the flexible connection of all the key sectors of strategic revival and critique. To avoid the discord of identitarian, anti-essentialist, pseudo-universalist or anti-communitarian discourses, whose interminable confrontation clouds construction of a shared alternative, the political and strategic articulation of all struggles against exploitation and forms of domination must be in the mirror image of their cause: irreducible, combined forms of oppression, all of them bound up with capitalist social relations and their social reproduction. The construction of this shared perspective is inseparable from an ideological struggle against commonplace fallacies and ruling ideas, a novel connection between mobilization and theoretical analysis. Its urgency is especially apparent on a terrain where the demonization of any critical thinking and the words that make it possible, starting with 'race' and 'gender', prevails. This critical dimension, which is not external to these struggles but immanent in them, initiating their mutual transformation, also contributes to their centrality at a time when collective consciousness is more necessary than ever for the purposes of radical social transformation.

Thus, gendered oppression is inseparable from capitalism. While it long predates it, far from being a mere vestige in the process of disappearing, it has been adjusted to capitalist logic, as have other forms of domination inherited from earlier modes of production, and then reconfigured in the framework of capitalism's specific social relations. The family, becoming nuclear, is not an alien or neutral institution,

having followed a parallel evolution. Within it, labour-power is reproduced, domestic labour performed, and roles and behaviours transmit-
ted. Yet it also affords forms of protection that alleviate the failures of the
social state. In recent decades, analyses of the social relations of gender
and materialist feminism have debated the question of social reproduction, endeavouring not to isolate it from production but without dissolving it into it, thus returning it to the centre of the fundamental logic of
neoliberalism.[84] For Cinzia Arruzza, the new global feminist wave is to
be regarded as a moment of the 'formation of a class subjectivity with
specific characteristics: immediately anti-neoliberal, internationalist,
anti-racist, obviously feminist and tendentially anti-capitalist', making
the strike its predominant form of struggle while avoiding the dual
pitfall of conceiving women as a full-fledged class or relegating the feminist struggle to culturalism.[85]

For their part, anti-racism and anti-colonial and decolonial thought
are experiencing an essential political rejuvenation.[86] It must be recalled
that the colonial roots of capitalism are 'dripping from head to toe, from
every pore, with blood and dirt', as Marx wrote.[87] The structural racism
that flowed from it continues to be perpetuated and reproduced at the
very heart of relations of production and the whole of social formation,
relayed by state policies on immigration and social segregation, repression of refugees and so on, tending to divide and create a hierarchy among
the dominated. Very much tied to contemporary imperialism and neo-
colonial policies throughout the world, the reality of 'race' does not pre-
exist racism but results from it, in the form of real relations of domination
that secrete their own justification. Use of the term does not involve the
slightest concession to its biological or cultural definition but registers its

84 See, for example, from very different perspectives, Daniel Kergoat, *Se battre,
dissent-elles*, Paris: La Dispute, 2012; Nicole-Claude Mathieu, *L'anatomie politique*, Paris:
Côté-femmes, 1991; Christine Delphy, *L'ennemi principale*, Paris: Syllepse, 2013; Sara
Farris, *In the Name of Women's Rights: The Rise of Femonationalism*, Durham: Duke
University Press; Silvia Federici, *Point zéro: propagation de la révolution. Salaire ménager,
reproduction sociale, combat féministe*, trans. D. Tissot, Paris: Ixe, 2016.

85 Cinzia Arruzza, *Dangerous Liaisons: The Marriages and Divorces of Marxism and
Feminism*, Talgarth: Merlin Press, 2013, 112.

86 See Hourya Bentouhami, *Race, cultures, identités. Une approche féministe et post-
coloniale*, Paris: Presses Universitaires de France, 2015.

87 Karl Marx, *Livre I* [*Capital* Volume 1], trans. J.P. Lefebvre, Editions sociales, 1983,
853.

objective social and political construction, whose effects are indisputable and powerful. These forms of discrimination, developed in particular by 'race management',[88] are inseparable from capitalist relations of exploitation and domination, deliberately impeding solidarity and common struggles. That is why political anti-racism and the struggles of working-class neighbourhoods, which are old, full-fledged components of national history,[89] can and must help to renew the forms and contents of political intervention,[90] extending it to those traditionally excluded from it and who either do not recognize themselves in the existing structures or scarcely do so.

Much is at stake in such a mutation. But it is often underestimated, to such an extent that anti-racist and anti-colonial thinkers have been relegated to the margins of the labour movement and its culture, despite the power of their analyses and their roles, from Aimé Césaire to Frantz Fanon, from C.L.R. James and James Baldwin to Malcolm X, among so many others. Fanon, exploring the inseparably objective and subjective dimensions of colonial domination, unmasks the principles of a hegemony that endures. He illuminates the stakes of a recognition that cannot be granted by others, consisting in a process of self-recognition, individual and political, far removed from any imprisonment in an essentialized native identity but tied up with a political strategy of emancipation that associates the fight against capitalism with the struggle against the colonial state. In a recent book, Glen Sean Coulthard attests to the richness of the struggles and analyses currently being developed by the indigenous people's movement in Canada, many of whose activists associate a challenge to the patriarchy and heteronormativity present in indigenous traditions with the development of demands focused on territory and fighting dependence on the capitalist market in accordance with this original perspective.[91]

Thus, it is strategically crucial to regard all social struggles as referring to the essential contradictions of the capitalist formation in the neoliberal

---

88 See David Roediger, *Class, Race and Marxism*, London: Verso, 2017.

89 See Gérard Noiriel, *Le Creuset français. Histoire de l'immigration, xixe–xxe siècles*, Paris: Éditions du Seuil, 1988.

90 Ahmed Boubeker and Abdellali Hajjat, eds, *Histoire politique des immigrations (post)coloniales. France, 1920–2008*, Paris: Éditions Amsterdam, 2008, Part 4.

91 Glen Sean Coulthard, Conclusion to *Red Skin, White Masks: Rejecting the Colonial Politics of Recognition*, Minneapolis: University of Minnesota Press, 2014.

era. But it must be added that the forms of domination subjectively experienced and rejected – first and foremost, racism and sexism – fuelling
anger individual and general, stimulating analysis and collective debate at
the same time as new forms of solidarity, are today among the most lively
sites of social and political riposte. Working at the intersection of multiple
determinants, concretely highlighting the ramifications of class domination and the exploitation of labour, these struggles embody to the utmost
the imperative of individual and collective reappropriation of social existence in its entirety.[92] Political feminism and anti-racism underscore the
necessity of a general dialectical approach, informed and militant, respectful of specificities. Maintaining the fundamental character of the labour-
capital contradiction, as well as that of exploitation and accumulation,
involves classing the proliferation of forms of domination among the
means of expansion and reproduction of capitalism. Such logical centrality does not lead to any strategic hierarchy; it requires the construction of
a unity that is not just rhetorical, but an active solidarity. Ramified and
articulated in this way, the political forces that contest the stratified, evolv-
ing complexity of the capitalist mode of production must be inserted,
propagated and proliferated at the heart of it.

---

92 The notion of 'intersectionality' was developed by Kimberlé Crenshaw to describe
the combination of various forms of domination and is at the centre of debates ('Mapping
the Margins: Intersectionality, Identity Politics, and Violence against Women of Color',
Cahiers du Genre 39: 2, 2005).

Conclusion:
Revisiting the Revolution

The perspectives with which the last chapter concluded merely outline some possibilities, which are of course easier said than done. They aim to help reformulate the contemporary question of the alternative in all its complexity. Whether called communism or socialism, it will perforce result from a determined, protracted break with capitalism – the sole escape from the unprecedented crisis that humanity is experiencing today. This project must rally the popular classes and their allies around a different choice of society and life, collectively elaborated. Only struggles in common will make it possible to construct as they go different social relations and a new relationship to nature. Approached from the unifying angle of re-appropriation, individual and social, existing struggles and the reflections that accompany them must also help define a different relationship between theory and practice, capable of overcoming the traditional division of labour but also the fragmentation of alternatives. On this condition a viable desirable and chosen future will be invented, beyond merely local solutions and yet distant from grandiose prophecies.

That is why, when it comes to the alternative, strategic reflection is primary, as long as we refuse its reduction to a subaltern technique or the instrumentalization of disparate demands. But its relative autonomy is to be dialectically attuned to its immersion in economic, social and cultural dimensions, of which politics must again become the instance of collective reflection and common management. Striving to continually adjust means to ends, which are both aimed at and constantly reworked as they are elaborated, only strategy in the broad sense can render the historical mutation required to escape the social and environmental catastrophes underway both credible and actual. In this sense, the word *communism*, while it retains its political pertinence, must above all refer to such a strategic construct, resolutely geared to superseding capitalism. Neither a compromise disguised as step-by-step pragmatism, nor dirigisme under the cover of democratic rhetoric, nor an ultimate vision for impenitent dreamers, strategy must be conjugated in the present around concrete demands that are from the outset bearers of a large-scale collective project.

Strategically harmonizing emancipatory struggles, giving them life within everyday solidarities, is not to search for their lowest common denominator, not to order them in a hierarchy, and still less to effect a synthesis of them from above. It involves forging with the utmost lucidity alliances and combinations, forms of proximity and cooperation, reconstructing a creative culture that is shared and multiple. Though not abandoning the party-form, the latter remains to be reinvented, to be joined with other forms of organization, collaboration and decision-making, capable of conferring true meaning on a dying democracy. In the absence of an active reappropriation of politics, the alternative is condemned to be written in the categories of the opponent. The abandonment of the divide between left and right, the denunciation of the 'caste' in place of a class analysis, the fetishization of millenarian hopes, the miniaturization of the alternatives, the apologia for flight and circumvention, secession to the philosophical Aventine – all these options are symptoms of strategic deficiency. From this viewpoint, the radical left is today profoundly affected not so much by fragmentation of alternatives as by the proliferation of internal divisions and quarrels. The reconstruction of an alternative to capitalism plays out at the intersections of its various lines of fracture, to make their concrete articulation possible without reducing or subordinating one struggle to another, or resigning ourselves to the dispersion of forms of emancipation and competition between them.

In André Tosel's words, 'it is up to analysis to clarify the articulation of these conflicts into totalities that are always open and non-totalizable.'[1] Such

---

1 André Tosel, *Emancipations aujourd'hui? Pour une reprise critique*, Paris: Éditions du Croquant, 2016, 69.

analysis must irrigate political activity and struggles, attentive to the complexity immanent in them. Only unitary labour, far removed from any homogenizing normalization, can obstruct the rise of nationalist, racist, sexist, Islamophobic, xenophobic and homophobic tropes, as well as the sometimes reactive forms of identitarian refixation, which echo this alienating, discriminating logic. A collective construction at once knowledgeable and active, attentive to the complexity of forms of oppression and domination, to their contradictory criss-crossing, bearer of its own auto-critique and continued transcendence – this is what can forge a profoundly political common culture, open to extension and enrichment, and hence counter the rise of exclusive filiations, without ignoring the invariably singular and particular motivation of the decision to struggle.

Rather than being the product of electoral logic, this unity, without neglecting institutional issues, must be fashioned on the practical terrain of existing mobilizations and struggles, but also in critical thinking, social sciences, debate and sharing of experience for the purposes of participating in the re-foundation of existing organizations. For we have to start out from the present and the history of the labour movement, as well as all emancipatory struggles, such as they are. This expansion from within, not from above, involves collective theoretical and critical work, able to break with the specialization of tasks as well as the vertical principle of pedagogy. This shared construct takes the form of unified historical, social and philosophical knowledge, formerly dubbed 'critique of political economy' by Marx, but also of the revival of debate, polemic, informed, rigorous confrontation, capable of relating this culture to concrete stakes, without reducing these two registers to one another. In this regard, it is a question of revitalizing not a Marxist politics seeking its line and slogan in the past, but a political Marxism drawing on the dialectical and strategic sources of a critique of capitalism that is to be constantly updated and compared with other critical traditions. The current absence of debate fuels dispersion of opposition forces, but also the proliferation of theoretical solutions intent on being ultimate, panaceas destined to prosper amid the crisis of concrete alternatives. This book hopes to contribute to that revived confrontation, identifying with the project of a collectively determined abolition of capitalism: what, yesterday as today, is called a revolution.